Better to Reign in Hell

Better to Reign in Hell

Published in the United States by The New Press, New York, 2005
Distributed by W. W. Norton & Company, Inc., New York

LIBRARY OF CONGRESS CATALOGING-IN-PUBLICATION DATA

Miller, Jim, 1965–
Better to reign in hell : inside the raiders fan empire / Jim Miller and Kelly Mayhew
    p. cm.
  Includes bibliographical references and index.
  ISBN   1-56584-890-X (hc.)
    1. Oakland Raiders (Football team)   2. Football fans—United States.
I. Mayhew, Kelly.   II. Title.

GV956.O24M55   2005
796.332'64'0970466—dc22   2005041564

The New Press was established in 1990 as a not-for-profit alternative to the large, commercial publishing houses currently dominating the book publishing industry. The New Press operates in the public interest rather than for private gain, and is committed to publishing, in innovative ways, works of educational, cultural, and community value that are often deemed insufficiently profitable.

The New Press
38 Greene Street, 4th Floor
New York, NY 10013
www.thenewpress.com

In the United Kingdom:
3rd Floor
18–20 Scrutton Street
London EC2A 4RX

Designed and typeset by Hiatt & Dragon, San Francisco, California
Printed in the United States of America

10 9 8 7 6 5 4 3 2 1

To Walt
and
In Memory of
James Albert Miller
and
Hunter S. Thompson
R.I.P.

Contents

Voodoo Man

Photo: Joseph A. Blum

Preface

Paradise Lost

If you have ever had to read *Paradise Lost* in school and found Satan to be a far more compelling character than God or Adam, you may be a Raiders fan. Sure, you knew that you were supposed to be rooting for the good guys, but they were boring. The teacher may have explained that Milton was on Team Heaven, trying to justify the ways of God to man, but Satan had a certain flair. When he said, "The mind is its own place" and "can make a Heaven of Hell, and a Hell of Heaven," you nodded along. After the archfiend asserted that it is "better to reign in Hell than serve in Heaven," you applauded his sneering eloquence. Here was a rebel outcast you could identify with. It was clear that you had an affinity for the dark side, and just what it takes to cheer for the team that everyone loves to hate.[1]

Imagine Al Davis and his Silver and Black legions as Satan and company recently cast out of Football Heaven after a brutal Super Bowl humiliation, devastating back-to-back 4–12 and 5–11 seasons, and two years of ugly, unsatisfying courtroom antics. "Thunderstruck and astonished," the Dark Prince rises to rally Raider Nation. "All is not lost," he begins, "the unconquerable will and study of revenge [along with] immortal hate" will give us "courage never to submit or yield: And what is not to be overcome? That glory never shall his wrath or might extort from me." Absolutely: We were robbed! Our rightful spot in the sun was taken from us and we're going to get it back through open war or covert guile! Fire the coach, slap the franchise player tag on Woodson, cut loose half the defense, pick up rebel castoffs Warren Sapp, Kerry Collins, and Randy Moss. Draft Gallery with the second pick. Get a dominant running back. Just win, baby! Don't rebuild, return to glory! That's the spirit![2]

And all of Al's army remembers the lost paradise, the golden era of the team's first stay in Oakland and the early days in Los Angeles, when the legendary rebels of old led the team to the best winning percentage in professional football. Raider Nation's retro jerseys recall Lamonica, Stabler, Plunkett, Van Eeghen, Branch, Otto, Biletnikoff, Blanda, Atkinson, Hayes, Tatum, Hubbard, Casper, Upshaw, Shell, Matuszak, Hendricks, Alzado, Allen, Long, and a host of other warriors of yore. Raiders fans chant the mantras, "Just Win, Baby," "Commitment to Excellence," and "Pride and Poise." The sounds of "The Autumn Wind Is a Raider" can be heard in the background. Raider Nation nurses the memories of three Super Bowl victories and curses a litany of epic bad calls. Despite the fact that the .780 winning percentage of the first decade of glory has sunk to below .500 over the last ten years, they all know that the Silver and Black will be back. Being cast down into the Black Hole of the worst back-to-back seasons in forty-two years is only a sign that their time is just around the corner. The air is thick with nostalgia and bitterness. Sweet revenge is on their minds. Raider Nation helped build Football Heaven and knows that someday they'll rule the place again.

If you know that the good guys aren't so good, you're a Raiders fan. If you know you've been jacked and are waiting for revenge, you're a Raiders fan. If you know your boss isn't any better than you are, you're a Raiders fan. If you flip off the guy who cuts you off on the freeway, you're a Raiders fan. If you root for your adversary to lose so you don't have to watch him celebrate, you're a Raiders fan. If you watch gangster films and root for the mob, you're a Raiders fan. If you hate piety, you're a Raiders fan. If you think Al is a player and he still amuses you, you're a Raiders fan.

We also like to imagine Al Davis as Al Swearengen, the venal, cunning, greedy, and skillfully brutal casino and brothel owner in the Social Darwinist HBO/TV western *Deadwood*. At first glance, he appears to be the most evil man in town, a man who'd sell his mother to make a buck (which he would), but as we learn more about the warts on the allegedly "high class" businessmen in town, Al's honest approach starts to look better in comparison to their hypocritical facades of respectability. In a town where everybody is a "cocksucker" on the make, it's the people with pretenses who are the most reprehensible. If Frederick Jackson Turner was right that the frontier was the proving ground that defined the American character, then *Deadwood* is a tough little allegory of community totally defined by market values. It's the war of all against all. The same could be said of the NFL, or corporate America as a whole. Hence, the joke isn't on the Raiders fans who root for the charming rogue, but on all the other people who think that their team is cleaner or that any of the corporations they entrust to entertain, employ, sustain, and protect them operates by some nicer set of rules. Like the stranger in Mark Twain's "The War Prayer," who comes to town and waltzes into the church to tell the good people that their prayers for "victory" over their enemies are really curses, we are here to tell you, dear reader, that Raider Nation is America. That said, everyone in town thought that the stranger was a lunatic.

Enter the Barbarians

The barbarians were at the gates. "What if You Threw a Party and Raider Nation Came?" a worried *San Diego Union-Tribune* front-page headline once asked. The answer, it appeared, was fear and loathing. Days before the Oakland Raiders even won the playoff to come to Super Bowl XXXVII in San Diego, the host city was already in panic mode with reminiscences of past atrocities. The Raider Nation: they brawl, bite the ears off innocent residents, stab local fans, and then proudly display video footage of the carnage on fan websites. Downtown businesses were desperately consulting security firms, and well-heeled residents were rethinking whether or not they wanted to bilk Raiders fans out of thousands of dollars for the privilege of staying in their swank bay-view condos. Waiters were dreading the influx of rude cheapskates and belching ruffians. Only the local bail bonds man, "King" Stahlman, was happy, brimming with anticipation that his profits would soar into the stratosphere with mass arrests.[3]

The *Oakland Tribune* paid back in kind with the headline, "San Diego Full of Raider Haters." It mocked the suntanned dilettantes to the south by observing of the Gaslamp Quarter that the "formerly rough, newly gentrified neighborhood" was "allergic to riff-raff." As another paper noted, the Super Bowl had "become a cruel nightmare for most residents in San Diego." "There is a general feeling that they are coming to destroy our town," said one San Diego businessman, pondering whether he should "duct tape his windows." "Their fans aren't our type of clientele," noted one snotty La Jolla restaurateur, "We want Miami or New York: rich people with lots of money." Raiders supporters had celebrated the AFC Championship by rioting and running amok in Oakland and now, yuppie San Diegans imagined, America's most hated fans were licking their chops at the prospects of pillaging an enemy citadel.[4]

The feared image of Raider Nation is part fact and part fiction. More than any other fandom in American professional sports, Raiders aficionados' devotion goes beyond sports. Like British soccer hooligans, it's in the blood. In a city that had 113 murders in 2002 along with a massive budget deficit and a troubled school system, the Raiders represent a chimera of hope and pride. As homeless Oakland resident Ben Ducksworth put it while collecting empty beer cans on East 12th Street, "The Raiders lift us all up. . . . I may be homeless and broke but I'm a winner. That's because my blood runs silver and black." The same holds true for "The Violator," the heavily costumed Raider NFL Hall of Fame fan, who despite being an unemployed construction worker from Los Angeles, still managed to make five games in 2002 and was personally flown up to the Championship by Raiders owner Al Davis. (There is little Al can do for the infamous "Raider Bandit," who, during the team's L.A. years, robbed a series of banks to pay for his football experience, only to be stymied when his TV privileges were cut off behind bars.)[5]

Raider Nation also includes the cops and firefighters who gather for Bloody Marys at the Fat Lady in downtown Oakland before games, the Brawley policeman who heads the Imperial Valley fan club, and a regular contingent of L.A.

gangbangers who make their way up to see games. The 66th Mob and the 66th Avenue Black Hole includes SUV-driving families who show up as early as three days before games to party on city streets just outside the stadium in anticipation of their game day tailgates. There they are joined by college professors, union longshoremen, peace activists with a secret vice, bikers in face paint, Baptist ministers, blue-collar pirates in full dress, and one-time wannabes. "It's an experience," observed CBS director Larry Cavolina after driving through a Raider tailgate traffic jam for an hour and a half, "It's like Woodstock."[6]

Cavolina's comparison is not far off base, since both Woodstock Nation and Raider Nation are imagined communities, which, in their own ways, paradoxically express the dominant values of the culture along with a utopian reaction against them. The semi-weekly masquerade in the Black Hole, the rowdiest, most notorious seating section of Silver and Black fandom and elsewhere throughout Network Associates Oakland Coliseum, is a display of intensely competitive tribalism accompanied by an equally deep longing for community. To outsiders, Raider Nation embodies the evil, animalistic "monster" that threatens much of middle-class America's heavily racist and classist imaginary. The multiracial, largely blue-collar Raiders fan-base is the "bad part of town" gathered en masse to menace fans accustomed to watered-down, Disneyfied corporate sports experiences.

That Raider Nation is a partial source of identity for two of the West Coast's most blighted communities, Oakland's flatlands and Southeast Los Angeles, only puts fuel on the fire. A gritty alternative to California's sunshine-and-granola image, Raider Nation has become a one-size-fits-all repository of rebellion for a far-flung national, indeed global, diaspora of fans smitten with their outlaw mystique. Real or imagined, the Raider Nation is an affirmation of blue-collar toughness, rebellion, and solidarity during a time that valorizes the lifestyles of the rich and famous. In an era that craves order and safety, Raider Nation offers chaos and fun. In the face of the new Puritanism, "Just say no" and "Watch what you say," the Raider Nation says, "Fuck you."

This is not a book about football, but a book about a fan culture that is unique in American society. We spent the abysmal 2003 season attending Raiders games in Oakland's "Black Hole," going to Ricky's sports bar in San Leandro and the Fat Lady in Oakland, corresponding with legions of rabid fans nationwide via mail and e-mail, and talking with them over the phone. We visited Raiders fans in the Los Angeles and San Diego areas, watching road games in living rooms, sports bars, and San Diego's Qualcomm Stadium, site of the Raiders unofficial ninth home game. As a result, this book gives the reader an inside-out look into the dreaded self-described Raider Nation. Our larger focus is on the various identities present in Raiders fandom: West Coast rust belt, Southeast L.A. gangsters, tough "Real Women" in black, virtual members of the Black Hole who form a global diaspora of TV watchers and website participants, obsessive tailgaters, "professional" fans, and various subgroups and hangers-on. Our role as participant-observers helped us delve into the interesting intersections of class, race, gender, region, and imagination that is Raider Nation.

While we suggest a number of theoretical and/or political ways to interpret Raider Nation, we allow contradictory readings to emerge through the voices of the various fans and observers we interviewed. Thus, the messy, amorphous nature of this imagined community is ultimately left unresolved. The fan interviews that comprise this book have been edited for brevity and readability and arranged in order to maintain the chronological and thematic coherence of the text, but not at the expense of the integrity of the individual voices of the fans. *Better to Reign in Hell* is a hybrid text, mixing together cultural studies, sports writing, sociology, historical analysis, political commentary, first-person reportage, and interviews in an effort to parse out the various meanings of Raiders fan culture. Some of the names have been changed to protect the innocent—and not so innocent. The introduction gives a conceptual map of Raider Nation, chapters 1 through 3 take the reader on a first-person tour of the Raiders' Super Bowl nightmare in San Diego, give a history of the postevent riot in Oakland, and explore the virtual and global reaches of the Raider Empire. Our 2003 journey begins in chapter 4 in training camp and continues through the rest of the book until the bitter end takes us full circle back to San Diego. Most of the writing is done from Jim's perspective with Kelly intervening in the latter part of chapter 7 on Ricky's sports bar and for the entirety of chapter 11 about real women who wear black.

This project should be compelling and informative for fan and nonfan alike, providing a window into the real story behind the media hype. As the riots following the Raiders' Super Bowl loss, the consistent brawling at the Raiders–Chargers games, and the die-hard loyalty and community of true Raiders fans show, this phenomenon demonstrates how sports fandom in its extreme form has become a site in which to express both the longing to be part of something larger, and the anger, frustration, and brutality that is the underside of American life for millions of people. While we will not shy away from the darker aspects of Raider Nation's story, this book is also a celebratory tale written by longtime Raiders fans who believe that, warts and all, "the living crowd" at Raiders games is one of the last surviving examples of Walt Whitman's rough, generous, egalitarian America:

Of every hue and cast am I, of every rank and religion,
A farmer, mechanic, artist, gentlemen, sailor, quaker,
Prisoner, fancy-man, rowdy, lawyer, physician, priest,
I resist anything better than my own diversity."[7]

The Oakland Lady

Introduction

Raider Nation as an
Imagined Community

> I root for the Oakland Raiders because they hire castoffs, outlaws, mal-
> contents, and fuckups, they have lots of penalties, fights, and paybacks,
> and because Al Davis told the rest of the pig NFL owners to go get
> fucked. Also they don't have a lot of Christians kneeling down to pray
> after touchdowns. Christians are ruining sports. Someday the Raiders
> will be strong again, and they will dip the ball in shit and shove it down
> the throats of the wholesome, white, heartland teams that pray together
> and don't deliver late hits.
>
> *George Carlin*, Braindroppings

Reading Football and Its Fans

How, an unschooled observer might ask, did American culture get to the point
where famous comedians and columnists along with ordinary fans associate their
loyalty to a football team so closely with prominent aspects of individual and
group identity? How did a professional football club come to represent the qualities of the antihero or, more incredibly, come to magically bestow upon their
followers a countercultural credibility and/or a gangster's swagger? How did the
act of collectively consuming the commercial product that is a slickly packaged
and sophisticatedly marketed professional football game come to bring people

together as "blood brothers" (or sisters, for that matter)? What in the world does any of this have to do with football?

Michael Oriard, ex–Kansas City Chief and trail-blazing scholar of the grid-iron, notes that football had "become a social event as well as an athletic contest" by the 1890s. After more than a century of changes, the social event that is football has evolved into a multibillion-dollar spectacle that is far more important economically than the athletic contest itself. With an $18 billion television contract, the National Football League draws larger TV audiences, attracts more million-dollar advertising deals, sells more merchandise, and has a larger influence on the culture than any other American sport. It even has its own round-the-clock channel, the NFL Network. Why all the attention? For Oriard, it is "beauty and chaos" that compels the fans to watch the game. More specifically, "It is not simply the violence that spectators . . . celebrate in football, but the human capacity to withstand violence and create something beautiful despite it, or even from it."[1]

In addition to the gorgeous brutality, Oriard argues that we watch our teams because of "personal connectedness or regional rootedness" or other narratives that we read in the "cultural text" of football.[2] In the case of Raiders fans, ties to Oakland and/or Los Angeles, racial tolerance, urban grit, working-class pride, cutthroat competition, rugged individualism, and rebel flair have all been central factors in drawing and testing the intense loyalty of their fans, who frequently embody the traits—real or imagined—that they associate with the team's image. Sometimes as "the Beast of Bourbon" puts it, Raiders fans ironically "revel in . . . notoriety," whether or not their "real self" fits their fan identity.

Oriard also discusses the perspective from which we watch football:

And imagine the fans watching these players and teams not as a "mass" audience but as actual people: European, African, Hispanic, and Asian-American; Catholic, Protestant, Jew, and nonbeliever; WASP and redneck; college graduate and high-school drop-out; conservative and liberal; racist and humanitarian; male and female, rich and poor, urban and rural, sick and

Raider-Gloria

well; ones just fired from jobs and ones just promoted; ones just fallen in love and ones just separated from a spouse; some pissed off at the world and some blissfully content. The possibilities are limitless.[3]

In the course of our journey into Raider Nation we discovered an equally diverse range of fans. While the Raiders' blue-collar image does have a solid base in reality (we interviewed longshoremen, warehousemen, firefighters, cops, members of the armed services, long-distance truckers, mechanics, concrete pourers, refinery workers, union pipefitters, waitresses, maids, and steelworkers), there were also white-collar workers (lawyers, doctors, teachers, businessmen, and bond traders) as well as those on the margins of economic life (unemployed and homeless fans). This socio-economic diversity went hand in hand with racial diversity and a multiplicity of political perspectives ranging from right-wing hawks with a Social Darwinist worldview to antiwar populists. As Raiders fan Randy Leppard puts it, "Silver and black fans are your neighbors, co-workers, friends, and acquaintances. We are black, white, brown, red, and yellow. Our Raider Nation consists of lawyers, students, doctors, garbologists, teachers, truckers, and the unemployed. We are everyone and everywhere. We did not emerge from the bowels of Hell, but the true fan would rather burn in Hades than cheer for the likes of the Jackasses [Denver Broncos] or Chefs [Kansas City Chiefs] or the Whiners [San Francisco 49ers]."

Randy's positive portrayal of Raiders fans is a direct response to what he calls "the haters" who defame them. His eloquent description of Raider Nation is an interesting mix of democratic populism a little reminiscent of Tom Joad's "I'll be everywhere" speech to his mother at the end of John Steinbeck's *The Grapes of Wrath* and an intensely competitive tribalism. This response was a common one among the Raiders fans we interviewed, and it shows that in addition to the predictable embrace of rivalry and competition that might be argued to echo the logic of the market which dominates American culture, it also displays the genuine longing for community that is its antidote.[4]

An Imagined Community

> Every game was a terrifying adventure, win or lose, and the Raiders of the
> '70s usually won—except in Pittsburgh, where cruel things happened and
> many dreams died horribly. You could see the early beginnings of what
> would evolve into the massive *Raider Nation*, which is beyond doubt the
> sleaziest and rudest and most sinister mob of thugs and whackos ever
> assembled in such numbers under a single "roof," so to speak, anywhere
> in the English-speaking world. No doubt there are other profoundly dis-
> agreeable cults that meet from time to time in most of the 50 states.
>
> *Hunter S. Thompson, "The Last Super Bowl"*

A useful way of addressing the meaning of fan communities comes in Dean
Chadwin's *Those Damn Yankees: The Secret Life of America's Greatest Franchise*.
While his book is mostly devoted to exploding the Yankee myth and exploring
its sordid corporate underbelly, Chadwin does spend some time discussing the
meaning of fandom. Specifically, he notes that "the identification with a team,
its uniform, and history involves baseball's most direct appeal to the gut. The
tribalism displayed by a community of fans has an almost immeasurable force. It
creates instant civic rivalries where none previously existed." In the course of his
skewering of the Yankees, Chadwin describes their fans as a "hegemonic nation
interested only in the claims of monarchy, a tribe set on domination . . . They
are the worst New York has to offer: loud, aggressive, unruly, unthinking, cocky,
self-absorbed, dictatorial, ungenerous celebrants of triumphalism."[5] Of more
interest than the condemnation here is Chadwin's use of the metaphor of nation.
"Yankee nation," as Chadwin calls the fans of the Bronx Bombers, is more than
just a disparate collection of individuals watching a baseball game; it is a group
identity, a site of shared meaning:

> Although the crowd in the bleachers will return home to their separate lives
> as soon as the game ends, for a few hours they inhabit a place where only
> one identity is acceptable: Yankee fan. Here Benedict Anderson's imagined

community is very real indeed. Any statement that violates the group's one idea can prove dangerous. Fans wearing hats in support of the rival Mets or Red Sox are hounded by hundreds of fans pointing and chanting "Mets Suck" or "Boston Sucks."[6]

Chadwin invokes the notion of an imagined community here as a way of understanding fan identity, but his discussion of fans is limited to their competitive tribalism. While many Raiders haters' image of Silver and Black fanatics might match up nicely with Chadwin's disdainful portrait of "Yankee Nation" as a bunch of vulgar homophobes who refrain from racial slurs only out of pragmatism, the concept of an imagined community is more nuanced than "a single idea" of exclusionary team worship and deserves a bit more attention.[7]

The term "imagined community" comes not from a cultural analysis of sports, but, as Chadwin notes, from Benedict Anderson's book on nationalism, *Imagined Communities*. Anderson sets out to analyze why people love, die, and kill for nations. Central to his project is exploration of the roots of people's sense of belonging to an "empty" philosophical concept. In an ironic statement given the subject of our book, Anderson claims of nationalism, "Like Gertrude Stein in the face of Oakland, one can rather quickly conclude that there is 'no there there.'" According to Anderson, a nation is "an imagined political community—and imagined as both inherently limited and sovereign." Nationalism, then, is not "an awakening of nations to self-consciousness; it *invents* nations where they do not exist." This phenomenon is not limited to political communities. In fact, Anderson tells us, "all communities larger than the primordial villages of face-to-face contact (and perhaps even these) are imagined. Communities are to be distinguished, not by their falsity/genuineness, but by the style in which they are imagined." The fictional nature of the nation is what allows it to supercede fundamental differences and conflicts of interest among its members. As Anderson puts it, "It is imagined as a *community*, because, regardless of the actual inequality and exploitation that may prevail in each, the nation is always conceived as a deep horizontal comradeship."[8]

Phil and Angel

While Raider Nation is not "political" in any overt sense, it is an imagined community nonetheless whose members' chosen identity, whether consciously or not, does hold some significant ideological content. Indeed, the parallel between the characteristics that Anderson claims for the political "nation" people imagine and the fan "nation" that Raiders fans dream of are striking. Just as people in a dying farm town in North Dakota, the Tenderloin in San Francisco, a Buddhist monastery on Maui, and a tenement in the south Bronx might all sport some form of patriotism (whether it be a flag on the front porch, taped to the side of a shopping cart holding everything one owns, on the bumper of an SUV, or on a t-shirt), Raiders fans from East Oakland and Washington, D.C., to Los Angeles and Liberia, Costa Rica, identify with and display the Silver and Black. The Silver and Black Attack website's map of Raiders fans shows them in every state in the union and more countries in the world than any other professional franchise; the map's heading proclaims, "We are everywhere."

What links these scattered legions of fans is not personal connection but a shared imagining. Most important, the fans we interviewed universally self-identified as part of "Raider Nation." How do they signify this identity outside of the stadium? Raiders fans fly team flags at their houses, trim their bushes into the shape of the pirate shield, put decals across the entire rear windows of their cars, stencil "Commitment to Excellence" on their vans, paint their living rooms silver and black, put helmets on their cats during games, walk their dogs with Raiders collars and leashes, barbeque on team-themed grills, make their little girls ride silver-and-black tricycles, and hang Raiders Christmas lights. They wear customized jerseys, t-shirts, boxer shorts, thong underwear (the hottest seller during Super Bowl week), watches, socks, baseball caps, earrings, necklaces, pajamas, pants, robes, aprons, jackets, and rain ponchos. They get Raiders haircuts and adorn themselves with Al Davis, "Fuck the Rest," and "Raider Nation" tattoos. Even their babies are outfitted in Raiders onesies, bibs, and booties while sucking on pirate shield pacifiers.

Indeed, as people's lives become more and more atomized and civic participation, like voting, universal military service, and other forms of community involvement, continues to decline, many people probably feel more connected to their team than to most other political and social institutions. As Robert Putnam puts it, "By virtually every conceivable measure, social capital has eroded steadily and sometimes dramatically over the past two generations." Putnam's study systematically outlines how "the quantitative evidence is overwhelming" that civic, workplace, religious, philanthropic, and political participation are significantly waning. Sadly, this trend has continued even after the wave of patriotism following 9/11. Citizenship is rapidly becoming a spectator sport that mimics the qualities of sports spectatorship—rooting and bemoaning without actually participating. Hence a unified Raider Nation is no more of a myth than "United We Stand."[9]

Sports sociologist Eric Dunning has explored the central role that sports has come to play in helping people construct (or "imagine") a sense of identity and belonging in contemporary society, whether it be through an association with a team's city or a particular class, race, or gender association.[10] Following Dunning, an imagined community like Raider Nation is a source of identification with Oakland or Los Angeles or California (depending on the fan) or a given subgroup (blue-collar, street tough, rebel, renegade businessman, black, Latino, etc.). It is also a source of identity and belonging in an increasingly fragmented society where traditional forms of community have long been under siege. As Dunning points out, the "deployment of the so-called 'new technology,'" "rapid social change," and global conflicts have led to the "disappearance across the globe of many older patterns of work and social integration and the emergence of newer ones." What sports does in the midst of these "anxiety-provoking imponderables" is "to give people a sense of continuity and purpose in contexts which are highly impersonal and beset by what many experience as a bewildering pace of change." Put simply, a fan might think, my city may be blown up by terrorists, my job may be eliminated because of a technological innovation or a budget cut, my kids' future may be in jeopardy, but at least there's the Raiders.[11]

Particularly for blue-collar fans in a city like Oakland, where deindustrialization has taken a severe toll on the job base and, consequently, on neighborhoods and families, sports can serve as an emotional life preserver. As cultural studies scholar David Rowe notes, when social institutions fail, a values vacuum emerges and sports can help fill the void.[12] Rowe sees sports as a way people compensate for the loss of meaning and community elsewhere in society. Interestingly, he notes that the power of sports is strong enough to get us to suspend our disbelief and cynicism in an era when they are, as he puts it, "abundant." Going even further, Rowe claims that we have seen sports "appropriate many of the functions of established religion, supplying the rituals and deeply held beliefs that have faded in increasingly secular societies dedicated to the worship of the god of conspicuous commodity consumption." Dunning makes a similar point when he argues that, "for the most committed fans, and perhaps for others besides, sport can be said to function as a 'surrogate religion.'" Clearly, the point here is not that religion has totally vanished from the world of all sports fans, but that sports (along with other consumer activities) have come to fulfill some of the same meaning-giving and identity-granting functions that once were the sole province of religion. After all, the games *are* played on Sunday.[13]

For some fans, religion and the Raiders actually go hand in hand. Despite George Carlin's assertion about the godlessness of the Silver and Black, a good number of fans overtly mix religion and the Raiders. As Mark Shelton, a corrections officer and pro wrestler explains:

> Another thing is that I'm a Christian. My understanding is that a great many Raider players are also. Both Napoleon Kaufman and Steve Wisnewski served and are serving God in a great capacity during and after they left the Raiders. People don't seem to make the connection with being a Christian and being a Raiders fan. Seems to be contrary to them. But taking castoffs and bringing them to glory is very harmonic to the scriptures and the teachings of Christ. I kind of dig the paradox.

Other Christian Raiders like Jim Freeman, who started a Christian Raiders club, agree: "You can't be weak or timid or wimpy to live your faith, and you can't be any of those things to be a Raider." A Southern Baptist minister, Brad Richardson, claims that "God is responsible for my being a Raiders fan" and that growing up near Arrowhead Stadium where the Kansas City Chiefs play was like "living in hell."[14] Unconcerned that some of their fellow believers might see devotion to the Raiders as well as the Lamb of God as contradictory, these fans simply marry their faiths.

So where then does the power of sports spectatorship come from? What could draw people in and seduce them into paying good money for games, gear, and the various other prerequisites for membership in Raider Nation? Michael Oriard claims that "a major part of football's appeal, expressed in a variety of ways" is "the intensity of experience—physical, emotional, psychological—" that the game offers "players and fans alike." Oriard notes that, as early as the turn of the twentieth century, writers like Jack London's friend James Hopper were penning tales about football as an expression of a "romantic primitivism." In the 1920s, Lewis Mumford attributed the rise of spectator sports to the reaction of a population "drilled and regimented and depressed to such an extent that it needs at least a vicarious participation in difficult feats of strength or skill or heroism in order to sustain its waning life-sense." By the 1950s, magazines like *Dissent* were arguing that football's popularity was a response to "the drudgery of everyday life," and an *Esquire* writer observed that the sport was an answer to the "decline of exuberance in daily life."[15] Dunning agrees, noting that the emotional arousal that comes from watching sports helps people fight boredom and pull themselves out of their deadening routines by surrendering to the "emotional contagion" that comes with being part of a large, expectant crowd.[16] It is not just the role of passive spectator that the fan plays but also, depending on the fan, the role of actor in their own show. In this way, fans connect not just to the players in the contest but to each other as well. The stronger this bond becomes, the more intense the loyalty to one's imagined community. Nowhere in sports is this bond closer than in Raider Nation.

The fans we interviewed frequently referred to fellow Raiders fans as "60,000 of your closest friends," "my tribe," "brothers," and, perhaps most commonly, as "family." Hostile observers inclined to see only machismo and violence in a gathering of Raiders faithful would be surprised to discover a loving community. "You will never get the full picture of Raiders fans until you visit the parking lot before a home game. My group has one of the best tailgate parties, which includes a DJ, full bar, and pigs roasting on spits. Race, age, gender, or socio-economic status means nothing. All people are bound together by their love of the Raiders," said Raiders fan Andrew Miller as he invited the authors to "come to our party and feel the love." Miller, who says he is "downright evangelical" about the "spectacle in the parking lot," views his attendance at the games as "one-third tribal gathering, one-third sociology experiment, and one-third football." As we spent the season wandering from tailgate to tailgate, we were fed, offered beers, given presents, and generally welcomed with open arms. In one of many instances of Raiders fan generosity, Kelly was given a "Raiders Girl" cap straight off the head of a fellow fan after she admired it on the wearer. "I'll get another," the woman told us after we tried to give it back. This gift was followed by a full course of carne asada and a Corona from her husband. Far from an isolated incident, this sort of Raiders potlatch is the norm in the parking lot. Come who may, no questions asked. What this clearly illustrates is that, for many fans, the social event of commingling with fellow members of their imagined community is equally or perhaps even more important than the game itself.

Dunning also points out that such emotional involvement stems from the fact that "one has to *care*" in one or more of three ways: about the sport itself; if one is a participant, about one's own performance; and if one is a spectator, about the performance of one's chosen contender. Fans have to identify deeply, or their emotional gears will not be fully engaged.[17] Nowhere is this identification with team and identity stronger than with Raider Nation. Even as the team's moves and political and legal battles drive marginal fans away, hard-core Raiders fans maintain a quasi-religious bond with their team. The fear that Raiders fans generate in opposing fans is as much a product of their intensity as it is any actual threat of violence. When Raiders fans speak about the nature of their connection to their team, their language is fraught with passion: their "gears" are clearly engaged. When asked to describe their fandom, Raiders fans almost universally referred to "passion" and "loyalty." Other descriptions included "intensity," "commitment," "heart," "rabid," "boisterous," "take no prisoners," and "totally nuts." As Raiders fan Michel Hines puts it, "I think Raiders fans are just a little over the edge most of the time."

Along with passionate identification with the team and its fan community usually comes hostility toward the other team and/or its fans. As Dunning notes, "It is easy to observe how frequently the very constitution of 'we groups' and their continuation over time seem to depend on the regular expression of hostility towards and even actual combat with members of 'they groups.'" The result of this is that "patterns of conflict appear to arise regularly in conjunction with this basic form of human bonding." In the vast majority of cases, the hostility of Raiders fans is limited to playful rivalry, heckling, and or some symbolic form of defamation. Fans in the Black Hole have been known to dress a blow-up doll in the jersey of a particularly loathed opposing player and pig roasting tailgaters at times robe the unfortunate swine in Broncos or 49ers wear.[18]

In a small minority of cases, fan rivalry escalates into violence that, as we shall see in later chapters, is frequently tied to insults that speak to identity. For instance, at a 1997 Raiders–Chargers game we attended in San Diego, the verbal sparring in the cheap seats was rowdy, profane, but harmless ("Chargers suck!" "Fuck the Raiders," etc.), until a Chargers fan sitting in front of six Raiders fans went from "fucking Raiders fans" to "low-class Mexican scum Raider fans." That transgression earned him a brief flight down the stairs. Fortunately for the racist Bolts fan, he emerged bruised but otherwise intact and, amazingly, the security guard ejected him rather than the Raiders fan who had hurled him halfway down the view section. The man and his friends who tossed the Chargers rooter were not gang members or criminal deviants, but rather carpenters from San Jose. I had spoken with them before the game and learned that they traveled to nearly every Raiders road game in the western United States, spending a healthy chunk of their income to do so. Hence, insulting the Raiders, already an integral part of their self-identification, was bad, but adding the racial slur made it a total assault on their identity—enough to turn a man who had struck me as a pretty nice, even gracious guy to an act of fairly extreme violence. What the incident illustrates is how when deeply felt fan identity is mixed with other forms of identity (race, class, region), the result can be explosive. "Raiders suck," can quickly get translated into "you suck," and in some cases it is unwise to cross that line.

It's All about Al

> Raiders fans are beyond description, literally, in some cases. They are wild and crazy, with outrageous costumes. They are safe and sane, Dockers and polo shirt types who happen to follow one of the unique organizations of sport.. . . . And, yes, most of them are employed, otherwise they wouldn't be able to afford the costs. . . . I grew up in Oakland, a Raiders fan. It is different now, a different fan base and a different level of devotion. Most were ticked off when Al moved the team to L.A., but some drove south for the games. When the team returned, it had to rebuild the loyalty. Mistrust remains.
>
> *Monte Poole,* Oakland Tribune

Just as imagined political communities transcend "actual inequality and exploitation," Raider Nation manages to do so as well. Perhaps the most obvious manifestation of this is the relationship between the fans and the Raiders organization. How, as one Cleveland Browns fan asked me in the course of my research, can Raiders fans forgive Al Davis? "He screwed them in Oakland *and* Los Angeles and now he's suing the city of Oakland. If [Cleveland owner] Art Modell had tried to come back to town along with the Browns, his life would have been in danger. Are Raiders fans just stupid or what?" The answer to this query is no, Raiders fans are no dumber than any other average sports fan who is willing to help further enrich millionaires who care more about luxury box revenues and their bottom line than about their fans or their host cities.

A serious look at professional sports organizations would not find a single franchise that puts loyalty to community over profit. As sports journalist Mel Durslag put it, "These guys aren't Eagle Scouts . . . You're dealing with cutthroat guys."[19] Indeed, decades before the Raiders left Oakland, Walter O'Malley crushed Brooklyn Dodgers fans by moving the storied team to Los Angeles. Of the Bay Area teams, the Giants, Athletics, and Warriors were all "relocated" from the East Coast and the Midwest. While Davis's heavily contested antitrust court victory and subsequent relocation are the most controversial example, numerous other National Football League teams have happily abandoned their hometowns as well (the St. Louis Cardinals for Phoenix, the Los Angeles Rams for Anaheim and then St. Louis, the Baltimore Colts for Indianapolis, the Cleveland Browns for Baltimore, the Houston Oilers for Tennessee, New York Giants for New Jersey, and the Dallas Cowboys for Irving, as well as a number of moves from old to new stadiums within the same city). As of this writing, even the Raiders' bitter gridiron and courtroom archrivals, the San Diego Chargers, are using the threat of a move back to their original home in Los Angeles as leverage for a better deal from the city of San Diego. And it's not just in the world of sports where loyal consumers and employees get screwed. In the new Gilded Age of Enron, there is hardly an area of American life where one's activities as a consumer do not inspire some form of cognitive dissonance. Sport is simply another part of our increasingly "cutthroat" economy, but many fans cling to the illusion that, except for "bad apples" like Davis, our games are somehow free from the taint of ruthless commerce. Other fans react ambivalently, cynically, or contemplate rejecting sports altogether.

Al Davis's decision to move the Raiders from Oakland to Los Angeles in 1982 was a crushing blow to the city, and to hard-core Raiders fans in particular. The reaction was frequently angry. As John Matuszak remembered it:

In Oakland, where the fans had embraced the team so warmly for so many years, it was an ugly time to be a Raider. People wore t-shirts that said FUCK THE RAIDERS and OAKLAND TRAITORS. The bolder ones shouted obscenities at us when they saw us on the street. Oakland fans turned on the Raiders and I don't blame them. They had been the greatest fans in the world, and now they felt like their team was getting stolen from them.

San Francisco Chronicle reporter Glenn Dickey recounts the remarkable fan protest at a December 7 (Pearl Harbor Day) Monday-night game where, "To protest the imminent move to Los Angeles, a large segment of the crowd—as much as a fourth of it—stayed out of the stadium for the first five minutes of the game. (One distraught fan brought a banner that read: WILL ROGERS NEVER MET AL DAVIS.)" Despite the large number of absent fans, Dickey notes that "the ABC-TV crew did not mention the fans' protest, nor did the cameras pan over the empty seats in the stadium." Former Raiders quarterback Jim Plunkett also remembers the boycott and adds that "at the two-minute warnings, the fans held up signs which had been passed out: 'Save Our Raiders.' The entire stadium looked like one big card stunt." Plunkett's sympathy with the fans was lukewarm, however, as he surmised that "the Raider fans deserve a team—not necessarily the Raiders." The *Oakland Tribune*'s Dave Newhouse, on the other hand, sided with the protesting fans, bemoaned Al Davis's "homicidal heart" and fumed, "Kick Al Davis out of football for good." In *Raiders Forever,* John Lombardo observes that "no one could have predicted that the team and the city would perfectly complement each other—a bond shattered when Al Davis dumped Oakland for Los Angeles in 1982, only to return in 1995."[20]

Lombardo, along with a good number of other Davis critics, argues that "Davis successfully sued the NFL for antitrust violations, winning the right to move the team to Los Angeles but tearing out the heart of the team's image." Davis's true feelings on the matter remain a mystery. After winning the legal battle that cleared the way for the Raiders' move to Los Angeles he said, "I don't look at it as a victory. I'm not emotionally elated. I have a lot of love for the fans in Oakland. The people are excellent, the community is excellent. They [the Coliseum Board] just ruined it; they destroyed it." Interestingly, a few years earlier in a bizarre *Inside Sports* interview, Davis's thoughts about "love" were somewhat different, "I only want to be loved by certain people—my players, the people I live with. No, not by humanity. I push it away because I don't need it. Maybe everyone else should work at it, but we need a few people to lead and dominate and get things done. I feel the role of love belongs to other people."[21]

Despite a Super Bowl victory in 1984 and a handful of playoff appearances in subsequent years, Davis began squabbling with the city of Los Angeles and the L.A. Memorial Coliseum Commission about luxury boxes and the team failed to emerge as the city's favorite. When rumors began to fly about the Raiders' possible return to Oakland in 1990, a *Los Angeles Times* poll placed the Raiders fifth in popularity among L.A.'s pro teams, and a poll in the *Oakland Tribune* showed that only 17 percent of Oakland residents thought it was "very important" that the Raiders return to the city out of the 39 percent calling it important. All the legal and political wrangling had clearly taken a toll on fan support. After negotiations to return the team to Oakland failed, loyal fans held public burnings of Raiders memorabilia.[22] When the team finally did return to Oakland in 1995 after the long-sought L.A. luxury boxes did not materialize, many observers were skeptical. In 2001, Lombardo noted the possibility of history repeating itself a third time:

> Once again Davis is disenchanted with Oakland. He is suing city officials for what he claims is lost season-ticket revenue and he wants to make more money through the already over-marketed NFL, catering now to the well-heeled fan willing to shell out big dollars for club seats, personal seat licenses, and luxury suites—all designed to make owners even richer. Raiders fans in Oakland haven't responded. The city lacks a substantial corporate base to financially support the Raiders. Home games in the Coliseum don't sell out, causing the Raiders to black-out local telecasts of their home games. The fans who've already been burned by Davis and face new threats that the team will relocate have put even more distance between themselves and the great teams of the 1970s.[23]

Disillusioned with Oakland for a second time, Al Davis went to court to seek recompense from his betrayers for the sellout crowds that he claims were promised him. Davis's testimony during the summer 2003 trial of the Raiders' $1.1 billion fraud lawsuit against the Oakland-Alameda County Coliseum

Board, Dublin businessman Ed DeSilva, and accounting firm Arthur Andersen did little to reassure Oakland fans that he was not looking for a way out of the East Bay once again. The *Oakland Tribune* reported that the 73-year-old Davis, clad in a black suit with a silver tie, "glared around the packed courtroom" as he denied any prior knowledge of problems with ticket sales and made his case that the Raiders had been "conned" into signing the deal that brought them back to Oakland. Of the Raiders' largesse toward the community he said, "I was signing to give the people of the East Bay a chance to see if they could do what they said they could do, and that is sell out the stadium . . . but it in no way bound me."

Indeed, the Raiders still claim that their 1989 $18 million settlement with the NFL gives them the rights to the Los Angeles market and are pursuing yet another new trial against the league for undermining their efforts to build a state-of-the-art stadium at Hollywood Park. Thus, as the *Oakland Tribune* reports, "The NFL may be faced with resolving the Raiders dispute through trial or settlement before being able to return a franchise to the nation's No. 2 media market." During his stay in Los Angeles, Davis felt conned by the Los Angeles Memorial Coliseum Commission as well. After the commission couldn't come up with the money to build luxury boxes in 1987, Raiders front office spokesman Irv Kaze claimed, "We question the Coliseum Commission's credibility. They have violated all the previous agreements. They have misled us."[24]

Meanwhile, back in Oakland in 2003 the Raiders deal had cost East Bay taxpayers $20 million more in public subsidies, $173.5 million since the team returned to Oakland in 1995. As the *Oakland Tribune* reported in May of 2003, "The $20 million will be plucked directly from the general funds of the City of Oakland and Alameda County, delivering another blow to the public agencies, which both have staggering budget deficits of their own." In the mid-nineties, East Bay taxpayers were told that the $350 million bonds floated by the city and county to revamp Oakland's sports facilities would be paid for by Arena and Coliseum profits. Revenues have not covered the bonds, however, primarily because of the Raiders deal. The Raiders, who pay none of the $2 million post-9/11 insurance premium costs or any of the $528,000 credit card fees for the sales of their tickets and personal seat licenses, cost the city and county $900,000 in legal fees for April 2003 alone. By the time Davis's case against the Oakland-Alameda County Coliseum, Ed DeSilva, and Arthur Andersen went to the jury, it had already cost the public $6 million.[25]

In late August 2003 the jury came back with a verdict that surprised many and pleased no one.[26] By ruling that the coliseum had acted negligently, but that none of the defendants were guilty of intentionally defrauding the Raiders, the jury granted the Raiders $34.2 million of the up to $833 million that Davis was seeking. According to the *Oakland Tribune*, Raiders attorney Roger Dryer "placed his head in his hands as the judge gave a summary of the judgment" and initially said, "We're disappointed with the verdict. We're disappointed with the numbers." Later the Raiders website quoted Dryer proclaiming, "It is a vindication and validation for the Raiders." The *San Francisco Chronicle*, on the other hand, headed its article: "Jurors reject Raiders' claims of fraud. $34.2 million award for negligence not what Davis wanted." For their part, Coliseum Board lawyers were celebrating and vowing to "never pay a dime." Clearly the spin and appeal cycle was kicking into overdrive.[27]

Immediately after the verdict the *San Francisco Chronicle* reported "Raiders Fans Unsure if Verdict Means Their Team Won or Lost" and featured an interview with Mark "Spike" Shadinger, who characterized the whole affair as "millionaires suing millionaires." The grocery store truck driver was not optimistic as he explained, "I think everyone is tired of the fights between Al Davis and the city of Oakland . . . I think everyone wants this thing settled so we don't have our town suing our team. But the scary thing is, this won't settle it. Davis will appeal, and it will just drag out." Hoping against hope that the Raiders' lawyers might take some time off their crusade against Oakland to "trademark him as the NFL's first official fan," Spike would be sadly disappointed as the lawyers for the Raiders and the Coliseum traded legal volleys for months to come until, in March 2004, Judge Richard K. Park of Sacramento put the parties in legal limbo. Ruling both that the Oakland-Alameda County Coliseum board was "essentially defunct" and that the Raiders could not seek city or county taxpayer funds until the court ruled on a joint appeal, Park kept the legal battle going for at least another season. Outraged by the ruling, the Raiders' attorneys pointed out that the award would be $6 million higher by 2005 because it earns 10 percent interest annually.[28]

In the meantime, Ed DeSilva, who was cleared (at taxpayers' expense) of any wrongdoing in the August 2003 verdict, sued the Port of Oakland over a business dispute. If that weren't enough for the good people of the East Bay, they were treated to the news that the Oakland Athletics had hired a businessman from San Jose to look for a new home for the town's baseball club. Oaklanders were then given the opportunity to watch yet another trial as the McGah family unsuccessfully sued their business partner, Al Davis, in an effort to remove him as the Raiders general partner for withholding financial records from them. As *San Francisco Chronicle* reporter Ray Ratto put it after the initial ruling in the Raiders trial in August 2003, "All this begs the question, 'Aren't any of these people even slightly worried that there might be a hell?'"[29]

Even before most of the 2003–2004 legal circus unfolded, longtime *Oakland Tribune* writer and Raiders observer Dave Newhouse had seen enough. When we interviewed him via e-mail in June 2003, we asked him for his impressions of the Raiders organization and its treatment of the fans and the community. His response was scathing:

The Raider organization? It has learned how to win again, but it hasn't learned how to stop lying. Pride, Poise, and Paranoia. That's how I'd describe the organization. You might admire Al Davis, but don't ever trust him. Oakland rescued him from a deplorable situation in Los Angeles that he created, and now he's suing us for $1.2 billion, possibly to return to Los Angeles since the NFL wants to put two teams in there. Some gratitude. For all his charity—Dr. Samuel Johnson said "Charity is the last act of a scoundrel"—and progressive thinking, Davis is the lowest of the low. He is as Pete Rozelle described him best, a charming rogue. Davis said he loves his fans; he turns his head at violence. Do for the community? How about trying to take his team out of here twice? What did Hunter Thompson say about Al Davis? Oh yes, "He makes Darth Vader look like a punk." Getting the picture?

Newhouse is also critical of what he describes as a "blindly loyal Raider Nation" that defends Davis unthinkingly. Davis biographer Mark Ribowsky, on the other hand, has noted that Raiders fans are "perhaps the only people in the country who could separate him from the substance of the team" because they had not "sanctified Al Davis." So how have fans reacted to the politics of football in Oakland and elsewhere? Clearly, a significant number of them in the East Bay and Los Angeles have rejected the team, but by no means all. Large numbers of Oakland fans traveled to games in L.A. and lots of L.A. fans now come up to Oakland, as shown by the early morning game-day shuttle flights packed with rowdy revelers clad in silver and black.[30]

Monte Poole, who covers the Raiders for the *Oakland Tribune*, told us that "as long as the team is a contender, the fans keep showing up. Not just locally, but nationally. Traveling with the team, I've grown accustomed to seeing Raiders fans filling hotel lobbies on the road, wherever the team happens to stay for the weekend. They come from far and wide." Thus the Raiders' moves have not killed their fan base in either town, nor had any negative effect on the hinterlands of Raider Nation from New York to Texas. They sell more merchandise than any other NFL club and draw huge crowds to road games. While Raiders fans may not have bankrupted themselves for personal seat licenses, they do sell out the big games, and the crowds are still the most frenetic in professional sports. The problem with attendance probably has more to do with the fact that, as Glenn Dickey observed of the new Oakland Raiders ticket prices, "The type of fan who used to come to Raiders games would be priced out of most seats." Fans from the flatlands of Oakland or East L.A. might still loyally follow the team, but mostly on television supplemented with a live game or two a year.[31]

Reading Al

> Many of us have been closet Raider fans for many years. . . . I always
> preferred the Raiders. They were rough, tough, rotten guys. The Niners
> were Mr. Clean—Bill Walsh was a rather God-like figure. . . . The Raid-
> ers were like the Grateful Dead.
>
> *Herb Caen,* San Francisco Chronicle

Our research shows that Raider Nation is not monolithic in its response to Al Davis and the Raiders organization. Some are "blindly loyal" to Al Davis, while others look at him like the hated president of their beloved country. These two extremes, along with those sprinkled between the two poles, happily co-exist in the imagined community of Raider Nation. Just as love of country can push real existing class differences and conflicts of interest aside in the service of America, devotion to Raider Nation allows fans to transcend the harsh socio-economic reality of the fan–owner dynamic, although not always in the same way.

Most fans don't blindly swallow the propaganda of their sports team's ownership wholeheartedly.[32] The fans who constitute the imagined community of Raider Nation aren't totally free to choose the context that constructs their community's meaning, but they *are* free to choose how to read various elements of the Raiders story. They are not mere dupes of a corporate plot to exploit them. Thus for most Raiders fans, Al Davis is not entirely synonymous with the Raiders, but rather part of the story that is the Raiders. The Davis myth means different things to different fans. Having worked hard to create his own myth, Davis has aided this process by ensuring his continued existence as a mysterious cipher into which fans can read a variety of meanings. Davis haunts the press box, brooding behind his oversized glasses, raising the hand bearing his Super Bowl ring to his mouth as if in prayer. Who knows what phantoms reside in the depths of his black-and-silver heart?

Davis is seen in a number of ways by Raiders fans. Some, like the webmaster at www.darthraider.com, defend Al wholeheartedly in the political arena as a loyal figure:

The L.A. Coliseum Commission screwed Al Davis. He brought the team here with the promise of them fixing the area up, adding parking and putting in Luxury Suites. They never followed through on any of it so he took the team back to Oakland. He had a better offer from Baltimore, but loyally kept the team in California. Now we find out Oakland screwed him too. Al Davis gets a bad rap from most of the media just like us fans do. But, look at what he does for his former players. Almost all of them that were elected to the HOF [Hall of Fame] asked him to do their induction speech. And Marcus Allen, Al Michael and Pete Rozelle are not some of my favorite people.

Mike Rosacker is also a big Davis fan:

The reason I became a psychotic Raider fan is because of Mr. Davis who I'm proud to have tattoos of him on both arms. I can't exactly summarize over 15 years of research into this man in a few sentences. But bottom line, he's done more for this league than anybody in this game. 99% of his players love him, and they are treated first class by Mr. Davis.

Darth and Mike, like the other Raiders fans who defend and identify with Davis see him as a battler, loyal to his allies, who wins against the odds and epitomizes the Raiders slogan "Commitment to Excellence." Rather than feeling screwed by the Raiders owner, they side with him and see him as synonymous with the team.

Other fans identify with the antihero Al. As Dan Bartolomeo puts it, "I really like Al Davis, even when I think he's dead wrong and lying through his teeth." Fans like Dan are adherents of the "Just Win, Baby!" (no matter what) ethos. These fans see Davis warts and all and proclaim, "He's a bastard but he's our bastard." What fans of this type recognize is that all owners are evil but at least our owner is interestingly evil. For the antihero crowd, many of the characteristics that Dave Newhouse bemoans are a badge of honor. The story of Davis bamboozling former co-owner Wayne Valley out of control of the team is seen not as a mark of shame by the antiheroes but as a badge of darkside honor. These Raiders fans are the ones who always rooted for the bad guy in the TV westerns. As Raiders fan Buck Allred puts it:

Al Davis represents the maverick inherent in the collective American psyche. He is many things: pioneering, progressive, a vanguard, while at the same time he is a throwback, or, some would say, behind the times. His kindness and generosity to "his" people (former players, etc.) is well known, yet he is perhaps more often remembered for his heavy-handed tactics with those who would defy him. He blazes his own path; he walks to the beat of a different drum. And, to Al Davis, at the end of the day, it all comes down to just one thing: Just Win, Baby! What could be more American than that? Besides, when I was a kid, I always rooted for the cowboy with the black hat.

Yet another group of fans see Al as "Davis the progressive and integrator." These fans rightly note that Al Davis let his renegade players dress and act how they wanted, ran a libertarian organization, was sympathetic to black players' concerns in the sixties, and has made a series of barrier-breaking hires. Tom Flores was the first Mexican-American head coach, Art Shell the first black head coach, and Amy Trask the first female CEO in the National Football League. Raiders fan Eugene Jeffers enjoys the "swagger" and "take no prisoners attitude" along with the antihero fans, but he also says, "I like rooting for a team that has an owner that is colorblind, gender blind and rallies the organization around winning. I like the fact that down and out people get a second chance with the Raiders." A large number of fans agree, forgiving Davis's other transgressions for this virtue.

Then there is the "Football genius/courtroom cad" crowd. Aficionados of this stripe point to Davis's undeniable mastery in turning the pathetic early sixties Raiders into the winningest team in professional sports. "He took castoffs and turned them into champions," said Jim. "Nobody else could pick these guys up like he did again and again. It was like magic." In the next breath, however, these fans dismiss Al's legal maneuvers, "Now he's too caught up in the endless legal stuff. He's lost his touch."

Other Raiders fans see Davis as "Shakedown Al." Stephanie Sandlin recalls "being devastated when they went to L.A. It was one of the most heartbreaking things Al could've done to Oakland. That town loved that team. All for cash and greed." Stephanie, along with many Bay Area fans, "lost interest in the 'L.A. Raiders'" but she says the team's return to Oakland "rekindled my passion." As for the Davis myth:

> Don't get me wrong, I love the Raiders but I also hate certain things about them . . . The thing I am displeased most about is Al Davis' tendency to litigate and never be happy with his lot. He is without a doubt one of the most storied men still running a franchise. He's done great things for the game, the league and the Raiders. He also in the past has been vicious and has bitten the hand that feeds him. That annoys me. In the last 20 years if I were to venture an opinion I think Al has grown a little more eccentric (it sadly can happen to brilliant people) and has surrounded himself with "yes men." This has prevented him from being kept in check and allowed the more negative aspects of his personality to come to the front. . . . With this trial that's going on in Sacramento, Al trying to shakedown the Coliseum managers. The "promises" of sellouts. It's crap. It's like the White Star line saying the *Titanic* was unsinkable. They never did (it was a shipbuilding magazine that actually said that) but it made it into the story. Same with the Raiders. . . . It's just Al going after more money. More notably, it's not like the Raiders are an organization in the red anyway. Also, Al needs to take some of the blame because the first few years back did suck. Sucking does affect attendance. Al got a good home and old loving fans when he returned to Oakland. Now, that old feeling of unease is coming back. I worry he'll pick up the Raiders and leave again. If he does that, I'm done with the team. It breaks my heart to say that. I truly do love them. I just can't handle Al breaking my heart twice.

Gorilla Rilla gets lucky

Photo: Joseph A. Blum

David, another Raiders fan who has tired of Davis's legal maneuvering, observes, "The Bay Area as a whole has had some trouble forgiving the Raiders for leaving Oakland." His list of "a few items that would help ticket sales in Oakland" includes "1) Time; 2) Less legal battles between City/County/Raiders; 3) [Lower] ticket prices/PSL [Personal Seat License] fees. The economy has been in a slump for several years—especially hurting the Bay Area. Fans currently pay some of the highest prices in the league. The worst of this section is known as 'Mt. Davis.'" David points out that Mt. Davis includes some of the worst seats in professional football priced "between $57 and $60 per [seat]!" Many of the other fans we interviewed agreed with this assessment, preferring to catch what David called a "pirate telecast" to being bilked for Mt. Davis privileges. As one Raiders fan put it, "Sell Mt. Davis tickets for 20 dollars a piece and you'll get sellouts."

Other fans' problems with Al Davis go beyond ticket prices to his management style. Kerry Smith says, "I'm not particularly fond of Al Davis because I feel he interferes with the coaches' responsibilities." Stephen Dixon is a big fan, but not because of Al: "I love the Raider Mystique. I have had serious doubts about Al Davis's competence over the years but have stuck with the team. I was very disappointed when [Raiders head coach] Gruden left as I felt he was finally a coach that could stand on his own without Al's strong influence." So what is there to be done? Stephen's radical proposal won't go over well in Raiders headquarters: "I still feel the franchise will be better off once Al Davis retires (or more like, passes on, as I don't think he will ever relinquish power while he still has a breath left)."

There are even moments when the bonds that hold the imagined community together break and fans revolt against their oppressors in the Raiders hierarchy and the Oakland Football Marketing Association. Perhaps the most extreme wave of fan anger came when the team had just returned to Oakland from Los Angeles and, as the *Los Angeles Times* reported, fans who were "frustrated over expensive 'personal seat licenses' and the failure of the team to offer season-ticket holders coveted seats for the Dallas Cowboys game" went nuts and "brandished guns, threw chairs and threatened the staff." Former ticket director Steve Ferguson remembers, "There was one incident in our office in which a fellow who was frustrated set a gun on the table and said to the customer service person, 'Are you going to take care of my problem, or am I?'" The wave of Raiders rage, according to the *Times*, had "employees crying in their cubicles" because they were "beginning to take it personally." In the end, crisis counselors and Pinkerton guards were brought in to deal with the emotional and martial needs of the staff. Although some of the ticket glitches have been worked out and such a wave of raw anger has yet to recur, getting the run-around from the ticket office is still a big fan complaint, though not big enough for most fans to secede from the nation.[33]

While some angry fans have rejected the Davis myth, other fans have resorted to irony. Part of this group sees Al as a fading eccentric who's in a kind of nutty decline. The big hair and the oversized jumpsuits are key for these folks. "Is that really club soda he's swilling up there in the press box?" asks one wag. Other fans of "Ironic Al" have invented their own narratives to explain the team's seemingly endless legal adventures. As Raiders fan Gary Glasser of San Leandro puts it: "It is often said that Al Davis is the anti-Christ. I merely say that Al died many years ago in Los Angeles. Disneyland took the likeness of him and made him an 'animatron.' Like those you see at Disneyland. He really has been dead for years. I am sure the commissioners of the NFL, past and present, will argue that."

A final subset of symptomatically postmodern Raiders boosters adopt Al's business strategies with tongue firmly planted in cheek. Laughing at the absurdity of the "third move," such fans discuss potential new homes in towns called Oakland across the United States or debate what truly constitutes "the Bay Area." Does Stockton count? How about Portland? Other places where they have bays? New Jersey? Thus, rather than creating cognitive dissonance for fans measuring the chasm between their own interests and Davis's interests, the existence of the Davis myth as a site of fan fancy, debate, and/or imaginative play actually helps strengthen the bonds that unite Raider Nation as an imagined community—everybody's got an opinion about Al.

Class and Subculture

> The Raider Nation is real . . . now you see other teams claiming nations, no one ever did before Raider Nation! We are globally represented and very well known for our love of our team. We are the Raider Nation and there is no other nation in any other sport or in any other team around the NFL . . . the Raider Nation stands alone!
>
> *Victor Cotto, Raiders fan*

Raider Nation does not just allow fans to transcend the exploitation of fans and the inequality between fan and owner, it also unites fans across class, racial, gender, regional, generational, and cultural lines. When it comes to class, as has already been noted, Raider Nation has solid working-class roots. Its geographic home is Oakland, and the tough flatland neighborhoods of the city and its blue-collar suburbs supply more fans than the affluent hills. As *San Francisco Chronicle* reporter and Oakland resident Jim Zamora told us, "Perhaps the highest concentrations of hard-core fans can be found in the flatland neighborhoods along International Boulevard–East 14th Street starting just east of Lake Merritt all the way to the far reaches of Hayward, and along San Pablo Avenue from downtown Oakland through Berkeley, Albany, and Richmond to El Sobrante." The perpetual poor stepsister to more fashionable, well-heeled San Francisco, the East Bay is more West Coast grit than California granola. Zamora observes, "These are parts of the Bay Area where pickup trucks outnumber SUVs and the team's pirate symbol is ubiquitous."[34]

The Raiders' Los Angeles fan base has frequently been mischaracterized by writers like Al Davis biographer Mark Ribowsky, who saw the team's move to "Hollywood" as a "forced mating of lunch pail and sushi" that traded its working-class fan base for "new fans from the rabid dens of Bel Air and Malibu." Others like Glenn Dickey note that "the area around the Los Angeles Coliseum has deteriorated badly in recent years," cite examples of fan violence, and claim that the Raiders "never developed a loyal constituency" in Los Angeles. Many others, including some Raiders fans hostile to Los Angeles or L.A. suburbanites afraid of the inner city, speak as if no one ever attended games in L.A. except for a gathering of some 50,000 Crips and Bloods. All of these characterizations are wildly inaccurate.[35]

Just as Raiders fans in Northern California are dispersed throughout the Bay Area, fans were and are widely dispersed throughout Los Angeles and Southern California. There are booster clubs in Los Angeles, South Gate, Torrance, Hawthorne, Carson, Covina, Highland, Anaheim, Orange, Canoga Park, the Eastside, and parts farther east and south. They range from the suburban San Fernando Valley in the north to suburban Orange County in the south and include the Eastside Raider Nation and clubs in the gritty industrial areas of the city. The area around the Los Angeles Coliseum is part of what the premier scholar of Los Angeles, Mike Davis, has called, "a vast city within a city" where the "browning of Los Angeles's industrial working class" has taken place. It is this part of the Raiders' L.A. fan base that came to associate the team's colors with street toughness. While some L.A. gangs did adopt the team's pirate logo and occasionally showed up at games, the assertion that gangs totally define the L.A. portion of Raider Nation is the product of fearful suburban imaginations. Much like Raider Nation in Oakland, Raider Nation in L.A. is a tough multi-ethnic blue-collar fan base, but it is not just a large extension of the street gangs.[36]

It is worth noting briefly here that there is a small subgroup within Raider Nation that has come to associate the team's "outlaw" image with literal outlaw behavior. Interestingly, the most notorious acts of Raiders fan violence were not committed by members of the Oakland chapter of the Hells Angels or L.A.'s East 14th Street Gang, but by regular fans who "overidentified" with the cutthroat image, perhaps as a way of compensating for powerlessness in other areas of their lives. The Raider Bandit was a bank guard from Sacramento, the Raiders nut who savagely beat a Steelers fan into a coma in Los Angeles was a white kid from the L.A. suburb of Augora, and the Silver and Black rooter who stabbed a Chargers fan in the stands in San Diego was a mechanic from Norwalk. This subgroup is a miniscule percentage of the overall fan base, and many Raiders adherents dismiss them as "not real fans." Raiders fan Terry Gartner's thoughts on the matter are representative of this view: "As for the fans . . . I'm afraid to say that there is an element of behavior that has attached itself to the Raiders and their games. Unfortunate, but true. And that, for the lack of a better word, gang mentality has given all Raiders fans a bad name." A distanced observer might also note the presence of violence and other forms of extreme behavior across the spectrum and see that other NFL fans brawl and break the law as well. Indeed, a serious comparison study of Raiders fans and British soccer hooligans would find Raiders boosters to be pussycats.

For those who hate the team and its image, though, violent fans have come to stand in for all Raiders fans in a way that frequently is little more than a thin veil for class prejudice and racism. As one "Raider hater" we interviewed characterized both Oakland and Los Angeles fans, "I think both are scum really. Oakland because of its middle- to lower-class people and L.A. because of [the] South Central environment. Hell, taking my kid to a Raiders [game] in L.A. was like watching *Boyz in the Hood* over and over and over." Another hater put it this way, "A book on Raiders fans? You mean a book on lower class criminals and idiots?" For people like these, hating "Raiders fans" is a good way to express general prejudices about race and class that they might perhaps keep to themselves in a different context. Raiders fan Mohamed "NOOR" Ahmed cites having to encounter such attitudes as the worst thing about being a Raiders fan. He recalls, "Getting messed with by the cops when we were younger. Cops think you're in a gang because you're sporting Raider gear. Today, it's snobby people who think you're some kind of low-class, like some of these clowns I run into at Stanford shopping center when I pick up my girlfriend at work. Sometimes I just growl at them." Hence much of the Raiders "we feeling" is fostered by a collective reaction to the way "they" demean Raiders fans. In this way, the imagined community of Raider Nation (from underclass to white collar) is a fan subculture that shares a sense of persecution and revels in its perceived "difference."[37]

Cultural studies scholar Dick Hebdige has pointed out that subcultures, "express forbidden contents" such as "consciousness of class, consciousness of difference." Clearly this is the case for a large percentage of Raiders fans though from varying perspectives. As one Indian fan put it, "Growing up, the Raiders, and Raiders fans have always been prejudged by the actions of a few. Throughout my life, I've drawn parallels to how the Raiders are perceived and how I'm perceived." Raiders fan Derek Ottman notes that "Raiders fans have a lot in common with kids who end up in alternative high school. Under 'the system' they don't fit in as a model student." Dave Kosta remembers, "My Dad, who was a biker back in the '70s, liked them because they were sort of the NFL's version of the Hell's Angels. A bunch of renegades and misfits, fun-loving guys who liked to drink beer and raise a little hell."[38]

Subcultures are, according to Hebdige, "profane articulations" that transgress "sartorial and behavioral codes" and sometimes includes the "breaking of laws." This explains the range of identification within Raider Nation, with a small minority engaging in law breaking (fighting, or peeing on 49ers fans sitting in front of them in the stands), while some others express their devotion with bootleg t-shirts that proclaim the wearer to possess a can of "100% Raider Whoop Ass" or denounce other teams and fans with a provocative "Fuck the Rest." Another subset of fans simply parties like maniacs and dresses up like pirates or evil skeletons, while others still might mildly express their "otherness" by frequently hanging out with this rowdy crew without doing much transgressive themselves.[39]

Hebdige also points out that subcultures are frequently met with "a wave of hysteria in the press" and elsewhere that is often characterized by "dread and fascination, outrage and amusement." Decades of press fascination, ridicule, and condemnation of Raiders fans attest that this is true for Raider Nation. *Los Angeles Times* columnist Bill Boyarsky bemoaned, "The Raiders have always viewed themselves as an outcast brigade, and their followers in the stands strive mightily to emulate." The *San Francisco Chronicle*'s Glen Dickey has portrayed Raiders fans as "a disgrace, drunken, and disorderly," who are no better than British soccer hooligans and who "look much like the Hells Angels." Jo Sparkes of the Arizona Sports Fan Network described an influx of Raiders fans at a 2002 Arizona Cardinals game as follows: "All we see are black and silver fans. Big ugly fans. Honestly, tattoos, gang scarves, teeth missing. Men and women alike. My season ticket holder lot is infested with Raider fanatics." Most recently, *Oakland Tribune* columnist Dave Newhouse lambasted the Raiders faithful as a bunch of "uncouth louts" and "a pack of drunken/stoned animals."[40]

A final aspect of Hebdige's subculture model that helps explain how the imaginary community of Raider Nation manages to hold groups with conflicting interests together (thugs and cops, white collars and blue collars, drunken heathens and sober Christians, and fans of all races) is how its symbols are both mainstream commercial properties (the Raiders logo) and pirated signs of rebel street culture (gangster, hip-hop, Chicano pride, etc.). Hence the multiple meanings of the Raiders' image form the glue that holds the nation together. Indeed, in the case of the "*cholo*-ization" of the Raiders logo (bootleg shirts that change the script to mimic *cholo* style for instance), the Raiders organization has reappropriated the latinized symbol and in turn sold it back to fans as "official" gear in Spanish or even in graffiti or low-rider style. In the case of the marketing of red and blue "Raiders" ball caps at some sports gear shops, even the gang use of the Raiders logo has been commercialized by savvy if unethical businesses. As Hebdige points out, the pirating of dominant cultural symbols and their subsequent "recuperation" by market forces is a part of the dynamic of subcultural style. Hence a white Republican from the Northern California suburb of Livermore and a black gang member from South Central Los Angeles might share an interest in football and some of the same "rebel" readings of the pirate shield, while their manifestations of "rebellion" would surely be quite different. The fact that many outsiders prefer to see the entirety of Raider Nation as a criminal underclass says more about the sordid political unconscious of the United States than it does about reality.[41]

While it is true that Raider Nation's heart is blue collar, it also includes physicists, doctors, teachers, lawyers, business executives, and a whole range of other professionals. As Raiders fan David Slack puts it:

Most non-Raider fans seem to have the impression that Raider fans are a bunch of crazy, heavy metal biker folks, but my impression is quite different. While there certainly may be some fans that fit that description, I think of all the sports fans out there Raider fans are the most diverse. I am a perfect example of that. I am a 38 year old, Ph.D. in Aerospace engineering who writes computer software for a living—hardly the stereotypical Raider fan you see on TV.

Many other white-collar Raiders fans we met made similar observations, but while some of them distanced themselves from the "criminal" image, no one felt the need to reject the blue-collar, working-class image. Indeed, they embraced it. Kris Snider makes that clear when he says, "The public would like to think that we are all drunks, rowdies, hooligans or gangbangers. Truth is a lot are professionals—doctors, lawyers, working class, normal people." For those who do not fit the working-class description economically, it stands in for grit, toughness, and authenticity. Daniel Chen, an oncologist and scientist at Stanford University, says, "Football is a tough sport and I like their tough, blue-collar, smash-it-up image.. . . I think having a Raiders sticker on my car, does 'protect' my car. It's sort of like being part of the Mafia."

Indeed, one might argue that in deindustrialized Oakland, the Raiders' blue-collar image is a throwback to the heyday of the great American industrial working class, a kind of nostalgic touchstone. While many of the men who built America may have had their unions busted and their jobs shipped overseas, in post-9/11 America the image of the noble beat cop, the heroic fireman, and the tough blue-collar guy is back (unless he's asking for a raise). Today, when the theme-parking, corporatization, and commodification of nearly every aspect of our lives threatens to make the American landscape into one big, antiseptic megamall, grit has an aura of authenticity that is otherwise lacking. As David Rowe points out, "A nation that has fragmented and lost any sense of common cultural identity," like the postmodern United States, "is preoccupied with the problems" that come with "capitalism and the erosion of authentic feeling and

It's all about the Raiders

cohesive, self-sustaining community." Hence, one central source of meaning in the Raider Nation is working-class authenticity and community, a commodity happily shared between actual working-class fans and their professional colleagues at the tailgate. Raiders populism is at the core of the imagined community of Raider Nation. You can check your elitism, racism, and class prejudices at the parking lot entrance on the way in.[42]

Raider Transcendentalism

> Raider fans are a surprisingly diverse bunch, despite their reputation as being mostly male swine with rap sheets and stunted vocabularies. I think many Raider fans revel in that notoriety regardless of their actual temperament or station in life; I know I do. There's a certain amount of personal satisfaction—perhaps it's just amusement—when fans of other teams find I'm not what they expected and they have to rearrange their prejudices. . . . [Raiders fans] are often wickedly funny and irreverent. They're loyal and optimistic even in the worst of times. And they bond like blood brothers.
>
> *Mike Sheehan, "The Beast of Bourbon," Raiders fan*

Raiders fans are downright Whitmanesque when it comes to the inclusive, egalitarian, democratic nature of their fan community. As Steve Lamoreaux puts it, "First, my impression of Raiders fans is that WE fans are a family." Marc Lein says of the Raiders and his fellow fans, "They taught me about life, that it isn't fair. The fans have been great, I have made friends of different ethnicity, religion, color, and creed." Mike Rosacker tells of a similar experience:

> The best part is going to Oakland. Wherever you go, you're hearing 3 different music artists AC/DC, Snoop, or 2Pac. The main thing I love about the Coliseum is the cultural fusion and the partying! Hispanics, African-Americans, white boys like me, and all other races join forces . . . The diversity, loyalty, and energy of the fans at the H.O.T. [House of Thrills] are something that you will NEVER find in any other NFL stadium.

Margaret Caraway, one of the many female fans we interviewed and a co-founder of a booster club, believes Raider Nation is notable because it is "accepting, friendly, and inclusive." She and other women fans attest to the fact that the imagined community of Raider Nation, though still predominantly male, is not hostile to women, as some feminist critics have claimed about football in general. James Shock notes how Raiders fans "are like family" where "all differences are put aside and people bond together," and Tim Bryner sees Raiders fans as a tribe remarkable for its "friendliness, camaraderie and common sharing of the tribal feeling . . . regardless of race, creed, color, religion, or whatever."

Mark Bryant, who is currently writing a novel on the Raiders and the city of Oakland, says of the city, "Oakland is a working man's, blue-collar mensch town." Raiders fans, according to Bryant, "see themselves as the underdog, the champions of the poor." Noting that "the East Bay is home to rich diversity, and people of all backgrounds," he holds up the "gritty" character of Raider Nation's place of origin in opposition to San Francisco, which is "only accessible to rich yuppies." Mary Anne, who is known in her family as a "Raider baby" because she was born just after the team's 1983 AFC Championship season, has feelings similar to Mark's: "I think for many in Oakland, the Raiders represent the little people, those of us that don't get any respect in society."

Raiders transcendentalism is what Mark calls "a state of mind, a religion, a daily sacrament." It brings with it a feeling of belonging and oneness. Bobby Davis remembers seeing his first game in Oakland as a pilgrimage of sorts:

I've always been a lone Raider kook for all these years, and suddenly I was part of a silver and black sea. It was like going to a secular Mecca. We parked next to some Latino guys from L.A. and became fast friends with them, talked all night with some guys sitting next to us in the stadium, and everybody was friendly and excited about the game. It was a big street party.

While being a part of "a silver and black sea" is not at quite the same mystic level as Ralph Waldo Emerson's "I become a transparent eyeball" musing in his

famous essay *Nature*, such expressions do show how the social event that is a
Raiders game transcends the contest and takes on a broader significance as site of
idealized racial and class harmony. Even while watching the Raiders on TV, fans
are small "d" democrats. Shawn Utterback recalls first meeting one of his good
friends in a sports bar in Richmond, Virginia, where they both went to watch
the Raiders: "We were completely different, ethnically, age wise, economically,
just about everything was different. But we had one thing in common. We both
loved the Raiders and ever since that day we became brothers and have watched
almost every single game of the last six seasons, together in that same bar."

Sometimes the game-day togetherness leads to other community-minded
activity totally outside the context of football. As Jan Frost says, "It is a real trip
to be part of something like the parking lot gang. Also the Black Hole group
gathers long before games, sometimes to eat and drink, sometimes to collect
food for Mother Wright and other groups. Everyone knows of the reputation of
the Raiders and their fans, but we're just regular people who love our team and
yes, we do charity work and donations also."

This sentiment was echoed by countless fans during our research who told us
about their work sending care packages to military personnel overseas in Afghan-
istan and Iraq, feeding the homeless, helping needy kids, or donating money to
help fight diseases. Stories of generosity abound. As one fan emphatically told us,
"Raiders fans will give you the shirt off their backs." While it is unclear whether
the sense of community that helps fans transcend their differences at the tailgate
or in the sports bar ultimately smoothes over racial, economic, regional, and/or
gender differences outside those contexts, it is certain that the experience, however transitory, of "one big family" is one of the most compelling and genuinely
meaningful aspects of Raider Nation.

The "one big family" of Raider Nation is held together and greatly expanded
by a sense of simultaneity and unity that transcends space and time. Today, the
ritual of the "simultaneous consumption" of media that Benedict Anderson says
gave birth to large-scale imagined communities centuries ago has gone into over-
drive. As Rowe notes, "Media sports texts" now have an "almost unprecedented

capacity to 'flow' across and around . . . 'economies of signs and space' in both local and global contexts." When these texts, "heavily loaded with symbolic value," are transmitted not just via the newspaper, but by radio, television, and the Internet, their consumers can be disconnected from the locality and/or the particular class, racial, gender, or other "necessary" aspects of fan identity and take on meaning independent of those things or adopt them regardless of any real connection to them. Hence the notion that one's team must be connected to one's city has been tossed into the dustbin of history by Direct TV and fifty-plus Raiders websites that make it possible to watch the game in real time and take part in the morning-after analysis of the big plays and bad calls.[43]

This shared consumption of Raiders football and the simultaneous rehash during the week that follows as well as the off-season are prime manifestations of what Rowe claims is the special magic of media sport: "It is able at particular moments to reconstruct symbolically disparate human groups, to make them feel at one with each other." According to Rowe, the feeling of unity created by this ritual of shared consumption goes beyond the game at hand to the creation of a shared myth that unites the past, present, and future: "Sport can connect the past, present and future, alternately trading on sepia-tinted nostalgia, the 'nowness' of 'live' action, and the anticipation of things to come." Thus members of Raider Nation from Poland to Maui who may never meet in the flesh can watch the game "live," confident of the fact they are doing so in concert with hundreds of thousands of their colleagues. They can also cite stories from the Raiders' historical canon of "great moments" and know that fellow chat room Raiders will recognize references to any number of Golden Era greats from Lamonica to Plunkett. Any member of Raider Nation worth his or her salt should also be able to hum the Raiders theme song, "The Autumn Wind," and know that AC/DC's "Back in Black" is the song that blares over the Coliseum speakers as the team takes the field. And if the team mantras, "Just Win, Baby!," "Pride and Poise," and "Commitment to Excellence," are not tattooed on his or her hindquarters, a Raiders fan should at least have them memorized. Thus a "massive" and "disagreeable cult," as Hunter S. Thompson imagines Raider Nation, is born.[44]

Señor Raider Man

One

Bin Laden Is a Raider Fan

Wartime Super Bowls are always dismal and lame.
Hunter S. Thompson, "The Last Super Bowl"

We are being plunged into a society where Big Brother has more control over what we do than we do and is jockeying itself into a position to have more control over what we think than we do.
Raiders fan Kim Nickel on the New World Order

RAIDERS GO HOME!
*Graffiti spray-painted on a billboard off Interstate 5
in San Diego during Super Bowl Week 2003*

I'm a life-long Raiders fan living in San Diego, so the 2003 Super Bowl seemed like a dream come true. After traveling to Oakland to see the Raiders clinch home field advantage for the playoffs with a 24-to-0 trouncing of the Kansas City Chiefs in a grueling downpour during their last regular season game, I returned again to see the Silver and Black destroy the New York Jets 30 to 10 and blow out the Tennessee Titans 41 to 24 to earn a trip to San Diego. Once I had displayed my loyalty by enduring a hideous monsoon for four quarters while sitting atop Mt. Davis and squinting downward for both playoff games, the Raiders had rewarded me by coming to win the big one in my own backyard. It was destiny. How could they not win? All that remained was the question of how *I* was going to make it to the Promised Land myself. At that moment, though, a faint but persistent voice in the back of my head started nagging me. "Every product represents the hope for a 'dramatic shortcut to the long-awaited promised land of total consumption'" it pestered. "But the fulfillment of this promise is possible only with the attainment of the totality of commodities," it continued. "A desire which excites the accumulation of commodities but which is ultimately insatiable," it nattered on irritatingly. I had another beer to drown the voice. Sometime in the midst of my alcohol-drenched giddy daze in the parking lot after the American Football Conference Championship game, my friends and I decided that we were going to the Super Bowl—by any means necessary.[1]

During that week, all of my postgraduate education and what little was left of my common sense deserted me to be replaced by an insane, self-destructive impulse to bankrupt myself and be publicly humiliated. I put off work and spent hours on the Internet and the telephone with ticket scalpers and my friends, who had also been dealing with scalpers for hours. Ranking somewhere below the amoeba on the hierarchy of living things, scalpers like to act as if they are doing you a great favor by *only* charging you twenty times the face value of a ticket when they could easily jack somebody else for thirty times face. Hell, if it weren't for their golden hearts, they'd be doing that very thing right now instead of waiting for you to come to your damn senses.

After days of this scuzzy form of psy-ops, we broke down. Rick, who had been checking with Jim, who'd contacted Chuck after he spoke to me, had determined that $2000 was a hell of a deal for 40-yard-line plaza seats under the overhang. That being close to one month's take-home pay after taxes, I checked my credit line—and bingo! Praise the Lord and pass the Visa card. Next thing we knew, Rick was blasting up the coast in his black Camaro to give $6000 to a rock star for his complimentary tickets. God Bless America, a country where state employees have enough credit to mingle with MTV executives for a few hours and supply tattooed alternative rockers with the cold hard cash for their decadent Super Bowl orgy. The imagination runs wild when pondering what use already rich rockers would put to a spare $6000. I'd like to think they gave it to charity, but something tells me those bastards were drinking a $500 bottle of champagne as they came on to ecstasy with a horde of heavily pierced but shapely naked groupies while we were suffering in Qualcomm Stadium.

Hunter S. Thompson captured the mood of that week better than any other journalist in the United States. He saw a "nervous American reality": "The 'war' in Iraq is all around us, like one of those San Francisco death fogs that never goes away. Your immediate instinct is to flee, but to where? It is a lot easier to just go back to bed than to get in the car and look for a place where there may be no fog. The odds are stacked against you, so why even try?" Thus, in the face of impending doom, the Raiders were my last beacon of hope, or at least that's how I'd framed the matter in order to justify my pathology. I know now it was just bread and circuses, but sometimes that's all we're left with. As Thompson proclaimed after casting aside his beloved San Francisco 49ers to jump on the Raiders bandwagon, "The Raiders will have fun. All the others will suffer." Unlike the chalk-eating Thompson, however, this week represented redemption for me. I was a Raiders fan during the pathetic Marc Wilson era, the excruciating 4–12 Joe Bugel year, the catastrophic Gulf War playoff implosion against Buffalo, the Baltimore debacle, the "snow job" in New England, etc. The Raiders *owed* me one, damn it![2]

While I was busy bemoaning the state of the union and getting bilked by scalpers, Operation Game Day was under way, putting fear into the hearts of San Diego's undocumented immigrant workers. In the name of protecting freedom, my government had audited more than 15,000 foreign-born security guards and taxi drivers in preparation for the Super Bowl, most of them from Latin America. From that list, the Immigration and Naturalization Service narrowed its search down to 80 people who were targeted in the sweep. More than 50 were arrested, a smaller number of those were actually charged with immigration violations. All of those initially charged were Mexican. Although some of those arrested had criminal records, none were linked with terrorism. One man, a Nigerian with British citizenship and no criminal record who is married to an American citizen, was threatened with deportation without a hearing for having a false social security number.

Most San Diegans happily ignored these suspect roundups and focused their attention on Super Bowl hype, but some civil libertarians noticed. Jordan Budd of the American Civil Liberties Union of San Diego observed, "This is being done in the name of national security. That's a farce. They're simply scapegoating the immigrant community while doing nothing to make us safer." Sam Hamod of the American Arab Anti-Discrimination Committee in San Diego noted that "many of these people have been working hard and living in this country for years. Now suddenly, they're considered dangerous. It doesn't make sense." The lawyer for one of those caught up in the sweep put it more harshly: "He's only a cabdriver. To protect the Super Bowl, the INS is destroying the lives of working people." Unfazed by such barbs, Edward Bell spoke for INS agents by crowing, "This is something we should be doing all the time." The shortage of cabs was not an issue for the NFL bigs and the corporate elite who sucked up the lion's share of Super Bowl tickets and leaving the real fans on the street. Why? Two words: stretch limo.[3]

Super Bowl week was not a good one for San Diego activists either. When peace groups pondered taking advantage of the huge national spectacle to get their message out, they found they were now on a par with terrorists in the eyes of local and federal law enforcement officials. Rent a plane to fly a peace banner over the stadium? No-fly zone. Pass out flyers in the parking lot? No public parking for fans, let alone undesirable peaceniks. Come on the trolley to protest in front of the stadium? Yes, maybe, but only if you stay in a tiny, fenced-off "free speech zone" under the trolley tracks that looked more like a holding pen for prisoners on their way to Auschwitz than a good place for a rally. Anyone wandering around in this little prison of democracy would look more like a zoo animal on display than a person with a serious political message. If that wasn't bad enough, free speech would be allowed only during certain allocated time slots—first come, first serve. If you got there after the Jehovah's Witnesses, it was tough luck. Even the streets in the vicinity of the stadium were restricted. It was a brave new world. Given this grim set of options, the Veterans for Peace decided to hold a vigil in Horton Plaza Park near the Gaslamp Quarter in downtown San Diego among the big Super Bowl parties. It was an ugly scene with men, one of them a friend and colleague of mine, who had served their country in combat in Vietnam being flipped off and cursed out by football partiers. It seemed during that grim week that even having put one's life on the line for one's country was not enough to buy officialdom's respect for the right to dissent. Quietly, amid the parties, ships loaded with sailors and troops cruised out of the harbor toward the Persian Gulf.

Having shelled out enough money already, I skipped the expensive Raider blowout at the beach and decided to walk through the Gaslamp and take in the spectacle for free on the night before the game. A bunch of us, all Raiders fans, headed toward downtown after eating dinner a few blocks away in Little Italy. On the way up Broadway, a cute kid who looked about ten years old leaned out of the window of a city bus and yelled, "Hey, fuck you! Raiders suck!"

Once we hit Fifth Avenue and turned right, we were in the heart of Super Bowl madness. The street was blocked off and jammed full of people, most of them in silver and black, with a smaller number of Tampa Bay fans and a large contingent of neutrals just there for the beer and carousing. People were very, very drunk. A pack of Raiders fans were screaming "Ray-duz! Ray-duz!" in a full throated frenzy at the corner of G Street, and we joined in as we passed. I high-fived a few more of my Silver and Black brothers who were standing in line outside a bar with an exorbitant cover charge. All the bars had exorbitant cover charges—$25 to $50 for the privilege of being crammed inside like a sardine with no live music and no place to sit: not a deal made in heaven.

We passed by a young man in a Tampa Bay jersey engaged in a three-way French kissing session with two girls. Eventually one of them staggered and fell. I looked around in vain for the *Elimidate* camera crew. On the next block, some Bucs fans were sitting on a patio outside a bar surrounded by a chain-link fence.

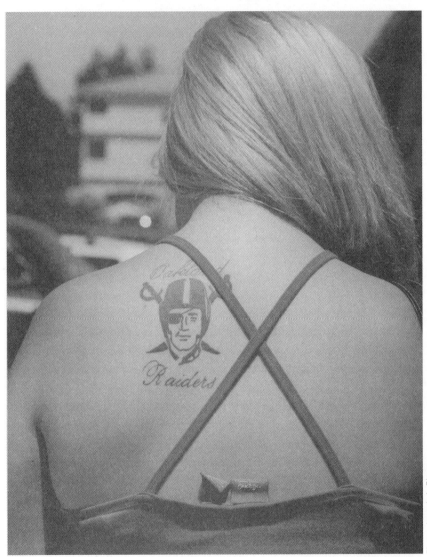

Die Hard

Chain-link fences seemed to be emerging as a theme. The Buckos were sur-rounded by Raiders fans who were heckling them from the outside. Beer-bottle fire was exchanged, but there were no casualties. We moved on.

We went in and out of the ad hoc Super Bowl gear shops without buying anything. There were Raiders fans from L.A., the East Bay, and all around the continental United States. We had friendly chats with some of them. It was like a big street party. People were happy just to be in the same town as the soon-to-be Super Bowl Champion Raiders. Most of them didn't have tickets. A guy in silver face paint drinking a beer out of a paper bag asked me if I knew where to get some. I told him my story and his face dropped. We watched the fireworks display, had a few beers, and listened to the free music inside yet another area behind a chain-link fence. Some kids ran through a crowd of Raiders fans with a Chargers flag chanting "Raiders suck!" and no carnage ensued. Outside of a few fistfights like you'd see at any big event filled with revelers, nothing happened, no riots developed. I saw a cab at the end of the blocked-off street and thought of the drivers being arrested to keep me "safe." Tonight, it appeared, San Diego was safe from both menacing cab drivers and evil Raiders fans.

I kept hoping, secretly, against the better angels of my nature that the paranoid *Union-Tribune* stories would be right and that barbarous Raiders fans would go positively medieval on the chi-chi tourist district. They could run the maitre d's through with their swords and raid the kitchens for raw meat. Then they could swing through the windows of wine bars on ropes tied to quaint balconies and chug all the best vintages like the real pirates of old. But alas, the avenging bar-barians had been priced out.

The next morning I woke up ready to win the Super Bowl. My partners in crime and I met at San Diego's oldest tavern, the Waterfront, for *machaca* and Bloody Marys. Established just after the end of Prohibition, the Waterfront is not only the oldest, but also the greatest of San Diego bars. During the heyday of San Diego's fishing industry, the bar was a hangout for the Italian and Portu-guese fishermen who worked the tuna boats. Its walls are covered with pictures of the lost world of blue-collar San Diego. Still a workingman's hangout despite its "discovery" by the community at large, the Waterfront has all the makings of a good Raiders hangout, except for the picture of former Chargers star Junior Seau hanging behind the bar. Other than that, it would seem to be relatively neutral territory. But, much to my dismay, upon entering my favorite local watering hole I was rudely greeted by "Raiders Still Suck" and "Stop Gangbanging for Uncle Al" signs. Then there was my favorite—a "Bin Laden is a Raider fan" sticker posted next to the beer taps. I should have taken this as a bad omen, but I entered nonetheless, proudly sporting my number 12 Stabler/Gannon jersey and Raiders cap.

The waitress, who should have recognized my face from serving me numerous times before, gave me no quarter and waited on our table efficiently but coolly. After checking my food for hidden objects, I concluded that the signs and the chilly reception were nothing more than harmless razzing, but the worst was lurking in the latter part of the day, waiting to pounce once I left the relatively safe confines of the Waterfront. At the time, I tipped generously while thinking to myself, "I'll come back and gloat later."

The rumor reached us on the trolley on the way to the stadium—Robbins was out. Was the Raiders' starting center hurt? No, word filtered back through the trolley. He was sent back to the hotel or kicked off the team or put in the hospital for an undisclosed condition. Others said that he'd been out all night drinking in the Gaslamp. Some had spotted him in Ocean Beach, others in Tijuana. I half expected it all to be lies and wild speculation. Another part of me wouldn't have been surprised to hear that Robbins had been kidnapped by G. Gordon Liddy and held in an anonymous Rosarito Beach hotel. It was all surreal. I should have taken it as yet another bad omen. A Raiders fan would later tell me that he suspects that the inability of a group of Raiders fans to perform a voodoo ritual at a Saints game a few years ago led to a shitload of bad mojo and possibly the entire Super Bowl nightmare. A plausible explanation, I suppose, but at the time I was still full of bravado. "We don't need Robbins," I said to my friend Chuck. "We've got it locked. Treu's a great backup." Chuck looked concerned.

Once the trolley pulled into the stadium, I expected our arrival four hours before game time to lead to a quick trip through security into the party zone. Instead, after we made our way through a baffling maze of switchbacks on the way to the main entrance area we were penned up like cattle for two solid hours. The crowd blindly swayed this way and that way, trying to find an opening in the security fence until the grim truth revealed itself: we were trapped. There were only a handful of entrances open and it seemed to be taking five minutes per person to enter the stadium. The longer it took, the bigger the crowd jamming its way toward the gates became. It appeared that the protectors of the homeland were banking on the fact that no terrorist would be smart enough to try to kill a couple of trolley loads of fans jettisoned between the station and the stadium rather than inside the stadium. Was the sense of drama of a halftime slaughter on a global television broadcast so important to the terrorists that it precluded going after a large group of sitting ducks like ourselves? Couldn't the bad guys throw us a curve? Or were we just expendable if the game itself was protected? I remembered the "Bin Laden is a Raider fan" sticker on the wall at the Waterfront. Could it be that Raider Nation had secretly been put on the list of twenty-five countries suspected by the Justice Department of harboring or sponsoring terrorists? If this was their plan, they were going to have to sacrifice a lot of "innocents" to get the few genuine Raiders fanatics who'd managed to crash the party. It was an inefficient strategy, but who knows?

It was a surprisingly hot sunny day for January, which was great when one was not pinned up against rich, slimy football fans. As the realization of the absurdity of our fate struck the crowd, people became angry, muttering under their breath or cursing security out loud. Men who looked like solid Republicans began to reconsider whether the tax cut was worth this absurd nightmare. As it approached midday, people began to pass out from the heat. An elderly man to my right managed to sneak his way in with this crafty dodge. I was surprised the police didn't search his unconscious body for weapons of mass destruction or ties to Al Qaeda. Later that night, only one local news station reported the two dozen or so people who had to be carted off in the name of national security. Such a negative observation might have gotten in the way of the booster pabulum official San Diego spits up every time anyone pays attention to it. I considered making a break for the free-speech zone to unleash a bitter tirade about the danger of voluntarily surrendering liberty for comfort or freedom from fear, but that might have meant trading in my piece of Raiders glory for a night in the slammer, so I held tight.

The mood became more profane and people began to heckle the security guards. A loud speaker was playing the song "Tequila" too loud and going over the blandly totalitarian security regulations over and over again in a closed feed-back loop. The draconian security regimen seemed to be comprised of several stages: a visual appraisal as you obeyed orders and stood behind a line, a pat down with your arms out as if under arrest, a bag and pocket search, a walk through a metal detector, and some undisclosed activity rumored to be an X-ray or a cavity search. Did I love the Raiders enough to endure a cavity search? I began to feel delirious from the heat. I thought I heard a wild rumor about a more thorough anal probe that resembled something from the *X Files*. This was not the utopian parking lot at the Oakland Coliseum where everybody is welcome and all is shared. It was a barren asphalt internment camp, a fascist military-prison-entertainment complex. We were at the breaking point, like a herd of nasty sweaty pigs on the way to the slaughterhouse. Where were the imaginary hoards of brutal Raider gangsters ready to mow down the Nazis with their handy Uzis and get this party started when you needed them?

Finally, we broke through the gauntlet, sneering our way through security and mercifully avoiding being pulled aside to room 101 in the Ministry of Love. As we made our way around the stadium, we noticed that there was no crush of humanity at the gate where the limos were dropping off the beautiful people. One world for the denizens of mass transit, another for the folks who brought you Reality TV and criminal tax shelters, I thought. We briefly engaged in the prerequisite bitter sniping at the errand boys for homeland security before performing the proper mental readjustments to prepare for the corporate tailgate. The rock stars had so back-handedly thrown in the tailgate tickets that none of us realized what a beggar's banquet awaited us. It was like entering another country, not the America where most of us live but the upper reaches of Corporate America where people are so blasé about luxury and abundance that it verges on terminal ennui.

The first thing we noticed was the free beer. Then there were free tamales and more free beer. As I sat down to stuff my gaping maw with tamales and wash them down with (have I mentioned it was free?) Dos Equis, my friend Rick tapped me on the shoulder to notify me that Bonnie Raitt was starting a concert behind me. As we walked through the crowd of affectless, coiffed, well-heeled revelers, I began to feel as if I had snuck into a secret society. Whatever you do, I thought, don't tell anyone that a week and a day before this moment you had seen Bonnie play at a massive antiwar rally in San Francisco and that your friend Alys had bumped into her afterward on the way out of a Vietnamese sandwich shop in the Tenderloin. If that comes out, they'll learn about the IWW t-shirt you bought or divine that you clapped for a speaker who blamed global capitalism for creating an obscenely huge gap between the affluent West and the dire poverty of the Third World, poverty that was, in turn, one of the conditions that fostered terrorism. Blamed capitalism? That would be it. I'd be finished with my new crew. I kept my peace and drank free beer as fast as I could swallow it, ate gourmet ribs and barbequed chicken, and strolled over to the swimming pool they'd constructed amid the normally desertlike environs of the Qualcomm Stadium parking lot. There was even a fountain and rows of lounges. I felt as if we had wandered into one of the parties in *The Great Gatsby* by F. Scott Fitzgerald where the colossal vitality of Jay Gatsby's vulgar materialism was at least ennobled by the raw power of his dream. On closer analysis, however, there was none of that there.

We took pictures of each other around the splashing water and made our way over to the tequila tent where open spigots of the powerful nectar lay unguarded. Open spigots of free tequila at a Raiders game! What kind of nihilist came up with this idea? But all was safe. There were few hard-core Raiders fans to be found in this bourgeois playground, and I felt as if my friends and I would be discovered and escorted out of the party and into some small cell in the bowels of the stadium at any moment. The possibility of a Raiders riot was small indeed among these corporate wieners. We took a couple of shots and ran into some Brazilian guys who "came up for the day" to see the game. They were wearing matching yellow soccer jerseys. It was a miracle of neoliberal corporate globalization. We took pictures of them and had a number of tequila shots. The more tequila I had, the more I began to like my new set. Rick suggested that we switch to beer in order to increase the likelihood that we would remember the game tomorrow. Good idea. Chuck suggested that we have one more round of shots, which we did before grabbing a final free beer and leaving our new friends and the Foo Fighters to rock out at the corporate tailgate.

Overfed and drunk as skunks, we headed over to the stadium, bloated and confident of victory. Inside we located our seats, and I noticed that of the two huge blow-up football players, the Raider was droopier. Another bad omen. Still, I pressed on in my unwavering faith that Gannon would slice the Bucs' defense to shreds and we'd be dancing for joy in the streets of the Gaslamp. With about forty minutes left until kickoff we walked around the stadium to say hello to our Raider buddies Jim and his father Hank. Jim was up at a concessions stand so we chatted with Hank for a bit and walked back around past the elaborate ESPN tent set up on the sideline. As we got back to our seats, Santana started up a brief set. Sting and No Doubt would play at halftime. Would there be a football game? Unfortunately so.

It started well with the Raiders picking off a Brad Johnson pass to put them in scoring position early. Chuck, Rick, and I were ecstatic. This was the start of it—a long raucous festival of Raider dominance. Points would be coming from the defense and the offense, falling off trees. The drive stalled and Janikowski hit a 40-yard field goal at 4:20 of the first quarter. It was all downhill from there, a horrifying free fall into the depths of depression. When Grammatica hit a 24-yard field goal at 7:09 of the first quarter, I thought, at least we stopped them. After his second field goal at 3:44 of the second quarter, I told myself the game might be closer than I had anticipated. Then Alstott's 2-yard touchdown run at 8:36 had me thinking it would be fun to see the comeback victory. Once

Gannon worked the kinks out, we'd really get this show on the road. The offense continued to sputter and the Bucs suddenly looked like a juggernaut. Just before halftime, at 14:30 of the second quarter, McCardell caught a 5-yard touchdown pass from Johnson. Can you say miracle comeback?

Halftime was a miserable blur. All the lifeless spectacle had been exposed as ridiculous decadence. The most noteworthy thing about the crowd was its utter indifference to everything. At one point during the first half, I stood up to cheer on the defense and turned around to a lifeless clump of silver-and-black-clad forty-somethings and yelled, "Come on, corporate Raiders, make some noise!" They seemed neither inspired, nor upset, nor even amused. Someone needed to go check the whole bunch to see if they had a pulse. If it was possible to embody the Platonic Form of affectlessness, they did. It was then that I noticed the tag hanging off one of their hats. The scenario was clearly this: fly in from Aspen or Miami or Manhattan and, once at your exclusive hotel, stroll up to the souvenir stand conveniently located in the opulent lobby and flip a coin. Heads it's Raiders, tails it's Buccaneers. As for the contest? Whatever. Do you want to dine at Morton's downtown or Japengo in La Jolla after the game?

Sitting through the second half was like enduring a ruthless beating that graduated into a meticulous torture session. If the Raiders' Swiss cheese defense and impotent offense were not bad enough, the interception returns for touchdowns added a particularly vicious angle to the experience. It was like knowing that you were slowly dying, with only the occasional sledgehammer shot to the gut to look forward to. I will spare you, gentle reader, the precise details. The comeback? It was a cruel hoax performed upon an already traumatized Raider Nation. Death is always more devastating when the dying patient is given a shred of hope to nurse only to have it ripped from his or her desperate, trembling hands. At one point during the apocalypse, Chuck turned to me and said, "After all we've been through, they're not even going to show up. I can't believe it, Jim. Two thousand bucks for this!" This hit me hard, since the whole thing had been my idea. I was with erstwhile Raiders fan Hunter Thompson who remembered, "The beating came close to utterly destroying my self-esteem. I felt smaller and smaller as the game went on. There was no relief, no mercy, no place to hide from it, and no sane way to explain it." I'll leave it at that. As the futile minutes ticked away, we decided it was no use staying to watch ex-Raiders coach Jon Gruden gloat and Chuck and I abandoned ship, leaving Rick to suffer alone. I left my free Super Bowl crap under the seat and gave myself license to stomp on the stupid little radio they gave us. Chuck tossed his against the wall by a garbage can and it shattered helplessly into useless fragments, an apt metaphor for the Raiders and our state of being. I went into the bathroom before we left and the ridicule came at me from all sides. The enemies of Raiders fans, fearing the fearsome thug myth, usually wait until they can pick you off in an isolated and vulnerable place to let you have it. I took it stoically. Outside, some guy was getting in Chuck's face, so we fled to the trolley station.

On the way there, we were greeted by some perverse Bible thumper who'd decided it was a good idea to greet angry, retreating Raiders fans with the message that we were all going to Hell. It was good for his health that he was behind a chain-link fence. I told him in no uncertain terms that he was the last person in the world that I wanted to hear from at that moment. In the back of my head, however, I did wonder whether God *was* punishing me for my hypocrisy in opposing war while shelling out an obscene amount of money to indulge my savage love of gridiron combat. The self-doubt generated by the victory of the Disney pirates over my beloved Raiders brought the whole bloated edifice of the Super Bowl down on my head. I saw myself as a creature driven by vanity and sustained by illusion.

Then, all at once, the crowd of defeated Raiders fans began to hurtle the absurd security barriers on the way to the trolley, ignoring police orders to continue weaving through the pointless maze like rats searching for nonexistent cheese. The cops issued sterner warnings, but nobody listened. It felt liberating until my friend tripped on the last hurtle and fell, gashing his arm badly, just above the elbow. He got up and we jumped on a trolley car and stood sullenly mute all the way home as people stared in horror at the blood dripping from his arm. It was there amid the lonely crowd on the trolley that the voice came back to haunt me, "The sole real status attaching to a mediocre object of this kind is to have been placed, however briefly, at the very center of social life and hailed as the revelation," the voice mocked. I tried to peer into the darkness outside the trolley window but saw only my own reflection in the glass. The voice went on, "But even this spectacular prestige evaporates into vulgarity as soon as the object is taken home by a consumer—and hence all other consumers too. At this point its essential poverty stands revealed—too late."[4]

Meanwhile, across town, the Super Bowl farce turned tragic. Greg "Griz" Jones, one of the few real Raiders fans who made it into the game, was blind-sided by an SUV as he crossed San Diego Mission Road while leaving the game. The hit-and-run assault sent Jones flying and the impact severely fractured his pelvis and cut open his head. Jones, the bear-sized linchpin of the "66th Mob," who camp overnight and tailgate on 66th Avenue by the Coliseum in Oakland, is known as an affectionate man who always makes enough extra food to feed the homeless at his tailgates. Witnesses said the accident sounded "like two cars colliding." At Sharp Memorial Hospital, surgeons had to insert a steel plate in Jones's pelvis. His recovery required months of painful rehabilitation. He had no health insurance.[5]

The Raiders' AWOL center, it turned out, had a tragic tale as well. Unlike the legendary Super Bowl drinking binge of John Matuszak, the Barret Robbins story was no light-hearted romp. The Raiders' center missed the game as a result of a bipolar episode. Later he revealed to ESPN that he had started feeling it coming on in the middle of Super Bowl week. "A real scared feeling started to happen, and it got worse," Robbins would later explain, "I didn't know what to do. What I did was started drinking. I felt that drinking was going to make it go away." Rather than the sex and drugs and rock and roll of old, this was no renegade Raiders myth but a real nightmare. Robbins recalled:

I left the hotel . . . I don't know what for . . . I wandered around aimlessly. I could remember seeing people that I knew. I could remember riding around with people that I knew, but I didn't know why I was there or where I was going or what I was doing. All I know is I was not where I was supposed to be. My brain had shut down. I don't remember Saturday morning. I remember being somewhere by the ocean and looking for a way home . . . or looking for a ride. I don't really know what I was looking for.

Robbins did not sleep all Friday night before the Super Bowl, made the team's 11:00 p.m. bed check, but was then spotted partying at an after-hours club called E Street Alley in the Gaslamp at 4 a.m. At one point early Saturday night, two Raiders fans spotted Robbins drinking, weeping, and muttering to himself as he sat alone in a booth at Moondoggies in Pacific Beach. "He looked lost," said one of the fans, who got Robbins a cab and gave the driver $20 to take him back to the Hyatt where the Raiders were staying. Robbins was then kicked out of the team hotel and is said to have spent the night in Tijuana. Eventually, he wound up at a local hospital with alcohol poisoning and was put on suicide watch. As Monte Poole observed, "Robbins spends part of his life in dark corners most of us never see and can't begin to understand."[6]

Two

Oakland's Burning

I believe there's really gonna be a riot here in Oakland. . . . I heard it over the radio that the police department was ready for anything, shotguns, blockades—I dreamed that a bunch of youngsters had started a riot and they had set Oakland on fire.

Luther Smith, calling for a police review board in
Oakland in Oakland's Not for Burning, *1968*

We *were* "representing" the town. Oakland is like this.
Greg Johnson, seventeen-year-old Raider rioter, 2003

In the wake of the Raiders' 2003 Super Bowl loss, a section of East 14th Street/ International Boulevard from 35th to 94th Avenues turned into what one police observer called "a war zone." "Oakland Police No Match for Street Mayhem," "Roving Mobs Surprised Police," "Disappointed Fans Vent Anger in Streets," screamed the headlines in the *San Francisco Chronicle* and *Oakland Tribune*. Whether the disturbances constituted a "riot," "mini-riot," or a mere outbreak of "Mob violence" was a matter of debate among observers, but the hours-long battle between 400 police officers and as many as two thousand mostly young Raiders fans was an indisputably startling event and yet another piece of bad news for Oakland, East Oakland in particular. In the late seventies, John Krich, in *Bump City: Winners and Losers in Oakland*, called the city a "modern ghost town" but still reveled in the life of "'funky East Fourteenth,' the world's second-longest gut, where six-pack and pick-up rule the strip" and one can see "the races uniting over a fat joint and the Raiders." By 1995, Gary Rivlin in *Drive By* saw less poetry and more pain as he relayed "the lures and dangers of East Fourteenth . . . one of the two main arteries running the length of East Oakland, a river of addicts, prostitutes, and down-and-outers drifting by the good people of the community." Jim Zamora, a current Oakland resident and *San Francisco Chronicle* reporter who covered the riots, describes East 14th (which turns into International Boulevard as it makes its way out of downtown, passes Lake Merritt, heads into Fruitvale and continues on by Elmhurst to San Leandro) as "the spine of Raider Nation." Zamora notes of East Oakland that "it's ethnically diverse, low-income, with a lot of crime and drugs. It's the home of many immigrants. This particular area [of the riots] is the home of the Hells Angels and was also Black Panther turf. East 14th is the oldest drag in Oakland. A lot of factories were on that street. The GM plant and other industries. It's the blue-collar heart of the city."[1]

Much has been done to break the blue-collar heart of Oakland. The working-class flatlands of West, East, and North Oakland have traditionally been cut off from the affluent hills by race and economics. As Beth Bagwell notes in *Oakland: The Story of a City*, posh areas in the hills were built, by both covert and overt means, as racially "restricted" areas: "Everyone knew what it meant when a district was 'restricted'; even if the racial restrictions were not spelled out in the brochures, they were in the fine print of the purchasing contract." Some well-heeled areas such as Rockridge openly advertised their exclusionary practices: as one 1911 pamphlet proclaimed, "It is probably unnecessary even to mention that no one of African or Mongolian descent will ever be allowed to own a lot in Rockridge or even rent any house that may be built there." While not restricted by race, economics kept blue-collar whites out of the hills as well. Still, as long as there was work in the sometimes booming industries tied to the railways, docks,

Photo: Joseph A. Blum

The spine of Raider Nation

shipyards, canneries, and auto factories, Oakland's multi-ethnic working class was able to carve out a piece of the American dream. The shipyard and wartime industry boom that came with World War II brought a large number of mostly southern black and white migrants, increasing the city's population and creating new tensions. Old timers were leery of the new influx of workers and, as historian Marilynn Johnson notes, federal housing policies "introduced new forms of federally sanctioned racial segregation that would influence postwar neighborhood development." These policies increased the urban density along the bay flatlands and later building loan programs planted the seeds for white flight to the suburbs. During the war, however, tensions between migrants and "native"

Oaklanders did not lead to a white exodus from the city's flatlands. Instead, while Oakland's conservative political establishment sought, unsuccessfully, to drive out the new migrant workers, a multi-ethnic working-class city thrived amid the conflict.[2]

After the war, Oakland began to lose shipyard and other blue-collar jobs it would never adequately replace. West Oakland, the heart of the city's black community, dubbed "the Harlem of the West" for its rich cultural life, continued to attract migrants even as economic conditions deteriorated. A brutal combination of factors led to West Oakland's decline. Some of the most damaging developments were the government's refusal to build adequate new housing, the destruction of old housing stock by urban renewal projects, and the construction of the Cypress and Grove-Shafter freeways. Another intrusion was the Bay Area Rapid Transit system. These thoroughfares sliced through the middle of a decaying West Oakland, and the Loma Prieta earthquake traumatized the city's poorest neighborhood even more, driving residents to the northern and eastern flatlands, with East Oakland receiving the lion's share of those fleeing the west side of the city. All the while, East Oakland itself was bleeding solid blue-collar jobs.[3] As Rivlin points out:

General Motors, Ford, Caterpillar, Mack, International Harvester—all shut down plants that had been operating in and around East Oakland for decades. The General Motors plant, in Oakland since 1916, laid off nearly 3,000 workers when it closed its plant at Seventy-third and Macarthur Boulevard in the early 1960s; a second GM plant, in nearby Fremont, laid off another 5,900 workers in 1981 and 1982. The Ford factory still stands at the edge of East Oakland, but now it is home to a bingo parlor and an indoor flea market. In its heyday Ford employed 5,000 workers.

Oakland and Alameda County lost 16,000 blue-collar jobs in the first half of the 1980s alone. By the year 2000, even a boosterish local history, *The Spirit of Oakland*, was describing flatlands communities by referring to "persistent unem-

ployment and its byproducts" like the city's 25 percent poverty rate, and the
"struggles" of a community "without an industrial base." When Ishmael Reed
toured the heavily Mexican American neighborhood of Fruitvale for his 2003
book *Blues City,* he noted, "Unemployment is up here because the source of
income, heavy and light manufacturing jobs, has relocated to cheaper labor markets or is being replaced by hi-tech industry." Chris Rhomberg in *No There There:
Race, Class, and Political Community in Oakland,* noted that in 2004, because
of this trend toward a two-tier economy, "80 percent of Oakland households
would not be able to afford a two-bedroom unit in the new developments" that
Oakland Mayor Jerry Brown is promoting to "redevelop" downtown Oakland.
As Rhomberg observes, Oakland rents rose by 65 percent between 1995 and
2000 and two out of five Oakland families had already been struggling to meet
housing costs before this surge in prices.[4]

Along with the loss of good jobs and rising housing costs in Oakland came
the flight of banks, supermarkets, and the white working class. For instance,
the number of banks in East Oakland south of 73rd Avenue, eleven in 1982,
had fallen to two by 1990. Without much capital, East Oakland, home to the
Coliseum where the Raiders play, has little with which to rebuild. Those who
fled the neighborhood left behind what one *Oakland Tribune* reporter called a
"no-store zone" where the Millsmont Certified Farmers Market, which opened
in the summer of 2003, was pushed by City Council member Desley Brooks to
compensate for "the absence of a major supermarket in the district and the need
for economic vitality that would boost neighborhood pride." Retail business has
also been hit hard as Rhomberg documents, "By the '80s, major retail stores
were rapidly leaving the central city for the suburban malls: In 1977, Oakland's
central business district could still boast seven department stores; ten years later,
there were only four across the entire city." As for white flight, in 1960, when
the Raiders were born, the East Oakland community of Elmhurst was 80 percent white, but by 1980 the neighborhood was less than 10 percent white. The
East Bay suburbs grew and prospered while Oakland suffered. As some affluent
whites begin to return, many fear that the result will be gentrification and dis-

placement of working-class minority residents rather than a bottom-up renewal of the city.[5]

This ghettoization of East Oakland along with rest of the flatlands, combined with the loss of industrial jobs, commercial services, and tax dollars, has exacerbated the decline of the area's schools. Before the state takeover of Oakland's schools in the summer of 2003, only five of Oakland's ninety-nine schools met state standards, with widespread failure in math skills and English proficiency.[6] In an insightful article in the *Oakland Tribune*, Jill Tucker explained how Oakland's poor kids are having the bar of expectations raised while receiving an education that is "among the worst in the nation" from a system that "favors white and wealthy kids."[7]

Hence, Oakland's flatland schools reflect the condition of their community and, as a result, only 25 percent of incoming high school freshman graduate, with 40 percent quitting and the rest falling off the radar screen of the Oakland school district altogether. These kids drop out into a dismal Oakland job market where the overall unemployment rate as of this writing is 10.4 percent compared to 6.9 percent statewide, and the unemployment rate for young people is 22 percent across the state and a stunning 56.3 percent among African American youth. If they get sick, the unemployed and uninsured can expect to go to a struggling county medical center that is underfunded and worse than most facilities because of a shortage of beds. The overall healthcare situation is bleak: as Rhomberg shows, "*Every* census track in East Oakland (and many in North and West Oakland) was designated by the U.S. Department of Health and Human Services as medically underserved, based on the prevalence of poverty, infant mortality rates, and the shortage of primary care physicians." Thus it is not hard to see why some of East Oakland's most marginalized young people, with the social fabric fraying around them, might turn to other sources of meaning and identity.[8]

As Diego Vigil, a scholar of "street socialization" puts it, "It is when social forces and influences do not function as they should that street subcultures arise to fill the void." For young people, like the twelve- to twenty-year-old kids on the street during the riots in East Oakland, "Socio-economic factors such as poverty, economic dislocation, divorce, single-parent households, and racism place severe stresses on many families, so that home life is regularly unstable." This leads to a situation where, as Vigil tells us, "Alienated youths whose lack of education and occupational opportunities preclude their entering the respectable status system face severe problems in establishing a social identity for themselves." In this context, "periodically acting *loco* elevates a youth's social status and enhances his street reputation." This might mean, in a small minority of cases, joining a gang or, more likely, going to a "sideshow" where you do donuts in the street in somebody's car, or simply feeling the need to act like a badass or crazy Raiders fan. As Jim Zamora put it, "A lot of people feel Oakland has a reputation to live up to. A tough, gritty, urban identity. The Raiders are a way to get in touch with your inner thug." What is surprising in the socio-economic context of East Oakland is not that young people sometimes get out of hand, but that people are surprised when they do.[9]

What happened the night of the Super Bowl was not on the scale of the Los Angeles riots, but a smaller series of flash riots that spread along International Boulevard for more than fifty blocks. The week before, rowdy celebrations of the Raiders' AFC championship victory occurred on International Boulevard as well. Jubilation had also veered into vandalism around Jack London Square downtown, leading to 25 arrests (compared to 55 at the Coliseum itself, which was 15 above the average of 40 per game). The Super Bowl week, however, the police had blocked off the gentrified area around the square, leaving East Oakland as the sole site for street parties. A crowd of 200 or so gathered at 37th Avenue and International after the game and started marching up the street yelling, "Raiders rule! Fuck the police!" Police in riot gear reacted with what some observers called a "zero tolerance" approach, making use of rubber bullets, tear gas, and flashstun grenades as their fellow officers in squad cars, on motorcycles, and in helicopters teamed up with California Highway Patrol officers, Alameda County sheriff's deputies, and a SWAT team to suppress the crowd of young Raiders fans.[10]

Some residents of the neighborhood hotly condemned the "Raider Nation

33rd Street off International

people" and welcomed the police, chanting "OPD! OPD!" as the riot troops passed by, while others resented having tear gas shot toward them as they sat on the steps in front of their homes. A week before, Liz Estrella had complained of a police overreaction in the *Oakland Tribune,* saying, "You never see this much police presence when there is a murder in this area. If the Raiders win the Super Bowl, it's going to be twice as bad." They lost, but even so she was right as the night yielded twelve car fires, numerous street bonfires lit in trash Dumpsters or started with discarded Christmas trees, some damage to businesses, and eighty-five arrests. Of those arrested, seventy-two were from Oakland and some were as young as twelve years old.[11]

At one point during the night, the small army of police was clearly outnumbered by riotous fans and had to retreat from a barrage of rocks and bottles. Other fans, however, did not fight with police, preferring to take part in sideshows or just stand on the sidelines and watch the chaos unfold. There was much drunkenness. According to Zamora, no businesses with "Raiders stuff" in the windows were damaged, but cars with 49ers stickers got trashed. He also notes, without claiming that the rioters were angry antiglobalists, that while the McDonald's at 64th Avenue was burned, the locally owned Kwik Way across the street was still open and serving burgers throughout the mayhem. Members of the multi-ethnic crowd (about half Latino and a quarter black, with the remainder whites and Asians) identified themselves as Raiders fans throughout the night, not just by wearing gear but by directing the battle like a game. "Raiders fans, roll it back. The tear gas is getting stronger," one man yelled to his cohorts in the midst of the fray. Neighborhood identification was also clear as one eighteen-year-old barked to a reporter, "You better take your shit home—it's East Oakland." Others proclaimed, "It's town business, it's what we do!" At least one other fan branded a police van with an anarchy symbol.[12]

While it might be wrong to attribute any conscious political agenda to these angry Raiders fans, Zamora does note that "there was a lot of venting at cops. Oakland police have a reputation for having a more aggressive strategy. In this case, it gave people something to engage. The cops may have been doing things that escalated the situation. It's hard to know in a situation like that. It's unpredictable." Some residents were also critical of law enforcement, complaining that the police reaction was over the top in response to what was just a rowdy crowd. One, by the name of B. Town, said, "It was just a gathering of people from Oakland having a good time. The police did too much with smoke bombs." A group of media students from a Fremont high school who had come into the city to hang out during the Super Bowl thought there were too many cops in the neighborhood and that, though the rioters had gotten out of hand, the police presence was a trigger. "The only reason people acted crazy was because police were harassing them," said Shakia Green of the anarchy on the street.[13]

There is clearly no excuse for random vandalism. However, such questioning of the motives and actions of the police is a reflection of long-held suspicions of law enforcement in Oakland's flatlands. As John Krich observed in the late seventies:

> It is not surprising that this city should be the unofficial birthplace of the word "pig"—at least, as that word applies to police . . . Oakland's "police services" have had a long record of brutality unmatched by any troop of a comparable size. Long before the Black Panthers popularized the jargon that described them as an "occupying force," Oakland's cops had amassed a well-documented record of harassment of labor. . . . With the growth of reported incidents of brutality against blacks in the early Fifties, a committee of the state legislature held public hearings on Oakland's force, the first and only time that has happened in California's history. Many of the men who enforced order in the ghettos were whites, recruited from the South, who lived in environs like San Leandro, which the NAACP once designated America's most segregated city.

Marilynn Johnson concurs, noting that during the forties in Oakland, "Police . . . hounded groups of black men congregating on street corners, forcing them to disperse or face arrest." Johnson also reminds us of how police routinely "rounded up hundreds of 'suspicious' individuals each year—typically non-whites in white neighborhoods" and "selectively enforced the draft law against black and Hispanic men." Years later, Ishmael Reed, who was concerned enough about drug crime in Oakland to condemn "black terrorists" and "crack fascists" and yearn for a "state of emergency" in the late eighties, was not uncritical of Oakland's police: "Thanks to the Panthers, the downtown establishment is black but that still doesn't prohibit the police from continuing to beat the shit out of black people." During the Jerry Brown era, the image of the police has suffered as a result of "the Riders" scandal, in which four rogue cops were accused of planting evidence, using excessive force, and filing false reports, with one having apparently fled to Mexico before a controversial trial in which the remaining defendants were cleared of eight charges while the jury delivered a hung verdict on twenty-seven others. Angry protests followed as the Riders walked. This scandal and similar problems have raised enough concern to spur reform in Oakland's underfunded and understaffed police department. Hence the tensions between police and youth on the street should not shock anyone.[14]

The mainstream media response to the riots was for the most part predictably scathing. Formulaic, superficial, and sensationalist local and national television coverage was the norm as reporters found the dramatic shots and hopped back into their news vans, and thoughtful reflection was subsumed by the image of a burning car accompanied by a predictable condemnation of the rioters. The *Oakland Tribune*, along with many Raiders fans, kicked the young people on the street out of Raider Nation, proclaiming, "Those thugs were not real Raiders fans." Upset at the damage to the city's streets and image, the paper pulled out all the stops, calling the rioters "hooligans," "outlaws," and an "unruly mob." Rejecting any attempt to understand the root causes of such outbursts as "excuses," the editorial proclaimed that "although society in general and Oakland in particular do have problems, that is no rationale for what happened."[15]

Monte Poole's column on the riots also took pains to distinguish the street revelers from the majority of "true Raiders fans," but did not cast them out of the imagined community entirely. Instead, he called them "the fringe element of Raider Nation." Noting of the kids on the street, "They are of this community, and they link themselves to the team," Poole bemoaned the fact that the Raiders organization had done nothing in the wake of the riots. Reminding Raiders players that "athletic figures sometimes fail to realize the impact they can make with even a token effort," he called on them to show up in East Oakland and help heal the city. It never happened. Laudable as Poole's sentiments were, they were based on the notion that professional sports teams have an obligation to the community in whose name they play, an idea which, if it ever had any currency, has long since been cast into the dustbin of history by corporate sports organizations throughout the country.[16]

Letters to the *Tribune* ranged from one that condemned the "low-life jerks" who rioted as, yet again, not "true and loyal" fans to another that went beyond recrimination to look at the bigger picture. "Aren't you tired of all these politicians, especially our City Council president, telling the police in his district, 'You should have used more force'?" asked Mickey Hall of Oakland. As for the fans, he chided, "It would be so much better if we used all this energy to fight the city for things that are more important than a football game. There are plenty to fight the city for. For example, education for our children is horrible. Let's help the ones who are actually fighting for us and our children."[17]

At the San Francisco Bay Area Independent Media Center website, one could find some interesting on-the-site reporting from Oakland residents as events unfolded. Rachael Montgomery contributed this post:

> I and a few of my housemates were also hit with tear gas while we stood in front of our door on International and 48th. A huge line of police were walking down the street with several rows of squad cars behind them and yelling at people to "GO HOME!" When they got to us, I began taking photos, and telling them, "I am home." They responded by shooting tear gas right at our feet, so we were forced to go inside. Three of us were stung by the gas in our faces, and I wasn't really able to see straight for about 20 minutes.

Another report from 38th and Foothill Boulevard also complained of tear gas, "despite the fact that the activity on the street (celebration) appears to [be] much more mellow than last week after the Raiders' playoff win." Yet another accused an unnamed journalist from a Bay Area newspaper of racism for telling someone on a cell phone that he was afraid to go into the crowd because he was white. This observer then lambasted "racist 'rich person's' reporting" and claimed that "patterns of corruption in the police force and police aggressiveness against poor or black/Mexican people were to blame for the violence that occurred, which was mostly some property destruction and a lot of violence against humans committed by the police." A good number of pictures were posted documenting massive police lines, vandalized squad cars, rubber bullets, and several arrests.[18]

When it came to analyzing the significance of the disturbances, the debate on the Indy Media website was over whether the Raiders riots were a manifestation of revolutionary class war, excessive police brutality, or reactionary thuggery by an unredeemable group of drunken, sexist, homophobic, lumpenproletarian gangs. One report by "black mamba" surmised:

> Pent up sub-conscious rage against the fascist police state we live in seems to me to be behind the violence. This display indicates that large segments of our society are at the point of revolting against the oppressive nature of our society, why else would people burn their own neighborhood? The propaganda and phyc-ops [sic] are so effective though that the rage is only related to state sanctioned events like the Super Bowl. If some one could only find a way to channel this rage to change the oppressive nature of our society, things would change quickly.

Another post said, "Revel in the beauty of a burning McDonald's," while still another asked why no banks were burned. This was greeted with, "To the person with the bank question—where are you from mutha fucka? Very, very obviously not Oaktown. If you were you'd know that in the free fire zone, along International/East 14th between like Fruitvale and the 90s there are hardly any banks—if there is even one." The rioters-as-revolutionaries crowd was assailed by people pointing out the absurdity of seeing "lumpen thugs" as revolutionary and others defending the Oakland woman who owned the McDonald's franchise or calling for the police to "unleash the beast" on the fascist football hooligans devoted to "corporate Raider Nation."[19]

Other responses went beyond condemning Raiders fans to rejecting and stereotyping Oakland itself. "People burn their own neighborhoods because Oakland is the shithole that EVERYONE in the Bay Area, and now the NATION, thinks it is. I have the misfortune of working downtown and it is a SCARY place! When five o'clock rolls around, everyone with half a brain GETS THE HELL

OUT!" One of the uglier posts not only mocked the pretensions of would-be revolutionaries but went on to say: "The bums and welfare clowns who rioted did so because they are ignorant cretins who were upset at their pitiful team getting its ass handed to it. Today they will get up (around noon), watch some TV (Springer), and wait for Friday (welfare checks). Have a nice day."[20]

While the worst nightmares of both the vast majority of law-abiding citizens who comprise Raider Nation and Oakland's boosters were embodied in the Super Bowl riots, the impulse toward the easy condemnation of a mythologized "mob of thugs" does little other than appease the pious. No matter how much Raiders fans might want to excise the young rioters from their imagined community, they will continue to exist. No matter what linguistic artillery is launched at them by the local press, they will still live in Oakland—and marginalized inner-city youth have been demonized for so long that one doubts that the papers' efforts did much damage to their sense of self, which was probably already dependent on *not* being respectable. Already outsiders looking in on mainstream American life and the Super Bowl show, the rioters' sense of agency came from their transgression of becoming participants in their own contest. Neither inhuman monsters nor angry revolutionaries, the young Raiders fans who got drunk and stirred it up on the streets of Oakland are a symptom of blight more than its cause. The reaction they provoked is instructive but not unique in the history of the city.

From Salon Culture to the California Barbarians

Headlines in the March 1943 *Oakland Tribune* announced the arrival of a major crime wave on city streets. Criminal activity and juvenile delinquency had become "intolerable," said the *Tribune,* and "decent citizens [were] afraid to got out at night." The city's evening newspaper, the *Post-Enquirer,* urged city officials to take immediate action, calling for a "drastic tightening and strengthening of the forces of law and order. We cannot allow rape, murder, prostitution, robbery and gangsterism to flourish and increase in our midst."

> Marilynn S. Johnson, The Second Gold Rush:
> Oakland and the East Bay in World War II

As early as the 1920s, the nativist Protestant white middle class in Oakland (many of whom were sympathetic to the Klan) were up in arms over the "saloon culture" that helped foster the ethnic machine politics of Mike Kelly. Rhomberg observes, "Opposition to booze went hand in hand with calls for greater controls over other forms of deviance as well. In March 1921, residents of 29th Avenue complained of gambling and loitering among young men attending night classes in Americanization" at a school in East Oakland. The police proceeded to arrest fourteen youths "with names like Gomez, Carelli, Cravalho, . . . and Prussino-vski" for "vagrancy." More violent forms of "law and order" were meted out in the 1920s when middle-class East Oaklanders beat, tarred, and feathered the editor of the iconoclastic *Free Press*. In yet another example of mob violence in the twenties, there was "a prolonged standoff between armed homeowners and the Streets department" over a sewage spill that suburbanites felt the city had not responded to properly. Such efforts to impose a nativist Protestant white middle-class hegemony by legal or extralegal means would ultimately fail to quell fears of disorder. By the time the forties rolled along, Rhomberg informs us that the "sudden mingling of groups in the shared space of downtown" had created new tensions: "Old Oakland residents were shocked at the unruly crowds and the seeming breakdown of moral order, yet for many workers the experience was a liberating release from social barriers."[21]

In 1944, the 12th Street riot left one dead and four wounded after an angry crowd of 5,000 black swing fans were turned away from the Oakland Auditorium where they had come to see Cab Calloway. Shut out of the sold-out show, the crowd smashed doors and windows and fought with white sailors on a city streetcar. Hundreds joined in and the anarchy spread down Broadway where truckloads of military police joined local cops to battle the angry swing dancers. Police cited no rationale for what they termed a "spontaneous outburst," ignoring the obvious racial undercurrent of the disturbance. At the time, the rioters were lectured by the *Oakland Observer*:

The riot on Twelfth Street the other day may be the forerunner of more and larger riots because we now have (a) a semi-mining camp civilization and (b) a new race problem, brought about by the influx of what might be called socially-liberated or uninhibited Negroes who are not bound by the old and peaceful understanding between the Negro and the white of Oakland, which has lasted for so many decades, but who insist upon barging into the white man and becoming an integral part of the white man's society. . . . Right there is where the Negro is making his big mistake. He is butting into the white civilization instead of keeping in the perfectly orderly and convenient Negro civilization of Oakland, and he is getting himself thoroughly disliked.[22]

In Oakland, and in other East Bay cities, the forties did not see just a racial panic but a wave of hysteria over crime, juvenile delinquency, and drunkenness. A good number of "the greatest generation," it appears, were out of control. The *Alameda Times-Star* was worried about "shiftless, irresponsible fellows who [do] little else but go out on 'binges' which usually land them in jail, at the expense of the city, after every pay day." In Richmond, the *Independent* was railing about a wave of "alcoholic playboys" and calling for a "concentration camp" to house them. As Marilynn Johnson points out, the urban conflicts and social anxieties of this era laid the groundwork for much of the turmoil of the sixties.[23]

In 1968, Amory Bradford of the Economic Development Administration of the U.S. Department of Commerce published the book *Oakland's Not for Burning* to tell the story of how Oakland avoided a Watts-style riot due in part to his (self-described) noble efforts. Despite his overly sunny view, Bradford does document the rage that many inner-city residents, who were threatening "to have a Watts here, and kill and bomb," felt over the lack of jobs in the city and urban renewal policies that looked more like "Negro removal."[24] East 14th Street was a flash point on several occasions as Bradford recounts an incident during the long hot summer of his stay in the city:

A group of youngsters had broken some store windows on East 14th Street. When the police arrived, a large crowd gathered, and moved into a construction lot nearby to pick up bricks and pieces of wood. More police came and dispersed the crowd, chasing some of them down side streets. There was no shooting, but a number of arrests were made. There were no serious injuries. There was some criticism by ghetto leaders of what they felt to be an excessive show of force by the police, who came in special riot cars, each carrying five men, equipped with crash helmets, riot batons, and shotguns.[25]

East 14th Street was the host of yet another disturbance that year when "several thousand high school students were out in the streets with nothing to do, looking for trouble. They began to form large groups and roamed up and down East 14th Street, the main thoroughfare of East Oakland, breaking store windows and shouting at passers-by." Not surprisingly, Bradford notes, "The police were ready and turned out in force. Holding their clubs ahead of them with a hand over each end, they formed a solid wedge and cleared 14th Street, pushing the students ahead of them." He also notes the famous shoot-out between the police and the Black Panthers where Oakland cops killed Bobby Hutton and wounded Eldridge Clever, taking two casualties themselves. Still, he asserts, Oakland made it through 1966, 1967, and the first part of 1968 "without a serious riot," but was still "on the edge of violence, until far more than is now in view can be done to improve life for those who dwell in the ghetto."[26]

For a contemporary observer sympathetic to the plight of urban America's poor, Bradford is depressing reading. He earnestly outlines the conflict between serving America's "urban needs" and "the expenditure of $30 billion per year in Vietnam" and proclaims:

We cannot afford *not* to spend what is required to solve the problems of the ghettos because the failure to solve them is endangering the future of our cities. . . . And even if, as some propose, we could contain this danger through repressive police action and limited welfare palliatives, this would merely postpone the day of reckoning. As a nation committed from the beginning to the principles of equality and opportunity, we could not for long continue to deny both of these to the large segment of our urban citizens now prevented from attaining them by historical and economic forces beyond their control.[27]

A year later, a *Los Angeles Times* headline would tell readers, "Oakland Minority Job Program Labeled 'A Pretty Big Disaster.'" The EDA program had created only thirty-three jobs. In 1973, Jeffrey Pressman and Aaron Wildavsky published *Implementation: How Great Expectations in Washington Are Dashed in Oakland*, where they argued that "the urban experiment had raised expectations but had delivered only meager results." Rather than saving Oakland, the jobs program never delivered a huge influx of capital. One of the only outcomes they could point to was the construction of the Hegenberger overpass to the Coliseum, which failed to provide a single job for the hard core of unemployed Oaklanders. Indeed, by 1969 only $3 million of the promised $23 million had been spent. Consequently, Pressman and Wildavsky argued, Oakland could look forward to being a "service center to the East Bay region" rather than a proud blue-collar manufacturing town. It was also, they concluded, a place where, increasingly, people of color lived and whites from outside the city worked. All of this was a far cry from a Black Panther Party plan, which, as Rhomberg reminds us, "called for a radical redistributional agenda, including a 5 percent capital gains tax on transfers of income property and the property of large corporations, a 1 percent tax on intangible stocks and bonds, increased rental charges and fees at the Coliseum" as well as "a residency requirement for all police and firefighters."[28]

The war on poverty, which, as Martin Luther King pointed out during the sixties, was never adequately funded because of Vietnam, gave way to a growing suspicion of the ability of government to solve social problems and an assault on "big government." With the rise of the New Right, poverty programs and other social spending were slashed and slashed again and tax cuts, the drug war, and the prison-industrial complex became the new holy trinity for America's inner cities. In California, Proposition 13, which has restricted the ability of the state to provide services since the late seventies, embodies the logic of the New Right. Rhomberg points out, "In its first year Proposition 13 cut the city's resources by more than $14 million, causing service reductions, closures of facilities, and layoffs of city employees." More important, this conservative counterattack continues to have a profound impact on economically blighted communities like Oakland: "The fiscal constraints imposed on local governments made any substantive redistributional agenda more difficult and reinforced public dependence on private investment in the city."[29]

By 1991, Ishmael Reed lamented how over a decade of "selfishness and greed" had affected Oakland as flatlanders and hill residents squabbled after the disastrous fire that devastated Oakland's more affluent sections by noting that few people "place the blame where it really belonged." The real enemies of the city's social fabric, according to Reed, were "the blow-dried, face-lifted commodities called politicians" and what he termed

The California Barbarians, who got through Proposition 13, created the conditions for the Oakland Hills conflagration when they passed a measure that told the poor and public school students to go stick it. These are the hoarding fatuous who have lynched our educational system, are in the process of destroying one of the world's great universities, and have closed libraries. They're the reason we don't have firefighters or the equipment. They're the reason we don't have enough police on the streets, so that our neighborhoods both urban and suburban, have been taken over by crack dealers, both the Nike-wearing type and the bankers who hold their money.[30]

Things would improve briefly for Oakland and the state in the mid to late nineties as the economic boom poured tax dollars into state and city coffers, but by 2003 the bubble had burst and a Republican minority had succeeded in recalling California's mediocre Democratic governor and jamming a draconian budget down the throat of the weak Democratic majority in the State Senate and

Assembly by refusing to vote for a single tax increase to help close the budget gap. On the federal level, the Bush administration was pouring billions of tax dollars into Iraq while the states were drowning in red ink at home. It was yet another defeat for "big government," and students, the poor, and those in need of healthcare and city services would continue to pay for it.

Even during the late nineties boom, California's marginalized inner-city young people have seen more stick than carrot. As Diego Vigil has pointed out, the "backlash against the Great Society, and all the rest of what the sixties represents" has led to a strategy of "unilateral suppression" of kids and young adults like the ones who rioted after the Super Bowl. Prison spending in California increased by ten times between 1980 and 1994, and with the recent passage of Proposition 21, a juvenile crime initiative, more teenagers can now be tried as adults and be sent to serve time in the state's burgeoning prison-industrial complex. Even Oakland mayor Jerry Brown, "governor moonbeam" image aside, was elected in 1998 on what Craig Thompson of the *East Bay Express* describes as a "four-point platform: ten thousand middle-class residents downtown; a no-nonsense crackdown on crime; remaking the city into Northern California's art Mecca; and, of course, liberating children from the shackles of their own public schools." Brown, who signed Proposition 13 into law in 1978 despite his reservations, has arguably failed on all four fronts, but his brainchild, the Oakland Military Institute, is still seeking to instill an "iron will" into "disadvantaged ghetto kids"[31]

Still, after decades of bashing the sixties, assailing government, and criminalizing and imprisoning inner-city young people, events like the Super Bowl riots persist. Consistently refusing to address the deep, seemingly intractable structural economic and social problems that are the breeding ground for events like the Raider riots, California has chosen instead to moralize and punish, mocking attempts to "understand" as failed liberal relics and speaking piously of "family values" and "personal responsibility." As a result, our society has become what Barry Glassner has called a "culture of fear" that blows events like the Super Bowl riots out of proportion, making demons out of young "Raider thugs" and blaming them for conditions not of their making. Glassner's analysis of our culture's fear of criminal youth is an apt explanation of why the fringe of Raider Nation has come, in the national imagination, to stand for the monstrous unruly other:

> Our fears grow, I suggest, proportionate to our unacknowledged guilt. By slashing spending on educational, medical, and antipoverty programs for youths we adults have committed great violence against them. Yet rather than face up to our collective responsibility we project our violence onto young people themselves.[32]

Hence voters continue to prefer funding prison beds rather than community college classes or antipoverty programs. Perhaps we can even pass a law making it punishable for kids under eighteen to wear Raiders gear on the street.

Terroristic Hyperrealism

Raider haters frequently like to point to events like the Super Bowl riots and claim that they are representative of Oakland as a whole (or Los Angeles before it) and show Raiders fans to be the worst of the worst. Nothing could be further from the truth. Indeed, such rampages are so common that sociologists have invented terminology to describe them. "Post-event riots" have occurred many times over the last forty years in North America in places like Detroit (in 1968, 1984, and 1992), Pittsburgh (in 1971 and 1975), Chicago (in 1992 and 1993), Toronto (in 1983), Montreal (in 1986 and 1993), Hamilton (in 1986), Dallas (in 1993), Vancouver (in 1994), Cleveland (in 1995) and many other professional sports cities. Post-event riots have also occurred after college sporting events in towns like Westwood, Madison, Columbus, East Lansing, and a long list of other places. One scholar counted post-event riots between 1960 and 1972 and found evidence of 313 incidents. If we go back further into North American history, the list is too long to cite. Many of these post-event riots make the disturbances in Oakland look like a tea party. In Vancouver, 70,000 people participated in a rampage. There were deaths in Detroit, and, in Pittsburgh, a crowd watched and cheered a rape. A look across the Atlantic shows us that the Raider riots, where no one was seriously injured, should not even be mentioned in the same breath as the soccer hooliganism in Heysel during which thirty-nine were killed in 1985. Equally horrifying "soccer wars" have erupted in Latin America as well. As the November 2004 brawl between Detroit Pistons fans (in the pricey courtside seats) and the Indiana Pacers showed, the world of sports fans, like it or not, is often a violent one. Hence the stereotype of the "Raider thug" or "hooligan" as an exceptionally violent fan is an unsupported myth employed selectively by critics, frequently as a way to lambaste their multi-ethnic working-class fan base.[33]

Some scholars insist that occurrences like post-event riots are best explained by pointing to socio-economic factors like those cited earlier in this chapter. Unemployment, poverty, or other forms of disempowerment are the triggers for such outbursts, they argue, citing examples like the Vancouver riot, where half of those arrested were unemployed. While it is clear that those socio-economic factors were indeed present in Oakland, it is also worth exploring other factors that some might say contributed to Raider rage. In *Among the Thugs*, Bill Buford seeks to explain British soccer hooliganism by exploring the meaning of the crowd. Rejecting a socio-economic analysis, Buford sees things in universalist terms. In the crowd, he claims, we are attracted to "the moment when consciousness ceases: the moments of survival, of animal intensity, of violence, when there is no multiplicity, no potential for different levels of thought: there is only one—the present in its absoluteness." Being part of a crowd, Buford argues, is a crossing of the boundary between self and other that has similarities to religious ecstasy, sexual excess, drug-induced states, and pain. It is "nothingness in its beauty, its simplicity, its nihilistic purity." This has nothing to do with our particular social or economic context because "the crowd is in all of us . . . the crowd holds out certain essential attractions. It is, like an appetite, something in which dark satis-factions can be found." While interesting, Buford's analysis essentializes crowds, narrowing their meaning to a "dark" surrender to "nihilism." For Buford, all crowds are, in essence, fascist.[34]

This suspicion of the crowd goes back to the father of collective behavior theory, Gustave Le Bon, a conservative whose fear of "the mob" was clear. According to Le Bon, the modern world was being taken over by the tyranny of crowds who were bent on replacing "the divine right of kings" with "the divine right of the masses." For Le Bon, "by the mere fact that he forms a part of an organized crowd, a man descends several rungs in the ladder of civilization." By entering the crowd, he argued, we become "unconscious" and therefore subject to "contagion." Crowds were, by nature, totalitarian because they murdered one's individuality. While Le Bon's ideas are still in vogue, they fail to explain differences in crowds (Woodstock versus Altamont, for example) and are fundamentally undemocratic in nature. Furthermore, the view that loss of self is inherently nihilistic relays a profoundly pessimistic view of human nature that lends itself perfectly to the culture of fear while ignoring the actual complexity of human collective behavior. "The people," even Raider fans, are not, to contradict Alexander Hamilton's views on the matter, "a great beast."[35]

Another, more provocative, alternative explanation for post-event riots comes from French thinker Jean Baudrillard. Trying to make sense of the same soccer hooliganism as Buford, Baudrillard argues that "political, sociological or psychological approaches are simply not capable of accounting for such events." The most significant aspect of the brutal events that resulted in the deaths of thirty-nine people at Heysel Stadium in Brussels in 1985, "is not their violence *per se* but the way in which this violence was given worldwide currency by television, and in the process turned into a travesty of itself." This is because, according to Baudrillard, "Today's violence, the violence produced by our hypermodernity, is terror. A simulacrum of violence, emerging less from passion than from the screen: a violence in the nature of the image." Hence, Baudrillard, not unlike Oakland Mayor Jerry Brown, who blamed "media hype" for the riots, claims that television's "very presence will precipitate a violent event."[36]

In Baudrillard's estimation, post-event riots are not "irrational episodes in the life of our society," but rather "something completely in accord with that society's accelerating plunge into the void." In a culture where "real events" have increasingly become mediated by the image, becoming part of the televised show has gained a quasi-religious significance. Thus sometimes fans follow the logic of the society of the spectacle to its logical conclusion. As Baudrillard puts it:

> There is another logic at work here, too, the logic of attempted role reversal: spectators (English fans, in this case) turn themselves into actors; usurping the role of protagonists (players), under the gaze of the media, they invent their own spectacle (which—we may as well admit—is somewhat more fascinating than the official one). Now is this not precisely what is expected of the modern spectator? Is he not supposed to abandon his spectatorish inertia and intervene in the spectacle himself? Surely this is the leitmotiv of the entire culture of participation.

By this logic, one witness of the riots, a high school student interviewed by the *Oakland Tribune*, had it right, "I think the media encouraged people, too. They wanted to put Oakland on the map. I guess people wanted to be on television." Thus, not unlike people who will endure any humiliation to be on a reality TV show, the rioters were simply following the logic of our media-worshipping culture by doing anything to become part of the show.[37]

And let us not forget that we like to watch them. As Francisco Perez told a reporter on the scene as he videotaped the riots, "Man, this is memories, even though it's a bad way." Baudrillard observes that the ancients were more honest: "The Romans were straightforward enough to mount spectacles of this kind, complete with wild beasts and gladiators, in the full light of day." Sports, he reminds us, "can be pressed into the service of any end whatsoever: as a parade of prestige or of violence." Furthermore, Baudrillard contends, violent fans are only mimicking the "state terrorism" inflicted on them, "For there is also a willful pursuit of draconian policies, policies of provocation with regard to a country's own citizens, attempts to fill entire sectors of the population with despair, to drive them to the brink of suicide: all of this is part and parcel of the policies of modern states." Of Margaret Thatcher, the British prime minister at the time of the slaughter at Heysel, he says, "She condemns [the fans], of course, but their brutality remains the very same brutality that she demonstrates in the exercise of her power." One might have said the same of George W. Bush if he had taken time out from rushing to war and bankrupting the federal budget to note the events in Oakland.[38]

So what to do about out-of-control fans, who, as Baudrillard says, "carry participation to its tragic limit, while at the same time daring the State to respond with violence, to liquidate them"? How do we deal with gangs of fans blocking intersections chanting "Raiders! Raiders!" and marching headlong into a phalanx of police in riot gear screaming "Raiders rule! Fuck the police!"? Baudrillard reminds us of a soccer match played in September 1987 in a completely empty stadium in Madrid where "thousands of fans besieged the stadium, but no one got in." Such punishment of unruly soccer fans, he argues, does much to "exemplify the terroristic hyperrealism of our world, a world where a 'real' event occurs in a vacuum, stripped of its context, visible only from afar, televisually." Perhaps, for our protection, this will be our future, with "events so minimal that they might not take place at all—along with their maximal enlargement on screens. No one will have actually experienced the actual course of such happenings, but everyone will have received an image of them." When one considers that the Raider rioters were already hundreds of miles removed from the Super Bowl and are economically excluded from regular attendance even when the Raiders are in Oakland, it becomes clear that they need to be excluded not just from games but from the "transparent form of public space from which all actors have been withdrawn." Someone must keep them away from their television sets. Otherwise, they might take the advice of the wag on the Indy Media website who, responding to a post that characterized the rioters as "a bunch of bored kids," advised: "Murder the organizers of your boredom."[39]

River City Boosters

Three

We Are Everywhere

Last time I checked, criminals do not do charitable work for their respective communities.

Steve Lamoreaux, Raiders fan

Dear God
Could you please speed up time? Friday is coming soon and people on our Raider list are starting (ok constantly) to annoy each other. The only remedy for this is actual Raider Football. A thorough A$$ whoopin' of the Lambs would be greatly appreciated so that maybe some sense of normalcy will return. Thank you.

Scott McCarroll, Raiders fan praying for peace on the
Listserve and conquest on the football field

Just Give, Baby

There was no "welcome home" parade in Oakland. The day after the 2003 Super Bowl nightmare, Raider Nation woke up with a hangover, licked its wounds, wondered what happened, and dreamed of next year. Fans on Oakland's East 14th Street picked up the wreckage after the riots, others went to work in the

East Bay suburbs, read the paper in Washington, D.C., checked the weather in Anchorage, got online in Manchester, England, or had *machaca* for breakfast and skimmed through a magazine in Mexico City. While the off-season certainly does represent a lull in the life of Raider Nation, the imagined community of fans does not go into hibernation altogether. In addition to fans in the Bay Area who may see each other in the flesh on a regular basis, the far-flung Raider diaspora goes to booster club meetings, attends occasional Raider events, and keeps the Silver and Black home fires burning online in the virtual Raider Nation.

On March 9, 2003, Bay Area fans held a raucous fund-raiser for the "Griz," the fan who was the victim of a hit-and-run by an SUV after the Super Bowl. More than a hundred people showed up at the Long Branch Saloon in San Leandro and paid a $7 cover charge, ate barbeque, and drank beer to help raise money for Greg Jones's medical costs. Banging their heads to live metal bands, or bopping along to rap and rhythm-and-blues acts, the crowd partied from one in the afternoon until two in the morning. Led by Rob Rivera and the Black Hole fan club, the silver-and-black-clad revelers (with some in spike-laden costumes) tailgated their asses off, altruistically. Jones, the injured insurance salesman, thanked the crowd gathered in the bar's parking lot and told the *Oakland Tribune*, "We have a common bond. It's something we're born with. It's in the blood."[1]

Raiders fans' charity activity extends well beyond Raider Nation. As booster club members like Larry Mastin of Vacaville explained to us, he and others send care packages to soldiers overseas. A veteran himself, Mastin remembers how difficult it was to be far away from home and how listening to Raiders games on the radio or reading about them in the paper brought him solace. "These guys appreciate anything that reminds them of home and being able to follow your sports team does that," he told us. Steve Lamoreaux of the Carson City Raiders Booster Club in Nevada is also proud of Raiders fans' communitarian ethos:

Our club members (all 150 of them) function as a family and I am very proud to be a part of that family. Our club has also done tremendous things for the Carson City Community over the last 10 years. Same could be said about the other 40+ booster clubs around the country. Last time I checked, criminals do not do charitable work for their respective communities. I believe Raiders fans have been given the wrong image by other fans and/or the media.

Tony Lara of the New Mexico Raiders booster club also emphasizes his group's good works and family values. "Our club is a family club," he told us. "Our club is involved in many community projects. We have gotten a very good reputation for helping on many charity fund-raisers and other community events."

Could this be true? Are all these do-gooders really bent on killing the Raiders' outlaw thug image? Apparently so. The Oakland Raiders Internet Boosters Club has generously contributed to a long list of charities. Some of the beneficiaries of their Raiders love and compassion have included the Children's Hospital of Oakland, the Women's Recovery Association, East Bay Habitat for Humanity, and East Bay Outreach Project, among many other groups. In addition to the Internet Boosters' efforts, another group of fans, the Skeleton Crew, buys tickets for poor kids who can't afford to go to Raiders games. Even the Malosos So. Cal. Raiders Booster Club with their menacing helmeted skull logo and tough guy image have a charity drive for an orphanage in Tecate, Mexico, with Malosos members heading down to deliver food, blankets, toys, "and a smile" to less fortunate kids.

What these activities illustrate is that the imagined community of Raider Nation has a life independent of football. Rather than simply functioning as sad bogus substitutes for "real" community, Raiders fan communities have, in some cases, turned their efforts back toward civic engagement. While hardly utopian in nature, these efforts do reveal a yearning for community that has survived the atomization of the postmodern era.

Virtual Raider Nation

While some fans devote themselves to charitable works and booster club activities, others feed their off-season hunger for the Raiders by taking to the Internet. Sometimes full of love and humor, other times seething with hatred or overcome by paranoia, the virtual Raider Nation helps form the glue that holds the imagined community together. Through things like Raider fan radio, fanzines, websites, chat rooms, and Listservs, fans can communicate with each other, debate football, flame one another mercilessly, give advice, discuss politics, share opinions about music or film, and argue over Al Davis's various legal battles. As David Rowe has pointed out, the Internet has allowed "the passive sports media consumer" to become an "all powerful media auteur." Fans can rearrange pre-existing materials, write their own texts, set up forums, arrange events, and network with other fans on the local, national, and international level. Completely independent of the Raiders organization in most cases, Raiders fan sites are a kind of do-it-yourself media world where fans rather than corporate elites determine the content.[2]

Raiders fan websites run the gamut of tones and styles. Many of them are football-only sites and post articles, statistics, and other Raiders news. Others, however, are more colorful, complete with animation (such as a cartoon Al Davis toasting the Black Hole with a foamy beer mug), theme songs (like "Raider Nation" and "C'mon Raiders"), video hookups, chat rooms, and a complex network of subject areas and links connecting the user to related Raiders sites or Silver and Black shopping opportunities. A tour of the highlights of the virtual Raider Nation starts for many fans at www.Raiderslinks.com, a site maintained by Peach that provides links to a wide range of Raiders-related websites. Peach's site has been visited by close to 200,000 fans since 2001 and lists most of the best but not all of the more than 100 Raiders websites, which range from Pirate Saq's Pirate Ship to Tufty's House of Pain.

Perhaps the most professional and comprehensive of the Raiders sites is "Nicole's Silver and Black Attack" at www.silverandblackattack.com. Maintained by Nicole Joyner, the daughter of former Raiders defensive back L.C. Joyner, Nicole's site provides the Raiders fan with a solid team history from the Raiders' dismal beginnings at Kezar Stadium, Candlestick Park, and Frank Youell Field through the team's glory years to the present. Here curious fans can learn that Western movie star Randolph Scott is rumored to be the face that inspired the Raiders pirate. They can also read about the history of the Raiders theme song, "The Autumn Wind," which is narrated by the former voice of NFL films, John Facenda. A list of "Raiderisms" explains to the novice that fans call the Coliseum "the House of Thrills" rather than "the suits'" favorite, "The Net." This section also decodes Raider nicknames like "Rainbow" for Lyle Alzado with his steroid-induced mood swings and "Horse face" for much-hated former Bronco quarterback John Elway. The best part of the "Fan" section is the map of Raiders fans that pinpoints the location of selected fanatics in all fifty states, Canada, England, Australia, Belgium, Costa Rica, Denmark, Germany, Greece, Italy, Jamaica, Japan, Mexico, Norway, Poland, South Africa, and Spain. If an intrepid fan is hungry for controversy, Joyner has included an analysis of the personal seat license/attendance/lawsuit fiasco that is filled with intelligent commentary.[3]

Other websites of note include Darth Freeman's Christian Raiders Page, which hosts a list of Christian Raiders from around the nation, Darth Raider's page and Darth Raider's Fan Galaxy, both of which feature fans dressed up as Darth Vader of *Star Wars* fame and lots of cool space graphics and Raider links. Raiders 'Till Death is Big Cory's "clean and sober" site, which features a menacing picture of the Grim Reaper and BlackHole Mike's Raiders for Life, which greeted the visiting fan with a swirling Black Hole graphic and a cartoon figure who dropped his drawers and peed on a 49ers logo (BlackHole Mike has meanwhile got religion and changed his site). A fan interested in still more Raider Nation craziness might head to the Raider Shack, where "Raider bones" will take you on a virtual tour of his house, complete with musical accompaniment. Then you might surf by the Bad Boys of Football, where a skeleton gives you the bird, before heading over to the Darkside. Not for the timid, the Darkside features gothic-style graphics and a thorough fan photo gallery as well as a "Hall of Vanquished Foes" featuring "cybersluts" and "cyberskanks."

As Robert Putnam has observed of virtual communities, "because of the paucity of social cues and social communication, participants in computer-based groups find it harder to reach consensus and feel less solidarity with one another." The result of this is that "participants in computer-based settings are less inhibited by social niceties and quicker to resort to extreme language and invective." This observation certainly applies in virtual Raiderdom, where posters on the Raider fan mailing list, Fans in Black, and elsewhere are far more likely to "flame" a fellow fan in a chat room than they would be to curse a fellow fan at a tailgate or in the stands. Consequently, reading Raiders cyberchat is at times a brain-numbing endeavor that requires you to sort through a myriad of petty insults and hateful vulgarity in order to read something about football. If the two years we spent lurking on Raiders sites on a daily basis is any indication, Putnam is clearly right that "cyberspace represents a Hobbesian state of nature, not a Lockean one." Neither an isolated "cyberghetto" where all interests are monolithically shared, nor a democratic "cybercommunity" based on an ethic of reciprocity, virtual Raider Nation is an anarchic free-for-all where the lack of physical proximity changes the rules. Thus, not just homophobia and sexism, but also racism and a whole plethora of other ugly aspects of Raider Nation's political unconscious surface on the Internet along with denunciations of such bigotry and genuine expressions of fellow feeling and solidarity. It is also important to note that the virtual Raider Nation is probably not different from the rest of cyberspace in that a kind of cyberapartheid exists, with more white and middle-class fans online than working-class or African American or Latino fans. Hence, it's likely that the foul-mouthed virtual thug assaulting your masculinity is not a genuine street tough from East Oakland but rather an overweight, middle-aged Willie Loman computer geek from Red Neck, Arizona.[4]

On issues of class the virtual Raider Nation is uniformly anti-elitist, but the forms of populism that inhabit Silver and Black cyberspace range from traditional blue-collar hostility to snotty rich guys (frequently from the more chic city across the bay) to what Thomas Frank has called "backlash populism." For the old school populists, economics still matter and it is bosses and corporations and the affectations of wealth that get skewered. For the backlashers, on the other hand, as Frank tells us, "It is primarily a matter of *authenticity*, that most valuable cultural commodity. Class is about what one drives and where one shops and how one prays, and only secondarily about the work one does or the income one makes." Thus the right and left wings of Raider Nation can unite in their hatred of the 49ers and their fans. The rightwing Raiders fans can hate them because they drink French wine, drive BMWs, and vote for tax-raising liberals, and the leftwing Raiders fans can hate them because they are the rich yuppie scum who are busting the unions and gentrifying every inch of the Bay Area. In either case, they are the enemies of regular folk variously defined.[5]

Divisions in the imagined community of Raider Nation also emerge during times of war or political conflict. In the wake of 9/11, many websites sprouted flags and earnest tributes to the fallen heroes of that day, but this unanimity did not hold as time passed. While our unscientific survey of the virtual Raider Nation leads us to conclude that many fans seemed to support the war in Iraq, others debated with them, and eloquent posts about the loss of civil liberties under the Bush administration were published as well. On one site, Raiders fans groused about CNN as the "Communist News Network" and slammed war protesters, while another site posted a link that led fellow fans to Vote to Impeach, a website devoted to ending George W. Bush's tenure as commander-in-chief. A Raider web surfer can find other political debates about the Supreme Court ruling on the presidential election in Florida, economics and class, affirmative action, police policy, and, of course, *Oakland Raiders* v. *Oakland-Alameda County Coliseum*. As opposed to the stereotype of all football fans as bigoted Neanderthals, the range of opinion in the virtual Raider Nation is far more diverse. Rightwing macho mingles with angry progressivism. In sum, the politics of Raider Nation are hard to gauge, but a heavy streak of anarchic libertarianism seems to unite posters from the Left and the Right. Whatever you do, just leave Raider Nation alone. This sentiment, and the love of Raiderdom, manages to hold everyone together. Football may not be outside history, but nobody checks your party affiliation at the tailgate. In Raider Nation, July 4 is Al Davis's birthday. Really.

Photo: Joseph A. Blum

Raiderhed

Every Track I Sizzle

> Time to paint the whole world silver and black
> Just like a freight train never looking back.
> *"Raider Nation" from* Waste of Life *by Dead River*

When not tuned in to Raider Fan Radio, Raiders fans like to rock out, and the virtual Raider Nation is also home to a number of Raiders bands. The Slacken-loader website introduces the visitor to a self-described "hard rock/metal/alterna-tive" band, which plays at the Black Hole tailgate party in the Coliseum parking lot, the Raider Rooter Booster Club in Tracy, and American Cycles in Hayward.

These gigs are supplemented by others at the Barbell Lounge, Vinni's Sports Bar, and Bob Dorn Harley-Davidson in Livermore. Slackenloader is joined by Raiderhed in the Oakland Coliseum parking lot battle of the bands as well as by My Hairy Brother, Ryan Roxie and the Silver and Blackouts, and Dead River. While Slackenloader plays mostly non-Raider metal covers, My Hairy Brother (which also has a website) transforms songs such as "My Sharona" by The Knack into a chronicle of the trials and triumphs of Al Davis entitled "Mister Davis," and the Beastie Boys' classic "Fight for Your Right (to Party)" into "Scream for Your Team." They have also created some topical tunes to celebrate various moments in a Raiders season. For example, in honor of last year's Super Bowl, My Hairy Brother changed Lynyrd Skynyrd's "Sweet Home Alabama" into "Sweet Home San Diego," and for the 2000 divisional playoff versus Miami they performed "Dolphin Killers," which parodied the Talking Heads' "Psycho Killer." Finally, on their latest album, *Rock Hard, Throw Deep* (which also includes "Scream for Your Team" and "Mister Davis"), they created the immortal songs "Holy Roller," sung to the tune of "Rawhide," which documents the 1978 game in San Diego that forever changed the forward-fumble rules in the NFL, and "They All Stink," a trash-talking song dedicated to "our" AFC West rivals all done à la J. Geils Band's "Love Stinks."

Another fun staple of the Raider tailgate scene is Raiderhed, the pride of Knumbskull Records. As their website explains:

> Raiderhed was the brain-child of one Van Dammit. A man for many years who has been a season ticket holder and fan of the Raiders through the good and bad. Inspired by last years AFC successes [in 2002], Van wondered how he could pay tribute to such a great team. Being a songwriter and musician it came to him one night watching replays from last season . . . a band completely devoted to the Raiders. Finding talented and versatile musicians, insisting that they be Raiders fans, Van was able to record the CD with the help of Dynomut and StonerDude.

In addition to the aforementioned three (the first two on vocals, Stoner–Dude on drums), the band also includes RaiderMace on guitar and Higher 1 on bass. Raiderhed, and its side-project, Bong, whose *Tokes* is also on Knumb-skull Records, describes its music as a fusion of funk, jazz, hard rock, and punk. Admirers of Fishbone, Bad Brains, P-Funk, Primus, Motown, and more, Raiderhed and Bong are more than just metal bands. Along with gigs at Ricky's, Raiderhed plays the South Shield's tailgate bash before every home game with plenty of energy and a good sense of humor and irony.[6]

Ryan Roxie and his fellow band members in the Silver and Blackouts have all adopted Raideresque stage names with Snake Davis (for Ken Stabler and Al Davis) on lead vocals, Johnnie Ottomatic (for Hall of Fame center Jim Otto) on guitar, Marc Stickum (for the hand goo worn by Lester Hayes and Fred Bilet-nikoff in the seventies) on drums, Dr. Assassin (in honor of Jack Tatum) on keyboards and "Smirk" (perhaps ex-coach Gruden?) on bass guitar. Front and center in the Silver and Blackout's repertoire is the theme song "C'mon Raiders," which announces proudly "I've got a commitment to/the animals at the Oakland Zoo/I've got a commitment to Excellence . . . Oi, Oi, Oi . . . Hey Raiders! You a fan? You better be . . . Cause they're the team the world loves to hate/You represent, the California State!" All of this is punctuated, of course, with searing guitar riffs suitable for head banging. For a listen of your own, dear reader, just stop by their website.[7]

The new kid on the block when it comes to the Raiders music scene is Dead River. Promoted as "Hardcore Rapcore Extreme Sports Music," Rude, Germ, Krank, and Ben Stone open their latest CD, *Waste of Life*, with "Raider Nation." "Just like the hounds of hell we're on your trail," they warn anyone who'll listen. "Try to stop us and we'll make you pay!" Rude growls into the microphone as Ben, Germ, and Krank grind out their best death-metal noise between verses. "Whatchu gonna be? Whatchu gonna be?," Rude asks menacingly. "Gonna be, gonna be, a Raider Nation!" comes the answer. While the response in the virtual Raider Nation was lukewarm at best, Rude and the boys have gotten airplay at 98 Rock in Sacramento and 101.7 Fox in Santa Rosa.[8]

By far the most famous and original piece of Raiders music apart from "The Autumn Wind" is "Oakland Raiders" by the Oakland rap duo The Luniz. The song is featured on the 2002 CD *Silver and Black,* whose cover features Yukmouth and Numskull sitting on the hoods of two separate Cadillac Escalades, one silver and one black, sporting Raiders and Oaktown jerseys. Behind the two of them and their Escalades is a mock Raiders shield painted on a brick wall with a sneering condom head wearing an eye patch standing in for the familiar pirate. As Yukmouth's "Smoke-A-Lot Records" website bio informs us:

Yukmouth is from Oakland CA. He started rapping in Jr. High School with rap partner Numskull and the group brothas with potential in West Lake Jr. High School in Oakland. Yukmouth being caught up with the streets was a hustler that stayed in and out of jail so eventually he stayed in jail for a yr, then he started getting serious with his rappin ability cuzz he was tired of slanging crack and going 2 jail [sic].[9]

Eventually the duo "turned the dope deal into a record deal" and put out The Luniz album *Operation Stackola,* which went gold in 1995. "Oakland Raiders" is "town shit" (Oakland rap) that maps and describes the tough flatlands of Oakland as the song begins:

Yo, yo I'm from da land of the playa, slick talkas, and colla poppas
Narcotics, and boss ballas, pit bulls and rot weillers
Niggas wit gold teeth, old schools on gold feet, killas, and O.G.'s
Task postil da police
Mac Arth to foothill, East 14th
Sobrante park, woodfield, Plymouth, and walnut street
From the ville to seminary to the rollin 20's.

Then the Raiders are brought in as a symbol of street credibility and gangster rap bravado that stretches far beyond the Oakland flatlands: "Rock residential slang crack and pack pistols / Every track I sizzle / Cuz I'm Raider, Oakland Raider / From da bay to L.A. to Las Vegas / Cuz I'm a playa, a boss playa / and if you wit me pop ya colla shake dem hatas / I'm a Raider."

The song goes on to salute a litany of other rappers like Tupac Shakur as fellow "Raiders" and takes the listener on a tour of Oakland: "From the Lake on Sundays, to the five O / Now we to Eastmont wit the sideshows" because "it's fun, and I'm famous, but I ain't trying to die tho." Survival is tough, because "I'm da city of dope, the town of the crack / I'm from the city of pimps, the town of the mac / East Oakland! . . . Where niggas get sideways / Shoot outs from the highways / Yo, East Oakland Bitch! I'm a Raider!"[10]

A listen to the rest of *Silver and Black* with songs like "Street Money," "Fuck You," and "Fugitive (Armed and Dangerous)" will give any interested party an unapologetic tour of life in the underclass of the Oakland flatlands. Surely not a favorite of the Oakland Chamber of Commerce, *Silver and Black* embodies all that has come to be reviled about commodified "gangsta rap" by conservative culture warriors, Bill Cosby, and concerned parents alike. Without engaging the uninteresting debate about whether rap causes criminality, it is worth noting that "Oakland Raiders" does give the outside observer a glimpse into Oakland street culture and shows how the symbol of the Raiders pirate has itself been pirated by a whole generation of kids who don't buy personal seat licenses but feel a strong sense of ownership over the Raiders image nonetheless. They uphold the debased underside of Oaktown as a banner of identity and neighborhood pride. If you don't like it, too bad. Beyond Oakland, "from the Bay to L.A. to Las Vegas," being a Raider has come to mean being a "playa" rather than the weak guy who ends up losing out. Other Raiders fans might be horrified by the news, but the kids at the sideshows in East Oakland imagine themselves as part of Raider Nation, too. We can't say that Al Davis hasn't cultivated the gangster image a bit himself in his own way. The kind of savvy underground entrepreneurial ethos one sees in much of hip-hop culture might easily be summarized with the phrase "Just Win, Baby."

Raider Empire

Beyond sharing music, debating politics, and, of course, talking tons of football smack, the virtual Raider Nation is a way to bring together members of the Silver and Black legions separated by vast distances. What a lurker surveying the wealth of Raiders websites will also discover is that the Raider Nation does indeed include a national and global diaspora. As Jim Zamora notes, "Raiders fans want to rule the planet. And they already have an active column in 20 nations from Norway to New Zealand to Nicaragua—not to mention all 50 states." During our research we interviewed fans from across the continental United States, Alaska, and Hawaii as well as Raider lovers in Italy, Australia, Poland, Mexico, Ecuador, Canada, England, Germany, Costa Rica, Scotland, and Spain. We also heard word of Raiders fan groups forming in South Africa, Belgium, Columbia, and Sweden.[11]

The Oakland Raiders are the only professional football organization to officially recognize booster clubs, and there are fifty-nine listed on the team's website, from the Raiders of the Far North in Anchorage, Alaska, to the South West Florida Silver and Black Attack. If the spine of Raider Nation is East 14th Street from downtown Oakland to Hayward and the heart is the Coliseum parking lot on game day, then Raiders fan groups at bars around the country constitute major arteries pumping Silver and Black lifeblood from west to east and north to south, sustaining the body of the Nation. Raiderheads gather at the Long Branch Saloon in Anchorage, Alaska; the Foundry in Aurora, Illinois; Brenn's Pub in York, Pennsylvania; Uncle Jed's Roadhouse in Bethesda, Maryland; and Hoots in Las Cruces, New Mexico, where they take over the bar on Sunday and grill in an enclosed patio area they have constructed specifically for that purpose.

In addition to these "official" fan groups, there is an unofficial legion of Raiders fans online and in sports bars and living rooms across America and across the globe. In the process of our research we heard from fans in Miami, Florida; Spokane, Washington; Portland, Oregon; South Windsor, Connecticut; Tulsa, Oklahoma; Easton, Maryland; New Orleans, Louisiana; El Paso, Texas; St. Louis and Kansas City, Missouri; Denver, Colorado; Atlanta, Georgia; Philadelphia,

Pennsylvania; Rapid City, South Dakota; and a long list of other cities and towns. From rural Kansas to the frigid plains of North Dakota, Raiders fans came out of the woodwork to tell their stories. From ex-Jets fans in New York City to those who have rejected the Steelers in Erie, Pennsylvania, the Raider Empire happily sprawls and proclaims its existence proudly. As Marc Gutierrez, a warehouse worker from El Paso, says, "We might live in Cowboy country, but we all live in Raider Nation."

Fans like Ron Snow of Colorado have found a bit of Raider Nation all around the country, "I have lived in five states and never been any place where there aren't any Raiders fans." His job on the rails has allowed him to spread a bit of Raiders spirit himself, "I do whatever the Union Pacific Railroad tells me to do . . . I have 34 years of railroading with 3 railroads." Similarly, Raiders fan Jeff Childs of Nova Scotia worked as a long-haul trucker: "My truck used to have Raider plates on it, and a huge shield painted on the back of the cab . . . which incidentally got me a few strange looks as I was unloading at the new Mile High Stadium a few years ago." On one trip to the West Coast Jeff remembers, "I joined up with the Imperial Valley Oakland Raiders Booster Club. [I am] member 175 . . . I still carry the card in my wallet!" In addition to rambling Raiders fans like Ron and Jeff, fans like Guadalupe Loera of New Mexico spread the word in other ways. Loera told us, "I own a Catholic book and gift store, I have never done drugs or been in jail. I am a normal guy" whose goal is to one day "go see the Raiders live."

Raider Nation includes single mother of two sons Amanda Briggs of York, Pennsylvania; Nancy Machiando of Aurora, Illinois, a currently unemployed former fund-raiser for Big Brothers and Big Sisters; Amin Badruddin, a systems administrator from Atlanta, Georgia; Dan Bartolomeo, a steel mill worker from Pittsburgh; and Clifford Bolden, an EMT from Springfield, Massachusetts. While many members of the Raider diaspora have made pilgrimages to Oakland, many others have never set foot in either Oakland or Los Angeles. Some tell harrowing tales of enduring abuse from angry home fans in Buffalo, Kansas City, Philadelphia, Boston, Denver, Baltimore, Seattle, and New York. Raiders fans told us of being drenched with beer in Buffalo, coldcocked in Baltimore, beaned with batteries and snowballs in Denver, threatened in Philadelphia, and verbally abused by hostile drunks in New York. Canadian fan "Bonesaw" tells of a game in Buffalo where "I must have had six beer cans thrown at me (empty) and my poor buddy got knocked right in the head." Steven Clark of New York, who has attended many games at the Meadowlands and the old Veterans Stadium in Philadelphia, says, "I can't imagine any crowd in L.A. or Oakland being any worse." He recalls a game in New York where boisterous Raiders fans took over the stadium as the Raiders crushed the home team: "There was even a chant of 'Let's go Raiders' that was louder than the traditional J-E-T-S . . . JETS, JETS, JETS one that goes on every game. It was that night that I realized how the Raiders were truly a 'national' team, rather than a regional one. The fans come from far and wide and wear their pride on their sleeves."

Such "road warrior" tales are central to Raiders fan lore, and they make the Silver and Black legions the closest thing the NFL has to the Deadheads who followed Jerry Garcia and the boys from town to town as if on a vision quest. Some fans even collect and trade videotapes of old games as if they were bootleg CDs of rock shows. Raider webmaster "Peach," who lives in Missouri and has been to only a couple of games in person, sees the Deadhead parallel himself:

Like Dead Heads, Harley Riders or Police, we take what we do seriously and it pays off in friendships and family, not in beating others and burning cities—no matter what you read in the press. Are all Dead Heads jobless dopers? Are all Harley riders thugs? Are all police on the take? No, no, and NO . . . Live and breath the Raider Mystique and you'll meet some very nice people. The Immaculate Deception, Holy Roller, Lytle Fumble, Sea of Hands, Heidi Game, and the Snow Job will all be a part of you. It's awesome stuff, it's all part of what being a Raiders fan is all about.

Separated by half the country from his beloved Raiders, Peach still feels part of something larger than himself. By creating the site that serves as one of the main gateways into the virtual homeland, he can be at the heart of Raider Nation, even in Missouri.

Being a Raiders fan in New Hampshire can be lonely. A fan of the Silver and Black since he was twelve, Dale Pendexter remembers watching games with his uncle at his grandmother's house and being impressed by how often the Raiders were able to come back from almost certain defeat. He liked the fact that they won a lot and has been a fan ever since. Dale goes to Oakland once a year, and when the Raiders play the Patriots he attends games at New England. Mostly, though, he gets his Raiders fix from his Sunday NFL Direct TV ticket and subscribes to *Silver and Black Illustrated*. He spends the off-season embellishing the "Raider room" in his house, which has black walls and ceiling and trim painted in a specially mixed shade of silver. Dale points out that "people think I'm obsessed" because of his black motorcycle, black Raidered-out pickup truck, and black lab named Raider (who, apparently, can say his own name), but he also believes that because he has a target for his intensity—he calls himself the "Number One Raider Fan in New England"—he stays out of trouble in other ways.

In Oakland and other parts of the United States, many Raiders fans are recent immigrants from Mexico, Latin America, India, the Far East, or elsewhere. Just as Raiders fans are coming from abroad to America, the increasingly pervasive distribution of the NFL product abroad is creating a Raiders World. We spoke to Canadian fans like Anthony Nardi of Toronto, whose cell phone chimes "The Autumn Wind," and Lee Hutchinson of Calgary, whose Raider couture got him in a bit of a pickle. Hutchinson recalls:

> I used to own a set of Raiders boxer shorts . . . so after drinking . . . a lot, we ran into a few of the Stampeders [Canadian football team] at a bar, and they are carrying on about how good they thought they were and I had to put my two cents in and tell them that they are simply rejects from the NFL and told them that a real team are the Oakland Raiders and as I proceeded to whip down my pants to show them the boxers of the Raiders I was wearing I pretty much took a shit kicking of a life time!! From a few of the boys from the

Stampeders!! A good night, a good ass kicking, and a few too many drinks!! But in the end they still suck and the Raiders are king!!

Across the Atlantic, the UK is home to the Raiders Fan Club of Great Britain. Brits like Steve Waite of Chester aren't ceding anything to their North American counterparts in Raider Nation: "I have a memorabilia collection that fills two rooms of my house! This includes signed stuff, Super Bowl stuff, programs, and game films going all the way back to the Blanda era." Steve has even made the trip all the way to Oakland to see a game and has a few good war stories to tell as well: "I was standing and yelling during warm-ups close to the Black Hole when this dude on the end of the line next to me throws up over the railing mid-sentence and then continues yelling as though nothing happened. You had to be there, I suppose, but it was funny as hell at the time."

Steve Poland, also from Britain, is a private investigator whose dream is to win the lottery and be able "to buy a season ticket and stay in the U.S. for the duration of the whole NFL season." A member of the British fan club, Steve has written articles in its fanzine about his trips to Raiders games in L.A. and his amazing memorabilia collection that includes over 9,000 items. As he told us, "I have cards that contain pieces of Game Used Jersey, Pants, Helmet, Shoe, Face Mask, Balls, and even End Zone pylons and Stadium Turf!" Derek Ryce of Paisley, Scotland (just outside Glasgow) works for a whiskey producer that bottles brands such as Chivas Regal and Glenlivet and follows the Scottish Claymores as well as the Silver and Black. Ryce, whose job is likely the envy of many a Raiders fan, wears his own "Rice" jersey in honor of the man who he calls "my idol."

Australian fans like Paul O'Shanassy of Melbourne get up at 4 a.m. to watch their beloved Raiders play while living down under, but also make trips to the heart of Raider Nation. One of O'Shanassy's trips to Raider Mecca almost ended in ruin. After coming a few thousand miles to see a frustrating loss, O'Shanassy and his friend were in a foul mood and almost got arrested after field-goal-kicking a beer bottle into a police car only to be released "after I was able to convince them that [we] were Aussie tourists" and "they felt sorry for me because of the look of terror on my face." The only kicking eighteen-year-old Polish student Artur "Fred" Chielowiec enjoys is that done by his hero, Sebastian Janikowski, the "Polish Cannon." "I follow the Raiders because I like hard game and faithful fans just like Black Hole," he told us. "I like Sebastian Janikowski" and thanks to him "I'm Raiders Fan." From Italy, Raiders fan Massimo Corsi told us, "I work for create the first Oakland Raiders Booster Club of Italy, I have sent the request to Raiders Booster Club and I waiting for the answer. My dream is to watch a Raiders match in the Coliseum Stadium." Mark Phillips of Liberia, Costa Rica, was born and raised there but has family in California. He was out of luck in terms of watching games until about ten years ago "when the cable companies took all over the country. So now we can watch the games, most of them, live, in Fox Sports, NBC, or ESPN." His football-watching crew, he explained, is a blend of locals and expatriates: "There are six Americans, four Costa Ricans (including myself) and even a Canadian."

In Mexico City, Barujo, an electrical engineer who works for the Mexican government, told us, "Obviously, I would rather watch a Raiders game than go out with a girl. If I do go out, I make sure that we go to a place where the game is playing, but for the most part I avoid dates when the game is on." He became a Raiders fan when he was seven years old and he "watched them beat the Eagles in Super Bowl XV." Barujo says that "the Raiders for me are more than a football team, they are a way of life, a way of being, because they represent liberty without reaching the extremes of licentiousness." The Raiders' "El Señor Al Davis represents a unique figure that is to be followed because he is a person that is vastly cultured and with revolutionary ideas." Also important for Barujo is the fact that Davis "has always given opportunity to people based on their qualifications thus becoming the first to hire a Latino coach, Tom Flores, and a black coach, Art Shell." As for the fans, they represent "liberty" as well but "also represent the working class, something that I identify with since my family is of this origin, without representing the hypocritical glamour of other teams such as the Dallas Cowgirls or the 49ers . . . the Black Hole is a must see, that is truly an atmosphere. You can truly feel the passion in that stadium."

Barujo has many memories of watching the Silver and Black in Mexico. When he was a kid and "would gather up all my action figures and have them watch the games with me so the Raiders could have more fans." As an adult he has watched games in "a hotel room in the Dominican Republic" as well as in the rural Mexican countryside:

> The strangest place I have watched a game was for the last playoff game against the Jets. I was in my father's small hometown in Jalisco for a town fiesta. I was sure that I would miss the game, but to my surprise I walked by a bar and could see that the game was playing. I went into the bar and saw about 10 Raiders fans watching the game with a lot of excitement, yelling after every play. I was very excited and happy to be able to watch the game with other Raider fans.

At home, Barujo's mother reports that "my son becomes unbearable and wants no one to bother him when he is watching the game. And when the Raiders score I think the entire block can hear him." His love of the Raiders actually drove him to seek a job at New Mexico State University, where "I will be able to travel and watch the games in person. That was one of my motivations for taking the job."

Moving in the other direction, Jon Cariveau of Guayaquil, Ecuador, grew up in Livermore, California, and spent many years as a Raiders fan in San Diego. Now that he has been transplanted to South America, Jon is happy to report that the Caliente sports gambling empire stretches through southern Mexico and Central America all the way to Guayaquil, where he can place bets on three-team parlays and compare notes with his friends in the East Bay, San Diego, Panama City, Panama, and Guayaquil. He can watch the games either in the sports bar or at home on the dish with his lovely wife, who, unfortunately, roots for the Rams. Together with a band of expatriate English teachers from the United States and Canada, Jon has not had to miss a crucial Raiders game in nearly a decade. "I've seen Raiders fans all over the country. In Guayaquil, in Quito, in Cuenca, in small towns in the Andes. It's a trip." Indeed it is.

MVP

Four

Training Camp

As a matter of general philosophy, the National Football League is the last bastion of fascism in America.

Ex-Raider Tom Keating

Any society that will put [Hells Angel Sonny] Barger in jail and make Al Davis a respectable millionaire at the same time is not a society to be trifled with.

Hunter S. Thompson, after visiting a Raiders practice

[When] a team plays for a city, it plays for the idea of a team and the idea of a city.

John Krich, Bump City

Our trip into the heart of Raider Nation started strangely at the Universal City Walk in Los Angeles, a mall attached to Universal Studios. After wandering through the bewildering maze of themed restaurants and specialty stores, we saw a man with a Raiders shield tattooed on the back of his shaved head. We followed him and he led us to pay dirt. Outside the Raider Image store, families were lining up to pose for pictures under the giant helmet that framed the door.

A man stood behind a headless number 00 Jim Otto figure for a portrait. We waited patiently, then snuck in after his wife got the shot. Inside we whipped out our handy notepads and began to document our experience. There were party-helmet barbeques, foam pirate swords, Raider thermoses, nutcrackers, flasks, billiard cues, dog leashes, license plates, tire covers, bathrobes, silk pajamas, beer mugs, shot glasses, baby onesies, silver-and-black hair color and face paint, and much more. I picked out a pirate shield binky for our incipient Raider baby and glanced over at the linebacker-sized fellow next to me, who smiled back at me sheepishly as he evaluated a onesie. We moved on to the wall of jerseys and surveyed the t-shirts and all the regular Raider gear, plus a whole line of shirts in Spanish "Compromiso a Excelencia," "Orgullo y Porte," and "Viva Los Raiders." There was even a cholo-style Raider Nation shirt. I noticed that Kelly and I were the only Anglo shoppers in the store and walked over to pick up a hat. In the city of angels, the Raiders clearly were still the Chicano team of choice.

After we bought our stuff, we spoke to Jim T., who helps manage the City Walk and other Raider Image stores in Los Angeles. Two days before, he told us, five thousand people had showed up to get autographs from Tim Brown. Starting at five o'clock in the morning, the Raider hordes had essentially taken over the mall with their sheer numbers. "Tim Brown came out on the balcony across from the store like Caesar with his arms upraised," Jim told us. "Imagine that." When we asked how it all went with such a huge crowd, Jim seemed relieved, "People get pretty angry when they don't get in, but things went pretty smoothly. You see some of the same guys at every signing," Jim explained. "Like one guy who comes in a wheelchair, every time. These guys are pretty hardcore." The day after the Tim Brown event, five hundred more Raiders fans were there for the second day of the grand opening weekend. Raider Nation was alive and well in Los Angeles.

Next it was time to deal with the Raiders organization itself. Here was my plan: get a press pass for our photographer for training camp and the entire football season, set up interviews with players and organization spokespeople, then angle for Al Davis. I had heard the stories about the Raiders' inept public relations, hostility to the media, and general paranoia, but how threatening could a book on their loyal fans be? We were fans ourselves, for that matter—not really media by any stretch of the imagination. We'd just call them and set it all up. When Kelly called the Raiders' front office they referred us to the public relations guy, whose immediate response was derisive laughter. "A book on fans? I'm not going to give you a press pass for a book on fans." We were, it seems, mere pissants to the Raiders hierarchy. After some explaining and cajoling, we were instructed to send the PR guy an e-mail describing our project and requesting a pass for a single game, perhaps in the preseason.

While our lawyers have instructed us that reproducing our correspondence with PR Guy would be ill-advised, let's just say that dealing with the Raiders' disingenuous doublespeak was a frustrating experience that left us scratching our heads. We were denied requests we had not made, generously granted permission to walk through the parking lot, told that the NFL and 9/11 were to blame for the denial of a press pass, and then informed that our requests had not been denied. PR Guy speaks with forked tongue, we thought. Still in limbo with regard to our photographer's press pass, we were, at long last, granted a one-day pass to the training camp in Napa to interview some of the Raiders players.

Hot damn! "Family Day" for fans may have been cancelled, but *we* were in. I e-mailed PR guy back and thanked him for his help. We had been all wrong about him. He returned my e-mail and requested that we call before we came. I decided to strike while the iron was hot and e-mailed yet more thank-yous and yet another "reminder request" about the press pass for our photographer. No response. Undaunted, we called and left a message for PR Guy at both the Raiders' headquarters in Alameda and at the public relations office in the Napa Marriott. Then we packed our bags and headed up to Napa, driving eight and a half hours to an affordable Travel Lodge about a mile from the nearly $300 a night Marriott where the Raiders were staying. After finding a Nation's Giant Burger where we ate our late-night dinner next to a psychotic homeless man who assaulted a napkin holder, we returned to our hotel where several groups of middle-aged wine drunks were stumbling around and yelling after a successful day of sampling merlots and cabernet sauvignons. Some of them had apparently forgotten to spit.

We didn't sleep well after the long drive and the loud drunks, but we managed to get over to the Marriott bright and early nonetheless. Outside the hotel a large bus awaited another gaggle of gauche winery tourists. Inside, the lobby was flush with affectless splendor. The well-groomed man at the front desk directed us to the room where we could pick up our press passes, and an amiable teenager leafed through a stack of envelopes and informed us that there was no room in the inn. My partner and I exchanged suspicious looks and got directions to PR Guy's office. Bleary-eyed, with coffee and notepads in hand, we made our way to the Raiders' PR brain center, a cramped, dimly lit hotel room where PR Guy and his colleague were hanging out in Raiders caps, t-shirts, and shorts.

We were received aloofly as PR Guy informed us that we should have called first. "We did," Kelly said as she glanced over at the other man she had spoken to on the phone the day before. He kept his poker face. PR Guy said he never got the message. The other guy asked why we needed to talk to players if we were writing a book on fans. "For their perspective on the fans," I explained, a little taken aback by the Raiders' official disdain for their loving admirers. Did they think that the Raiders were a public service organization, selflessly donating their time to the ungrateful masses? I smiled at him. He seemed utterly unmoved. It was then that the Raiders' PR strategy crystallized before my eyes in a moment of football *satori:* Fuck you, we're the Raiders. I mentioned that we had driven all the way up from San Diego, and it seemed to break the standoff. PR Guy folded and told us to sign in, and we got our passes—even one for Joe, who was driving in from San Francisco as we spoke. I asked again about Joe's press pass for the preseason game, and PR Guy told me that we'd know by the end of the week. That was the last we heard from him. So much for the interview with Al Davis. For the time being, however, we had done an end-run around the royal Raider blow-off.

To be honest, once we had the press pass, I found myself feeling strangely blessed to have been touched by the Raiders' notorious official paranoia and rudeness. I could now take perverse satisfaction in knowing that I was being tolerated for a brief period of time. After years of loyally following my team and shelling out thousands of my hard-earned dollars, I would be allowed to stand in their godly presence for three hours. Sure the Raiders granted "special privileges" to the booster clubs and occasionally gave tours of Raider Mecca to deserving fans or made their players show up to sign autographs, but I was Dr. Nobody from Nowhere and managed to get in just like Hunter S. Thompson did during the glory years. Now that was an accomplishment only to be surpassed by my brief interview with Raiders great Tim Brown, who responded to my request for a thirty-second chat with, "No, no, no, leave me alone! It's my day off!"

After we got our credentials, we walked back out to the lobby, and I was struck by how ungritty the whole setup was. There was a huge display of fresh flowers in the middle of the lobby and a stack of brochures outlining the advantages of the Amadeus Spa. I cringed at the thought of my beloved Raiders getting aroma-therapy, a mud bath, and a manicure. I glanced over at the faux library and tried to imagine the Tooz driving down the freeway in Oakland shooting at road signs. Could this corporate utopia really be home to the Raiders' working-class rebel mystique? We got another cup of coffee and waited for the 8:45 practice to start. As I sipped my java, I cycled back through the Raiders glory years' legends.

Back in the day, the Raiders camp was not in the sumptuous Napa Marriott but in the El Rancho Tropicana in Santa Rosa, a now defunct lodging described by former team doctor Rob Huizenga as "a funky one-story motel complex" that was affectionately nicknamed "El Roacho Turpentina" by the players. It was "El Roacho" that Pete Banaszak recalls the Hells Angels visiting each summer with the tacit approval of Raiders "everyman" coach John Madden. There, in more humble surroundings, the camp was, according to Huizenga, "one part celebra-tion, one part M.A.S.H. unit, one part riot." By all accounts, when camp was in Santa Rosa, what went on in the Bombay Room before curfew was as important to the team spirit as what happened on the field during practice. "The Raiders are back in town. Lock up your wives, daughters, and house pets," the local paper once proclaimed. There were Raiders orgies, sexual escapades with maids, and "high-tower Johnny" was arrested while attempting to score one night on top of the cherry-picker the team used to film their practices. John Matuszak would kidnap Raiders staffers and make them drive him around as he had sex with his girlfriend.[1]

Ken Stabler, whose long hair was, according to John Lombardo, "the perfect example of the message of fuck-you Raider independence," would study game plans "by the light of a jukebox" in between bouts of his legendary womanizing. Stabler's Raiders dug their hands into "the candy jar" for speed pills, which they called "rat turds." Snake's "wild-eyed" Raiders "would be so wired they couldn't stop moving their jaws." Of the Golden-era Raiders, Ted Hendricks quoted the visionary British Romantic poet William Blake and remembers, "I didn't have to answer to anybody." Gene Upshaw used to rap with Black Panthers Huey Newton, Eldridge Cleaver, and Bobby Seale in Oakland bars, and, as Cliff Branch recalls, "We were very liberal and guys partied, but that never stopped us from getting the job done . . . If you wanted to be a hippie or a Hells Angel, that was fine as long as you played Raider football. John [Madden] gave us a lot of rope, and breaking curfew was encouraged." Ben Davidson with his Harley-Davidson motorcycles and handlebar moustache was, as Mark Ribowsky puts it, "a sixties generation icon of anti-heroism." Chip Oliver, professional football's first hippie linebacker, is alleged to have played on psychedelics; he eventually dropped out and joined a commune. Ex-Raider Tom Keating recalls, "We had people that did *everything*." As George Atkinson puts it, "Shit, when we came to town it was lock up the goddamn kids and the dogs. We had the skull and crossbones on our helmets, the black jerseys, and the whole bit, and we lived it." Jack Tatum's nickname was "Assassin." The Raiders were labeled the "criminal element," and they reveled in it.[2]

The sound of Bach and the antiseptically clean aura of the Marriott tried to break through my badass Raider reverie, but I fought it. Even in the L.A. years, guys like Lyle Alzado kept the craziness going, and Raiders partying and coke use continued to scandalize the league. In recent years, Darrell Russell's ecstasy-fueled fall from grace and Sebastian Janikowski's GHB-induced floor dives have kept the outlaw legend going. Wasn't there even a Raider pot bust last season in San Diego? I struggled to keep the Golden-era rebel outlaw myth alive in my head. Cognitive dissonance? No problem. Wine tourists were heading for the bus in front of the hotel. I thought I recognized Vivaldi's "The Four Seasons" playing in the lobby. Kelly nudged me and told me it was time to head to practice.

As we padded through the posh halls of the Marriott toward the practice field behind the hotel, I clung to my press pass with a strange sense of disbelief. Joe Queenan has observed of such moments that seeing a professional athlete up close and personal is like seeing a god whose feet are not supposed to hit the ground. While fans love their team forever, athletes come and go. I had never been keen on meeting a Raider because I was not deluded enough to think that they wanted anything more from me than my loyal dollars and distant adoration. As for my desires, I wanted them to win. When they didn't win, cut 'em, trade 'em, see you later. No Raider or rock star or Greek god of any other sort was bound to be coming to dinner at my house anytime soon, nor was I heading up to Mount Olympus. Hence, I was emotionally opposed to shattering the aura, but here I was nonetheless.[3]

I passed by the rope that would keep the unwashed masses from getting a peek at the boys in silver and black and stepped onto the magic turf of training camp gazing up at the "Commitment to Excellence," "Pride and Poise," and "Will to Win" banners that hung all around the field. The team was lying on their backs, stretching. We were instructed by security not to sit on the field or step toward the sideline. I glanced over at the blocking dummies. Was I really here? All the exercise equipment at the end of the field was painted silver and black. Coach Callahan was standing at a distance watching the whole field full of prone players. I surveyed the far sidelines—no Al Davis. Indeed, Tim Brown, Jerry Rice, and Bill Romanowski all had the day off as well. As Callahan watched, the other coaches walked through the sea of bodies, all in silver and black except for the kickers and quarterbacks, who wore red. "On your backs! On your butts!" barked one coach. "If you quit wearing those heels you'd do all right!" yelled another. Kelly noted that, at the moment, she was the only female on the field as another coach scolded a player for being a "woman."

Once the drills started, I glanced up at the men high atop the cherry pickers filming the practice. They looked serious. Indeed, the whole affair was a model of corporate efficiency as the players broke into various skill groups to work on footwork, kicking, blocking passing, receiving, and so on. Walter Camp, who saw the football coach as a kind of Taylorist factory manager, would have been happy. "Play with your eyes!" a coach yelled. We watched a scrub who would soon be cut throw a few passes. Jerry Porter was wearing Tim Brown's number 81. Security guards paced back and forth giving the practice an aura of Homeland Security. Nobody looked hungover or wired. There were no fights. I walked back over to the hotel to go to the bathroom and saw Tim Brown talking to a man in a "2002 Wine Tasting Triathlon" t-shirt and a straw hat. It must be a fan, I thought. So I waited patiently for my turn, and, as noted previously, got blown off by Brown. The next day, however, I would discover that the man was a reporter for a Bay Area newspaper who was asking Tim how he felt about getting fewer catches this year. I thought back to Jerry Porter, his competitor, wearing 81 and it seemed clear that I had haplessly stumbled into a Raiders soap opera. Jerry was the only other Raider who refused an interview that day. In this case, being a nobody with a "media" badge on was a distinct disadvantage.

Back out on the field, I met Joe, our photographer, who'd shown up with his camera in a Boilermakers Local 6 hat and t-shirt, just in from taking shots of ironworkers on a Bay Area bridge project. With his long gray hair and beard, he was a strange sight on the Raiders practice field. Any picture we took, we were informed, was the property of the NFL. After watching another few minutes of drills, we noticed a group of fans standing next to us under the cherry picker. We walked over, introduced ourselves, and got their stories. As opposed to the aloof demeanor of the Raiders' public relations guys, the fans were friendly and accommodating. All members of various booster clubs, they had gotten in to see practice under a special deal the team has with its official fan groups. Composing a class of fan royalty, these booster club members get to come to camp, attend official Raiders events, meet players, and get occasional tours of the Raiders' facilities. "Get out of the drill!" yelled a coach to a Raider who wandered out of his area as one of the boosters told us that the Raiders were the only NFL team to officially recognize fan clubs. Indeed, ex-Raider Morris Bradshaw helps coordinate activities, we were informed. While the idea of "officially recognized" fans seemed a bit odd, Jeff Haldeman, Jeff Clark, Larry Mastin, and Dave Laughlin were all very nice guys who told us some great road warrior stories about surviving the hostile confines of the Meadowlands in New Jersey and Veterans Stadium in Philadelphia as well as tales from Baltimore and Buffalo. Jeff showed us pictures of his elaborate Raiders room back home in York, Pennsylvania, and Larry talked about following the Raiders from overseas while he was in the military. He also had a pretty cool Raiders watch. We would meet Dave again the next week at the first preseason game as he tailgated beneath the River City Raider Boosters tent. We talked about Santa Rosa camp lore and exchanged e-mail addresses. No Raiders thugs here, and nobody from Oakland.

Once the practice ended, we strolled over toward the entrance of the weight room where coach Callahan was having his press conference. Almost immediately he was surrounded by a pack of reporters holding cameras, tape recorders, camcorders, and one or two with old-fashioned notepads. He went through the litany of injury reports and comments on rookie performances. We stood outside the cluster of ravenous sports journalists and took pictures of them taking pictures. Kelly lingered by Callahan's escape route to try to snag him for a brief question about fans, but he was too quick, bolting past her and a tubby fellow from a small Bay Area publication. With no Callahan to query, we were left to loiter around outside the weight room and compete with reporters and a throng of fans for the players' attention. Being elite members of the "media," we didn't have to stand behind the white line with the privileged fans or behind the rope like the outsiders. Instead, we jockeyed for position with the *San Francisco Chronicle,* the *Oakland Tribune,* the *San Jose Mercury News,* and other Bay Area news media types. After losing out to all of them, we repositioned ourselves at the end of the line of fans. It was clear that the players had developed a sophisticated system of media/fan avoidance. Player after player emerged from the weight room and suddenly got a call on his cell phone. It was either a spontaneous miracle of coincidental mass communication, or a handy postmodern dodge.

The cell phones allowed the players, almost all of whom stopped to sign balls, helmets, pictures, and other Raiders items, to do the rounds while still managing to maintain an aloof celebrity cool. Player after player came out, cell phone in hand or just about to ring. Deciding that it would be impolitic to try to penetrate the players' protective cell phone bubbles, we watched them head down the line of fans, waiting for a conversation to end or a technophobe to emerge from the weight room. We felt a little bit like birders waiting patiently for a majestic specimen to land on a proximate branch or spectators at an overcrowded zoo hoping for a rare glimpse of a reclusive tiger.

Fortunately for us, not all of the Raiders were plugged in. After security shooed us away from blocking the exit from the practice field several times, we hit pay dirt. Roland Williams stopped and greeted us with a grin before telling us what he thought of the fans: "They're the best fans in the league. The most committed fans in the league." He stopped briefly with a playfully devilish look in his eyes. "They have the highest number of tattoos on elderly women amongst all NFL fans." We laughed, and he continued: "I once saw this guy with a bald head and the shield tattooed all over the back of his head. It was amazing." Beautiful. We thanked him for his time and quickly jotted down some notes. Next came Mo Collins. Mo spent a *long* time signing autographs and spoke with the fans in a very gracious and friendly manner. It reminded me of stories of the old days when the players would come out and stop by fans' tailgate parties after the games or meet them in local bars to hang out. "Raiders fans are very intense and very loyal to the Silver and Black," he told us. "It's great to have that kind of support behind you." We thanked Mo and took notes as a couple of players on cell phones stopped by. A few of the lesser known rookies looked a little daunted by the attention and snuck by quickly with their eyes to the ground as the line of fans failed to recognize them.

Our luck with the big guys was consistently good. If our day in camp was any indication, for the most part the nicest guys on the team are the offensive and defensive linemen. Less glory, fewer cell phones, more smiles. Tackle Brad Badger stopped by briefly and told us, "On game day, it's incredible. Compare it to Halloween. I played in the Coliseum as an opponent and those fans will find anything to pick on you. The intensity of Raiders fans stands out. It's more than with fans of other teams. You know some of those guys would get down on the field and make the tackle themselves if they could." A few more cell phones went by, and, just when I thought Raiders attitude was dead, Jerry Porter came back from the lunch room holding a piece of pizza. When the rush of autograph requests were shouted out he said, "Fresh out of autographs. I ain't got none." "Oh, is it that way now?" said a sassy, flirtatious woman behind the ropes. Jerry kept walking.

Eric Johnson stopped by next after spending a lot of time with the fans, chatting and signing, and said, "Raiders fans are the best. They really help the momentum. Especially the Black Hole fans. On third down and five or fourth down and five they get so loud that other teams can't hear their calls. There is no other stadium like Oakland—except San Diego and that's because it's filled up with our fans, too." He smiled and headed for the lunch room. A reporter was asking Adam Treu a question about Barret Robbins. A lot of the reporters were asking questions about Barret Robbins, that and the Brown/Porter "controversy." Rick Mirer came out and asked us to head over to the shade to talk. "Having played for five other teams I can say that there are passionate fans everywhere, but these fans take an especial pride in the intimidation factor. It's interesting to see it from the other side. Word around the league is, don't take your families to Raiders games. Players get things thrown at them." Comparing Los Angeles Raiders games with games in Oakland, Mirer noted that both were tough venues, but, "The stadium in Oakland is more intimate than the L.A. Coliseum. The fans there try to make it hard on opposing players. It's the things they say." He paused for emphasis and then continued on with a wry smile, "And *the way they say them.* You don't look them in the eyes."

As Rick finished up his comment, Matt Stinchcomb came out and one of his teammates recommended we speak with him. He looked at us as if we were

Photo: Joseph A. Blum

East 14th/International Boulevard—East Oakland

about to try to sell him an overpriced lemon in the back of a used-car lot. "Are Raiders fans good fans?" I asked tentatively of the man who could squish me like a grape. "Of course," he said curtly as he turned his back to us and signed a few obligatory autographs. John Parella, on the other hand, was more talkative: "Raiders fans are some of the greatest fans in football. The most passionate. They don't just come to cheer, they know the game. When I was in San Diego, they were okay. But here, they have a terrible week if we have a bad game." I asked him what he thought of Oakland and/or the East Bay community and he said of the East Bay outside of Oakland, "I live there. So I like it a lot." After we spoke to Parella, we let a few backups and cell phones go by unmolested before we spotted one of our favorite Raiders, Frank Middleton, wearing a t-shirt they sell at Ricky's Raiderland in San Leandro: "60 Minutes of Hell." Frank got right to it, "Raiders fans are crazy lunatics. It's all good. They're not like San Francisco where they drink wine and eat cheese. They really are the twelfth man." When we asked Frank about Oakland, he said, "I don't know much about Oakland. Where does Oakland begin and end? People don't bother you. They show up for football, but they don't bother you." Jerry Porter came back out and signed some autographs, stopping at the end of the line to lean over a very little boy who was playing a Gameboy and ignoring the wide receiver. He had no comment for us. "I'll check you later," he said.

It was hot and most of the team had come out of the weight room, but star quarterback Rich Gannon was still in there. We sweated and waited and Bill Romanowski came out. Just as he was headed our way, a reporter stepped in front of us and grabbed him. It was the wine tour triathlete! There was not much time to mourn the loss of the Romo interview, however, as Gannon appeared in the distance and stopped to speak to a camera crew. When Gannon paused, Charles Woodson came out, went down the line, and spoke to Kelly as he walked: "Raiders fans are the best in the nation," he told her amiably. "In Los Angeles, in Oakland, all over. A few fell by the way because of the switches [between cities], but they come to rallies and are more emotional and a lot more into the game than other fans."

Kelly thanked him, and he disappeared down the hall. Gannon, the big fish of the day, awaited. I watched as he wrapped up the TV interview and, minus cell phone, started signing autographs. Then, two steps away from us, his phone rang. Undaunted, I lurked behind him as he walked over to the fans behind the rope and signed autographs. I would not let the man who represented half of my unnamed number 12 Stabler/Gannon Raiders jersey get away. Who was he talking to? His contractor, it appeared, as I thought I overheard, "I don't want those spindle things put in downstairs, okay?" I kept hanging around. Behind me, players were getting in tricked-out SUVs with perfect black paint jobs and fancy silver rims. Gannon paused, turned his back to the fans, and listened intently to his cell phone. It must have been a home decorating emergency. I think I caught his eye, but he darted away quickly, losing me as he made his way down the hall. Short of tackling the NFL's Most Valuable Player, I was out of luck.

In the meantime, Kelly got in a good interview with Tom, a really nice security guard for the Raiders. "It's beautiful to get to interact with crowds," he told her. "When the Raiders first came back in 1995, the crowds were rowdy. The practice was closed to the public, but people made holes in the walls to watch. They tried to sneak in, too. We had to have security twenty-four hours a day. Sometimes the players would throw their room cards out their windows to girls." Tom stopped and pondered what else to say. "Every now and then we get a Raiders fan out there [behind the ropes] in full gear. Some crazy guy who believes he's an actual Raider. These guys will yell and scream and we'll have to tell them to calm down." Still, Tom loved his job and had great praise for the Raiders family. "Fans in Napa are great. People bring cakes and pies. Family day for the fans gets crazy. I've been to almost every stadium in the NFL and there is nothing like the Raiders fan. The tailgating is something else. It's one big happy family." We thanked Tom. Joe walked over and took a picture of a blonde girl, Amanda Logan, with a Raiders tattoo. I thought about what Frank Middleton said, "Where does Oakland begin and end?" It was time to find out.

We went from mingling with the official boosters with money to spend on plane tickets, vacations in Napa, and wine tours to the center of unofficial Raiders fandom in the heart of East Oakland. Driving down East 14th Street/ International Boulevard, licensed and unlicensed Raiders symbols abound on shirts, jackets, cars, store windows, rugs, blankets, and banners draped on the sides of buildings or hanging in storefronts. These fans who bleed silver and black might be lucky to come up with the cash to make the trip a few blocks down the street to 66th Avenue, turn right and pay a minimum of $47 for a ticket once a year. Their passion is just as strong as that of the official boosters, but, in this case their identity has local roots, tied as it is to the funky poetry of the boulevard. Clusters of kids in Raiders gear who may never have heard of Daryl Lamonica or be able to recognize Al LoCasale, adopt the Raiders' tough image and pirate swagger because it says, "I exist, I'm tough, I can take it."

As we drove along, Joe, our photographer, commented on the character of International Boulevard, "East 14th is a very interesting place. It's a real interesting racial mix, a distinct area where things have changed a lot over the years. It seems to me like it's very much of a melting pot—Vietnamese, Chinese, immigrants from Latin America, Chicanos, and blacks, all along the boulevard. It makes you think of the number 7 subway train in New York City." In the beginning of our journey we passed by the Alameda County Jail near Lake Merritt. Joe glanced over at a building by the lake and told us how Huey Newton had gotten a penthouse there after returning from prison. "He went to Vacaville and came back a different person," he said. "He bought a telescope and used it to look back over at the jail." Joe, it turns out, had a long history in the Bay Area Left:

After my best friend got shot to death in New York City, I dropped out of NYU and came out here. Before going to UC Berkeley I did penance by first going to Oakland City College, which was on Grove Street (it's Martin Luther King now), not far from Eli's Mile High Club. This was 1961. I got an apartment on Alcatraz Avenue and went to Oakland City College, which was a hotbed of activism and the birthplace of the Black Panther Party because both Huey and Bobby Seale were students there. So there was all kinds of activity going on. I also met some radical folks and became involved in the Civil Rights Movement. Friday nights were spent picketing downtown Oakland restaurants in Jack London Square that refused to hire minority workers. Ex-senator William Knowland, who owned the *Oakland Tribune*, was a real right winger and he would come with his entourage and a police escort to whatever restaurant CORE [the Congress of Racial Equality] was picketing, push through our line, and go to dinner there.

I eventually went to Berkeley, graduated in 1965 and got recruited to be on the editorial board of the Movement Newspaper, which had started out as the Northern California Friends of SNCC [Student Non-Violent Coordinating Committee] newsletter, but grew into a national monthly newspaper in the late sixties. I had a strong relationship with Huey Newton in that I had known him peripherally at Oakland City College, where there had been a fierce struggle between the cultural nationalists and a group who were more revolutionary nationalists, led by Huey. When I became editor of the *Movement* newspaper (around the time when the famous picture of Huey sitting in the chair came out before he was shot), I got to go interview him when he was in Alameda County Jail. When I first came in there was a whole line of people in the public visiting area, but he saw me in the back and said, "Let me talk to that white boy for a minute." So I spent a lot of hours with him, which of course he loved because he could be out of his cell. He could come down there and sit and smoke cigarettes and talk about politics. Over the course of several weeks we did an extended formal interview that was eventually published in the *Movement* newspaper entitled "Huey Newton Talks to the *Movement* about the Black Panther Party, Cultural Nationalism, SNCC, Liberals and White Revolutionaries."

East 14th turned into International Boulevard, and we passed by Cambodian and Vietnamese restaurants, Wonderful Boutique, New Saigon Supermarket #2, the Lineman's Club, Tacos Sinaloa, Oakland Bait, and Bui-Phong Bakery. There was a black pickup in front of us with a Raiders shield taking up the entirety of the back window and a van passed by flying a pirate shield flag. In Fruitvale we went by Discolandia, The Gold Key Club/La Llave de Oro Club, and stopped when we came upon Paris Wig and Beauty Supply, where the owner had lovingly painted "Go Oakland Raiders" beneath the announcement for "Human Hair on Sale!" The owner, W.S. Song, has the sign painted every year at the beginning of the season. "It's just my way of supporting the team," he told us. Unfortunately, Mr. Song is always working, so he doesn't get to go to games.

After talking to Mr. Song, we kept driving down International Boulevard, now behind an old Plymouth with a Virgin of Guadalupe on the right side of its back window and a Raiders shield on the left. There were Mexican flags flying in front of some of the shops, and trucks occasionally stopped to unload produce, bottlenecking traffic on the street. We passed by open-air fruit stands and pulled off on a side street to take a picture of a big Raiders shield painted next to the front door of United Auto Body, where a "Raiders Drive" sign was also posted beneath the hours. Back on International, we headed past the Eritrean Ortho- dox Church and continued on, at one point glancing over at the now-repaired McDonald's that had been vandalized the night of the Super Bowl and noting the Kwik Way and the "Men of Valor Academy" across the street. A homeless man was wandering aimlessly in the middle of the road, ignoring the honks and shouts of motorists. A Mexican woman on the sidewalk was strolling with her two little girls in white dresses, a daughter holding each hand. A block or so later a black lowrider with customized silver flames painted across his car's hood was parked by a storefront displaying a Raiders shield. Cruising past Chen's Restaurant, Holiday Fish and Soul Food, and Mandy Ruth's Shelter, I couldn't help but see the street as an ever-unfolding Whitmanesque catalog. The lack of chain stores had kept it from becoming yet another endless, bland, standardized strip mall zone. International Boulevard bristled with life and danger. It was, I thought, one of the last great American streets. I thought of The Luniz song, "East 14th . . . Cuz I'm a Raider, Oakland Raider." and remembered passing a church that proclaimed, "Jesus es el Señor de Oakland."

The distance between the odorless chi-chi halls of the Napa Marriott and the teeming streets where young kids joyfully run and weave back and forth through traffic on bicycles in the summer heat was palpable. Still, something tells me that despite the protestations of more "respectable" fans, and perhaps some of the players themselves, that this is the spiritual heart of Raider Nation, the place where a new generation of fans has transformed the Raiders' aura born of the sixties and seventies into a far more edgy moniker of street polyglot.

Those who say that the tough kids on the corner are "not real fans" hold to the illusion that cultural signs, like football logos, are dead, stable, fixed sites of meaning and cannot be multiply rewritten by whoever chooses to claim them. The world has changed beneath the radar screen of the older generation of fans, and commentators who fail to see how the dramatic disparities between the largely white middle-class suburbs of America and the miraculously diverse new immigrant and old native working- and underclass inner-city neighborhoods has widened to a chasm. Membership in an imagined community, however, is not determined by exclusionary socio-economic barriers, but rather is forged in the mind's eye of the fan. Thus, on this bright day in July, it was clear that Raider Nation lived in the imagination of East Oakland.

We passed by the Bethlehem Christian Center (J.E. Bobo Senior, Pastor) and the Zodiak Motorcycle Club with a crowd of the Wicked Wheels outside by their bikes. I glanced over at a burned-out Victorian, and Joe talked about what used to be here in East Oakland and what happened to the solid working-class jobs that originally supplied the Raiders with their "blue-collar" image:

> There was a fleet of auto plants that are all gone. In addition to places like the Chevrolet assembly plant, Oakland had a strong manufacturing base with plants making electrical machinery, metal fabrication, food production, canneries and, of course, the shipyards. Since the early 1960s, the whole Bay Area has suffered from deindustrialization. I joined the Boilermakers, Local 6, in 1971 when it was still pretty large and vibrant. It has shrunk by 90 percent. There were large shipyards both here and in San Francisco, where I worked. During World War II, when the union was still having a battle about being a Jim Crow union, there were shipyards that employed 250,000 to 300,000 workers in the Bay Area. As late as 1971, passing on the job as a boilermaker to your son was still something you could do. You could still earn a decent living. By the time I retired, my local had to merge with Local 10 in Oakland to retain the name of Local 6. I believe the two locals together had at least 5,000 members when I joined. Now they have less than 500 because so much of the work has gone to lower wage areas, many of them outside the United States.
>
> On the waterfront the Longshoremen still have a great union, but the work is containerized, so the number of people you need, which is the other part of the waterfront story, is considerably less. So the cities have actually changed in

their class character. We have all sorts of people not doing well and homeless on the streets and in the projects and the ghettoes, but the rest of the city [both in San Francisco and Oakland] is much more upscale.

As we cruised by the nineties, the street got a tougher, edgier feel. There were more young men on the corners and the feel of the area was meaner. I looked down a side street and saw what looked like a drug deal. A lot of the guys were sporting Raiders gear. I looked at a little boy, about eleven, proudly wearing a Woodson jersey while waiting at a bus stop with his dad wearing a Raiders cap.

The fact that these fans, many of whom are very young, may be less knowledgeable about the team's storied history and less able to shell out big money for personal seat licenses does not make their expropriation of the Raiders' image as a source of personal, street, and neighborhood identity less meaningful. Football has played a role in the "Americanization" of immigrants in the United States throughout the last century and has always been a site of class struggle with regard to who owns the game. This was true when immigrant coal miners and other white ethnic working-class players like my grandfather and his brothers in Pennsylvania took up the game of the Ivy leaguers, and it is true today. What a drive down International Boulevard shows is that economic exclusion from the luxury suite set has not negated the community's love of the Raiders as a symbol of the "thereness" of Oakland, independent of whatever happens in the courtroom or on the field. Until the "corporate base" completely replaces the "fan base" in American professional sports, these "undesirables"—in the eyes of the elite who think they own the game, and the world—will continue to crash the party in their unlicensed, bootleg gear. As for the real "gangsters" amid the wannabes and plain old fans, one might ask whether in a culture where violence is as American as apple pie if it is not totally understandable that kids shunted to the margins would prefer to be feared rather than ignored. Make your fellow citizens tremble in your wake rather than pity you.

We headed out of Oakland and into San Leandro past an old auto plant that now houses bingo and sofas. Joe recalled that in the sixties the line between the cities "was a real demarcation." East Oakland was largely black and then you had "the very white suburbs." The Panthers, Joe told us, used to talk "about the occupation of the ghetto by an occupying army of white policemen, a lot of whom were apparently recruited in the South, and I don't mean South San Leandro." Today though, we noted, San Leandro is far more diverse. It's still a blue-collar suburb, but not a lily white one. I noticed more trees and a park as we rolled on past Sam's Super Burger and City Hall. We stopped to take a picture of the "Trailer Haven" sign, a bit of pure Americana, and continued on by Ernie's Sea Food and Pring's Coffee Shop before finding the turn that took us to Ricky's, the Raider fan Mecca. It was closed, but we got out and snapped some shots of the bar and the parking spaces playfully reserved for Al Davis, Ken Stabler, and a long list of other Raider greats. Afterward we sat on the hood of the car, and Joe voiced some us his reservations about the meaning of fandom:

> This kind of fan phenomenon, even if it's not a sellout, where you get 50,000 hard-core people to show up, some of them staying overnight beforehand, troubles me. Well, these people would never show up at a union meeting. It reminds me, too, of the sixties when I was a member of the Hayward worker's collective and I went to work for Kellogg's while the Vietnam War was raging. These workers were obviously being squeezed economically, and they were definitely contributing to the cannon fodder being sent to Vietnam. I had been a bit of a sports fanatic before politics took over, but what struck me was that there would be these really incredible things going on in Vietnam, and we were getting close to having a strike at our plant, and people would come in and the entire conversation would be taken up with which person ran for how many yards for the Raiders or whatever. That's how the hegemony works in this country, keeping workers from talking about what really matters. I was really struck that people could work themselves into such a frenzy and show an intellectual capacity for analysis of football, but not for their own economic or political condition.

I think this is part of a larger conversation about the role that sports play, which you are exploring, and we probably have some differences about the hegemonic aspects of keeping males fanatical, sometimes to the point of violence, about something that doesn't have any real connection to their lives. I had my flirtations with the rebel nature of the Raiders, but the idea that young men, and not such young men, whether they're on drugs or alcohol, would actually shed each other's blood over whether they were Raiders fans or 49ers fans when they should be united because they have shared class interests has always been something I find extraordinary. What is it that really divides Raiders and Packers fans? They're all really working people. You take the big rivalries in the olden days, the Packers or the Steelers. You couldn't find two more working-class cities than Oakland and Pittsburgh. And people would be ready to kill each other over some allegiance to highly paid professional athletes. It staggers the mind sometimes to think what a big mountain we have to climb to get people to see what their real interests are.

It feeds a lot of jingoism. And in the Raiders' case you have this illusion that you are being rebellious when, in fact, you are just fitting in. I mean I'm not pushing this to the point of saying that people are totally duped, but there is something powerful about being involved in allegiance to a team. It's a yearning for community, I know. Part of the reason I'm pushing the other thing is to have a discussion about what it all means. I also realize that as soon as the game is over the bills are the same, whether you have a job or not is the same. Nothing in your life of any consequence has changed.

After awhile, we noticed somebody walking toward us. It was Bob Ricardo, the co-owner of Ricky's, who greeted us warmly and told us to come back later once the season started to check out the whole scene. Bob was a handsome fellow in his mid-fifties who looked like he'd just gotten back from fishing. He gave us a brief history of his family's business and agreed to do an interview later. We headed back into Oakland, this time weaving through Elmhurst, Eastmont, and Seminary Park before returning to downtown as the afternoon bled into twilight.

Death don't have no mercy

Five

What a Long, Strange Trip It's Been

Raiders fans ate, drank and laughed together, cheered their team together, and won or lost together. The bonds of camaraderie that tailgate fans create for each other go far beyond what is experienced in the workweek world. Because of Raider love, every Sunday is a family reunion.

Craig Parker, Football's Blackest Hole

Raiders fans are the most passionate fans alive. Now honestly, that doesn't mean they are the most intelligent, straight-laced, sober, nonconvicted of felonies or misdemeanors fans, but loyal and energized they are!

Mark Wilson, Raiders fan

Sometimes the light's all shining on me
Other times I can barely see.

The Grateful Dead, "Truckin'"

On the day of the first preseason game, Kelly and I got off the freeway on 7th Street near Mandela Shipyards and made our way past the public housing alongside the train tracks under the freeway to downtown Oakland. At Broadway we turned left and cruised past bars, tattoo parlors, Chinese restaurants, and the newly gentrified ornate storefronts of Old Oakland. It was early in the morning so we kept going past 10th Street and rolled by the ornate *Oakland Tribune* tower, DeLauer's Newstand, Frank Ogawa Plaza, and the Paramount Theatre, an art deco masterpiece complete with an elaborate mural of dancers. At Grand we noticed that the old Hofbrau Restaurant was closed down before we drove on through auto row toward the hills. We passed the Sawmill, passed under the freeway, and turned left on MacArthur and left again on Telegraph where we cruised by Nordic House, Holistic Acupuncture, a Portuguese church, and an athletic club in an old mortuary building. We noticed a quaint red wooden church and saw the old Sears building with closed businesses inside. Past 24th Street the city got grittier and I noticed a pool hall, a Giant Burgers stand, and a gothic-looking Baptist church. In Koreatown we saw the Bear's Cave bar and rolled by the beautiful old Fox Theatre at 19th. Coming full circle we made our way back to Broadway, turned right on 10th, and parked in the Convention Center lot before tossing our bags in our room in the Washington Inn, built in 1913, which at the moment was packed to the gills with a boisterous Chinese wedding party.

After donning our Raiders gear, we walked to BART and rode the escalator down to the platform, where a very angry janitor was screaming at people to get out of his way as he swept up some broken glass. The woman standing next to us shot me a glance and said quite audibly, "He's got some issues." Once our train came we were on our way to our first game, an insignificant preseason contest with the St. Louis Rams, as official participant-observers. I glanced at the papers I'd picked up on the way to the station. The Terminator was campaigning to recall pallid Governor Gray Davis and get himself elected and, of the 130 candidates, the *East Bay Express* had endorsed former *Diff'rent Strokes* star Gary Coleman. In the world of sports, *Oakland Tribune* columnist Dave Newhouse opined, "Let's hope the jury hasn't been fooled by Al Davis." The Raiders trial had gone to the jury, and Newhouse informed his readers:

> We are about to learn who are the most gullible people on Earth—Oakland Raiders fans, East Bay politicians or a Sacramento jury. Raiders fans are

gullible because they continue to believe Al Davis is without fault, even if he yanks their beloved team out of Oakland once again. With feigned sincerity Davis says he cares about the fans. And they believe him because they are lambs and he is their shepherd, and he can lead them anywhere. They refuse to believe he cares only about money and power, and he'll stomp on anyone to get what he wants. Even those fans who worship him.[1]

I put the paper down. Clearly the season was off to a fine start. Our train was zooming through Fruitvale, and I looked out the window at a $1 Or Less store and a giant Goodwill. As we glided along, we passed a burned-out house, a junkyard, a taxi yard, a body shop, the old Oakland Cannery, plumbing supplies, more junkyards, vacant lots, and a goodly amount of industrial wreckage. We were five hours early for the 6:00 p.m. game as the train pulled into the sparsely populated Coliseum BART station. Kelly and I strolled over to the empty pedestrian bridge above Coliseum Burger on one side and Coliseum Steel on the other. The Raiders shield on the Coliseum itself loomed ahead. We walked up to a lonely vendor and bought our first program for the 2003 season. Not seeing any fans, the first person we encountered on the way to the parking lot was an Alameda County sheriff's deputy, whose assessment of what it was like to work Raiders games was given on the condition of anonymity: "Some days can be tough and some are not. Raiders fans love to drink, so it's drunk fans who are the problem. In fact we almost lost an officer last season. A fight started and the police handcuffed a Raiders fan who then kicked an officer in the face, which caused him to have a brain hemorrhage. We almost lost him. But the guy who did this represents only a small minority of fans." With that grim start, we kept moving.

Once we made our way down the ramp to the parking lot, we could see that it had recently opened and that a lot of fans had already set up impressive tailgates—five hours early. The first group we encountered was Bonnie McDonald and friends. They were flying a Raider Nation flag along with a Mexican flag above a big white canopy covering their elaborate spread. It was a large, multiethnic gathering of people ranging in age from their twenties to their sixties. We

Singh Shady #1

Photo: Joseph A. Blum

were greeted warmly as we took a picture of their setup and introduced ourselves to Bonnie. "What irritates me the most—I really hate it—is when people say they're for the 49ers *and* the Raiders because they live in the Bay Area," she told us. "In my mind, you're a Raiders fan or not." As for the fans' image, she said emphatically, " I called a radio show years ago because they were beating up [on] Raiders fans on the air. To me it was obvious what was going on. The Raiders have had to deal with a lot of media bashing. Some kids get rough, so every Raiders fan is labeled an outlaw. But most Raiders fans would give you the shirt off their backs. We bring a lot of food. If you're a Raiders fan, help yourself. We have a friend who works his way down the tailgate line." Back in the glory days, Bonnie remembered that "90 percent of the players lived in Alameda. The Raiders were everywhere you went. They didn't make as much money then. You knew them."

Cars continued to stream into the lot. I noticed that there were Raiders flags flying alongside the flags of not just Mexico but also Brazil, England, Australia, Ireland, Jamaica, Puerto Rico, the California Bear Republic, and, of course, the United States. Raider Nation, it seemed, had a variety of sister countries. We met up with Joe and his friend Ilene, who had never been to a Raiders tailgate before. She noticed that there were many people in wheelchairs as well as elderly people and small children. "It's a real family event, and that surprises me," she informed us. We walked by a black pickup blaring AC/DC, and I was struck by a visage that seemed to have been plucked straight out of a Grateful Dead show. There before us was a Sikh with a very long beard, swaying and drumming away on his bongo. On closer inspection the drummer was wearing a number 1 Raiders jersey with "SINGHSHADY" inscribed on the back. Singh Shady, it appeared, was fulfilling his dream of playing in the Black Hole for the first time. Hailing from Vancouver, Canada, Singh Shady took up drumming after a visit to Venice Beach, California, at the ripe old age of thirty-two. "After my weekend in Venice, I went back to Vancouver and went to drumming school where a kid there gave me a drum. I practiced for two years in my basement, thinking about this day. My dream has been to drum in the Black Hole." Unfortunately, Singh's ticket (which he has posted on his website) was in section 338, two decks above the Black Hole—but it was serendipitously in row 8, seat 8, on 8/8/03. Still, the experience seemed worth the nonstop drive down from Vancouver for some pre-season drumming action. Singh was happy to pose for several photos and gave us his e-mail address and website information.

Singh's website, we would later discover, greets the viewer with a large "WOW" with a picture of the Earth standing in for the "O" and the motto: "You Gotta Believe, Before You See." One is then treated to a Singh Shady poem:

> In Singh Shady's World
> It Takes a Lion's Heart,
> To Love The Mysterious Ways
> Of The ONE Cosmic Energy.
> The Game is KARMA
> The Goal is to TRANSFORM
> > Negativity to Positivity
> > Darkness to Light.

Then the interested shopper can click on "Wear the Lion on the Heart" and choose from a wide range of Singh Shady sweatshop-free apparel. Search further and you will find "Shadyz Nation," where the photo of our favorite "sports drummer" appears above the heading, "Ever See a Team Lose The Championship Game, And Their Fans Dancing in the Stands!" The viewer learns that "I figure if I go to Oakland, Play my drum at The BLACK HOLE, Sooner or Later, I Gotta Get Noticed! . . . Around Every DARK CLOUD, Is a SILVER LINING!" This is followed by a tribute to other Raiders fans complete with links to their AMIAFAN.COM web pages and a copy of Singh's famous first ticket to the 8/8/03 preseason game with the Rams. If all of this is not enough, you can check the Venice Beach Drumming Circle schedule and learn that "Singh Shady is a Capitalist Communist [whose] goal is to Make Money, Share Money" and has made his name a registered trademark. Wow.[2]

After we bid adieu to Singh Shady, we wandered a few parking spaces farther on until we came upon Phil Ramirez (AKA "Raider Phil"), his wife, daughter, and son Angel. Phil and Angel were wearing silver-and-black face paint and had skulls and spikes on their shoulders. We stupidly declined their offer of *pollo asada* and admired their big silver truck with a giant Raiders shield painted on the hood. They had dragged a Rams doll to the game on their trailer hitch. I looked over and Joe was taking a picture of a Raiders fan being interviewed by a TV news reporter. The interviewee was Traci the Raiders Cat. Traci had been dressing up as a Raiders Cat for two years now. Although she couldn't afford to buy tickets to most games, she comes "because it's like a family." Traci was saving up to buy season tickets next year. For now, she enjoys doing karaoke at Ricky's and hanging out in the parking lot before games. Traci, it turned out, was not the only Raiders fan who came to the parking lot before games they couldn't afford to go to. Larry the "Raiderman," who looked vaguely like a Raiders hobbit, told us that he'd been a fan since the late seventies. He had lived on "the east side" of Oakland in the same house since 1969. Currently unemployed, Larry could scrounge up enough money to get his silver face paint and shoulder spikes at the Halloween store, but the game tickets were out of reach. He was hoping that someone would give him an extra. As we walked away, I thought of what ticket-less fans say at Dead shows: "I need a miracle!"

About this time I remembered that we actually had one official "appointment" to meet BlackHole Mike, one of the many Raiders webmasters. We met up with Mike next to where Slackenloader was setting up to play. "I saw my first game in 1978 on TV with my grandfather. What struck me was the mystique of the Raiders, especially Stabler, but all the greats," he told us. Mike, who is a mortgage broker, lives in Fremont. "The core of the Black Hole met in 1995 to 1996. I actually sat in another section and tried to get people going there. I pointed to the Black Hole and said, 'I belong there.'" He also told us that the Black Hole does a road trip every year. "Contrary to what people might think," he elaborated, "There aren't many fights. I remember in New Orleans in 1995 the Black Hole broke up a fight. We actually break up more fights than we cause." As for the music, Mike said, "It's my job to bring the band in. It's Slackenloader this

I need a miracle

Photo: Joseph A. Blum

year." We thanked him and noticed that Slackenloader had started to tune up.

Once our visit with BlackHole Mike was over, we kept wandering through the rows of tailgaters. It was only a couple of hours until game time now, and the barbeque smoke was thick and people were getting considerably drunker. We stopped and admired an industrial-sized kettle barbeque that had giant slabs of brisket and ribs; whole chickens and a turkey; and a rope of sausage links all hanging from wires over the coals. A big bear of a man, also named Mike, got up to greet us and gave Joe and Ilene some ribs. Mike and his girlfriend Jenny were working on a bottle of tequila, but it was love not war that the cactus juice inspired in them. After the ribs we strolled by a big group that was roasting a whole suckling pig over coals laid on top of metal sheeting. The unfortunate swine (we later learned) had been hunted down, captured, and killed by the Raiders fans themselves somewhere near Petaluma. From there we strolled on past the River City Boosters and met back up with Joe and Ilene, who had briefly disappeared into the ribs.

At the southwest corner of the parking lot by one of the main gates we met Donovan and Jack, the first fans in the lot. Arriving the night before at 6:00 p.m., they had set up shop in front of the gate and waited overnight for the privilege of getting their prized spot. According to Donovan, they usually get to the game twenty-four to thirty-six hours before kickoff. "Sometimes we'll have two hundred people out there all night," he told us. "The earliest we have shown up is Friday morning for a Sunday night game." Donovan and his friend Jack have been the first in to tailgate for three years. Jack, who grew up in Richmond and has been a fan since 1966, explained, "It's a Silver and Black thing. I go to games stone-cold sober, but I'm on a high from this." He gestured toward the extensive tent setup the two had erected behind their Raidered-out trucks, complete with a customized Al Davis banner. Jack's strategy for getting in first was elaborate:

I always get stall one, row one. I got here at 6:00 p.m. last night, but sometimes I'll come two or three days before the game. I have orange cones I use to mark off my area in line, and I have a deal with the guys behind me to guard my spot so I can go home to take a shower in the morning. I have to be fresh and clean. There are twenty-two people now who have negotiated around the tailgate rules and prohibitions so they can stick together once they are inside the lot. The police have tried to get me to take down my stuff, but I stick with it. This is my life. I love this team. This is what we do.

Donovan and Jack both pointed out that people they have met in the parking lot are some of their best friends in the world, and that this is the only place where they see them. It was, I thought, like a temporary migrant camp, a weekend experiment in collective culture.

Strangely amid the odor of searing beef and charcoal smoke, I smelled elephant dung. It was very hot and I was wearing a heavy black football jersey, so I thought this might mean I was having a seizure of some kind, but as our trek through the parking lot continued I discovered that the circus was literally in town: part of the parking lot was cordoned off for the Ringling Brothers and Barnum & Bailey's Circus, the Greatest Show on Earth. I was surprised that the circus thought there was much of a market left for clowns with Gary Coleman running against Arnold, a porn star, and a host of other tongue-in-cheek wannabes to occupy the State House. It was getting even closer to game time, so we circled back to where Slackenloader was covering head-bangin' favorites. I laughed when I saw that the singer was wearing a "Slackenloader for Governor" t-shirt and that Gorilla Rilla, yet another costumed Raiders celebrity fan, was kicking up his heels with a leggy blonde woman.

After a dance or two we interviewed the Gorilla, Mark Acasio, who was currently in the fourth year of his tenure as the Raiders Gorilla. Why be the Raiders Gorilla? "To do something different and get a lot of attention," Mark told us. "I've been on the Jumbo Screen in the Black Hole." Mark, who has lived in the Bay Area his entire life, has a Gorilla Rilla website as well as business cards. An entrepreneurial gorilla, he does parties and other events for pay and Raiders games for free. After chatting with the Gorilla, we ran into another group of celebrity fans: Azel, Kimmy, and Melvia, the Oaktown Pirates. Clearly the most fashionable of all the costumed Raiders fans, the trio bought personal seat licenses in 1995 when the team returned and, inspired by the Raiders theme song "The Autumn Wind," began attending the games as pirates in November 2001. Azel was originally an Eagles fan, while Kimmy and Melvia were born and raised in Richmond and Oakland, respectively. After Azel bought the hats, they started getting a lot of attention and have been chasing TV cameras and news photographers ever since. Not surprisingly, once we shot their pictures they gave us their card and web address and were off to the next shot, striving to keep themselves firmly enshrined in the heaven of the spectacle. Less driven by fame was Thomas, a pencil salesman who rolled up to us in his wheelchair, oxygen tank strapped to the back, to offer his wares. We bought one that said, "With God on the Raiders' Side They Can't Lose. God Bless. Go Raiders." Kelly and I said goodbye to Joe and Ilene. It was time for the game.

Inside the stadium we made our way through the hallways echoing with chants of "Ray-duz! Ray-duz!" On the way to our seats, Mario Garcia was nice enough to stop and model his "Aztlan Raiders" t-shirt and when I asked him what it meant, he replied, "Chicano Pride and the Raiders, man!" We headed down the stairs to the Black Hole and found our seats in the second to the last row from the top. They were not down next to the field with the costumed crazies, but they gave us a nice panoramic view of our fellow Black Hole denizens nonetheless. Right off the bat we met the couple behind us, Art and Karen and their friends, who made us feel right at home. Art, we soon learned, had recently been a judge in the Raiderettes tryouts. Many of the aspiring Raiderettes, Karen gleefully told us, had trouble following directions to move right to left. We laughed and continued chatting. When we told them we were coming up from San Diego, they offered to let us stay in their motor home overnight. Once everyone found out Kelly was pregnant, they asked for updates at every game. As Bonnie had said earlier in the parking lot, they would have given us the shirts off their backs.

Sitting next to Kelly was Madison, a polite, soft-spoken man in his forties who frequently came to games with his wife and, unlike the rowdies all around us, rarely spoke. Jack and Bill usually sat in front of us. Jack wore a Raiders construction hat and actually worked in construction, unlike the many who have adopted workingman's gear as a fashion trend. He is a large, gregarious guy with a booming voice and a big smile who looked like he could play linebacker himself. We asked him how long he'd been coming and he said, "Ever since they came back we've been to every game. It used to be a lot rowdier about four or five years ago. I haven't seen a fight for the last year, when there had been maybe one or two per half. So it really has gotten a lot better." Good to know, I thought.

Back in the seventies, Hunter S. Thompson described the fans in Oakland Coliseum as

> a sort of half-rich mob of nervous doctors, lawyers, and bank officers who would sit through a whole game without ever making a sound—not even when some freak with a head full of acid spilled a whole beer down the neck of their gray-plastic ski jackets. Toward the end of the season, when the Raiders were battling every week for a spot in the playoffs, some of the players got so pissed off at the stuporous nature of their "fans" that they began making public appeals for "cheering" and "noise."

It was the old Kezar Stadium where the 49ers played that Thompson described as a half-full "drunken madhouse" so mean and crazed that "10,000 of them were out there for no other reason except to get involved in serious violence." How times have changed.[3]

Looking around our neck of the woods and the Black Hole in general, the crowd was diverse racially and, it appeared, socio-economically. Hells Angels and housewives, gangsters and garbage men. What united the crowd, however, were ten basic commandments that you had to tolerate, even if you did not obey them: 1) wear black; 2) stand all game long or sit and miss the game; 3) be loud; 4) drink heavily; 5) curse like a sailor; 6) flip off opposing players; 7) fuck with opposing fans until they request a police escort; 8) fuck with the police escort until they request a police escort; 9) laugh a lot and have a hell of a good time; 10) be nice to fellow Raiders fans unless they are openly flaunting the ten commandments (in which case they should be fucked with).

Although the stadium was only about half-full (the attendance was 37,341, to be precise) and the game didn't count, the Black Hole threw itself wholeheartedly into the game for most of the first half. AC/DC was blaring, and the thrill of the first few snaps of the new season got us all going. We could finally put the Super Bowl nightmare to rest. The game defined crappy—a sloppy 7–6 Raiders win, which, despite the baseball score did not even have much defense to speak of. Three words defined the game: missed field goals. If the teams had had any dignity, they would have given the fans their money back, with interest, or at least displayed some shame that people had paid to watch them stink up the joint. By the second half, the Black Hole was largely disengaged. Old friends were catching up, and people broke one of the commandments and sat down. I saw one man ejected for an undisclosed offense and another man fall asleep in his seat. Far more interesting than the feeble contest on the field was the voodoo priest whose sharp costume made him look just like the character in the James Bond film *Live and Let Die*. Kelly got a beautiful shot of him with his cute young son and daughter, a nice mix of menace and innocence. We also saw a guy dressed up like Peter Krist in Kiss, with black-and-white makeup, a black leather vest, skull shoulder pads (the Raiders touch), silver-studded leather gauntlets, and dark, flowing rock-star hair. Some people a couple of rows in front of us were drinking whiskey out of a binocular flask. I couldn't help but think again of a Dead show or Mardi Gras or carnivale. For now, the costumes were a hell of a lot more interesting than what was transpiring on the gridiron. Nonetheless, the Black Hole was jubilant in victory.

On the way to the BART station somebody started a call-and-response chant, and the happy crowd followed along: "I say Raider, you say Nation." "Raider!" "Nation!" "Raider!" "Nation!" Somebody was selling buttons with multicolored lights flashing blue, red, green, and yellow. "Look at all the pretty lights," said a little girl somewhere on the dark pedestrian bridge. On the train back downtown a gaunt, elderly black man turned to an old white guy with bushy white hair who was wearing a Jerry Rice jersey and asked, "Did they win?"

"Yeah, seven to six," he replied.

"It's the rebirth of the Nation," the old man shouted like a biblical prophet as he left the train in front of us at 12th Street. "The rebirth of Raider Nation!"

The next evening we met our friend Scott and his girlfriend Megan at Yoshi's for sushi and a Pharaoh Sanders show. Originally opened in North Berkeley in the early seventies by Buddhist artists Yoshi Akiba, Kaz Kajimura, and Hiroyuki Hori, Yoshi's moved to Oakland in the late seventies, eventually ending up in Jack London Square in the nineties. It is heads above the best jazz club in the western United States and the cultural jewel of Oakland. I had called Scott to help me flesh out my bizarre theory about the Deadhead/Raiderhead parallel. Having seen over two hundred Grateful Dead shows and a good number of Raiders games live and on TV, he was, I felt, the man for the job. He and Megan also worked in Oakland and lived in Hayward, the far end of the spine of Raider Nation, so I thought they might have some insights on local culture to share as well. In between pieces of seared albacore and raw salmon, Scott warmed to the subject: "You know, there are obvious differences that both sides would probably emphasize. A Deadhead would probably say, 'Oh that's ridiculous. You know, we're not like Raiders fans. Those guys are carnivores and crazed.' And Raiders fans would probably say, 'Oh, that peace and love hippie shit, come on.'"

"You mean the suckling pig roasters wouldn't see a common interest with spinning, dancing hippie girls?" I asked.

"Right, that probably wouldn't happen, not unless you had a giant eggplant that was slowly turning over the flame, getting ready to be turned into veggie burgers."

I asked for confirmation: "So, the one big difference would be suckling pig versus eggplant?"

Scott explained:

Yeah, I would say suckling pig versus eggplant, if it makes any difference. And yet, when you think about it, no matter what they're eating, if they're carnivores or vegetarians, they are there in the same spirit. They're there to have a good time. They are there to be communal, talk with the people next to them, the people walking around them. People often see old friends at events like these. They are not necessarily friends you hang out with in real life. They're friends you see at these events.

At my first game I remember thinking, "Here I am coming to this place where I'd seen maybe over 100 Dead shows. Oh, this will be a completely different event, more like a baseball game." I was in baseball mode because this is a sports stadium, but once I got off the BART and into the crowd, into the throngs of it, I couldn't help but be reminded of being at a Grateful Dead show parking lot because here are all these people all over the place drinking beer and sharing food and everybody is having a good time. It seemed just as important to be in the parking lot as it was to go to whatever event was going to happen. There was a community feeling that isn't typical. It wasn't like, "Okay, we're here, let's park the car and go into the stadium. Watch our event." It felt like the community aspect of the whole thing was far more important.

In the Dead community, you would often see people at each show, but you wouldn't see them at other places. It was all about the show. That community existed as a kind of free, anarchic community with no government or whatever. You were just with your people. At the Raiders game it seemed the same way. They were so many people recognizing other people and/or welcoming in strangers. I don't know if they want us to say this, but there is a counterculture edge to the whole Raiders phenomenon. It helps that they are called the Raiders because they have the pirate outfit image and the fans gravitate toward that. It seems similar to me in that no matter how big the Dead got, they were never a mainstream rock act. No matter how many people were there, it was still a countercultural event on one level or another. And with the Raiders it seems like they're always fighting against, you know, the fans and the team, even the owner, the mainstream of football. And sometimes they get in trouble. They can be bad boys. They can get into the newspapers in the same way the Dead would get arrested on a drug crackdown or something like that.

There is even a Hunter S. Thompson parallel: he covered the Raiders and the counterculture, the Hells Angels, too. I don't have to stretch too far for this because you've got Hells Angels and other bikers and some pretty mean, nasty-looking guys in both scenes. People who haven't been to a Dead show probably think they're just a bunch of hippies and tie-dyes only, but especially in the early eighties there was a very strong biker scene at Dead shows. I mean it would have actually scared off a typical nineties Dead fan. There it was— you had your bike, your dog, and the wife—hanging out behind you—ready to go. So the scenes share that element, and yet somebody who looks mean and scary just might turn out to be the friendliest guy in the world once you start talking to him.

Interestingly, once I got into the stadium, there was this giant poster of Jerry Garcia as I'm walking in. The average sports stadium does not have huge portraits of Jerry Garcia and Bill Graham. So just when I was about to dismiss the comparison of Deadheads to Raiders fans as a frivolous thought, there it was again. Once I got to my seat I could tell I was at a football game, but when halftime came and I started milling around, God, I felt like I was between the first and second sets of a show. Everybody had to stock up in between. They had to go get their beers, their food. They had to walk around and meet people. I ended up talking to all kinds of people that I never would talk to if I were just walking around the street. But you're in line and suddenly they are your best buddies in about five minutes.

There is also the level of extreme inebriation. That is the fascinating thing about both kinds of events—some people are going up and others are coming down. At the Dead shows it might literally be coming up and going down in a drug sense, but at a Raiders show, it is those people who started drinking really early in the parking lot, and you don't think they are going to make it through the third quarter. Then there are the other ones that got in late and really want to start piling on now at halftime. Alcohol actually plays a bigger role in the Dead scene than many people think. There are probably a lot more people drunk at shows than on acid, if you took a poll of everybody. There can't be too many Raiders fans on acid. That's a very interesting concept. It looks like this year there'd be some pretty bad trips going. There is a lot of speed in the speed metal scene. That seems to fit. And I did smell a lot of weed in the hallway. I would say it's a positive thing that there is weed going on at Raiders games overall. It might actually take the edge off.

Speaking of people being "out there," the costume thing is another parallel. I'm sure you've come across a lot of that. At a regular concert you would hardly ever see people in costume, unless you were going to a Halloween show or something. But at Dead shows it was common to have some guy walking around in an Uncle Sam thing or running around like some kind of gnome. Wizards were quite common. There were always wizards. And Yoda. Yoda was a big favorite for a while. We always had a Yoda spotting. People just did whatever struck them. And it's the same with the Raiders. Some of the costumes are influenced by the silver and black and all that, but some of the others are just out there. They really don't have anything much to do with the Raiders. It's just creativity going on.

"You mean gorillas don't have anything to do with the Raiders?" I interrupted, laughing.

"As far as I know, there weren't any gorillas who were active pirates—or Raiders," Scott replied.

"What about Señor Raider Man?" Kelly interjected. "The guy with the silver-and-black sombrero?"

"Yeah, I met that guy in a bar once, and he's something else. I mean, he's got it all going at once, you know. He's worked really hard on that exterior, but I'm not so sure about the interior. Of course, he seems like a nice enough guy, firm handshake." Scott ate another piece of sushi and continued on:

There is this whole carnivalesque thing. I was an English major so I occasionally have to use a word like "carnivalesque." I won't say Bakhtinian or anything like that. But anyway, "carnivalesque" is a term that the average English professor was using even if they didn't know how to party. Still, I always liked going to places like Key West or New Orleans or a Dead show, places or events that had elements of the carnivalesque. Mardi Gras is probably the ultimate example in the United States. Every Dead show and every Raiders game has a Mardi Gras edge in a way. They play with death symbols. If you look at the Grateful Dead, of course, death is symbolized but the skeletons are happy. And at the Raiders games there are a lot of death symbols—in the makeup, the skulls and things like that. It's actually similar to the Mexican Day of the Dead, in that people at Dead shows, Raiders games, and in Day of the Dead festivities all use death symbols positively. These events are rituals. They're actually not afraid of death; they're celebrating life of which death is a part. It's a mockery of pretense as well, a leveling of sorts. We're all it in together, nobody's any better than anybody else in the face of death. It's a healthy awareness of death. These symbols that might usually be purely negative or would be used in some stupid horror movie or something like that are transformed. It's like, "Hey, we're partying like crazy here, and yet we know we look like skulls and death faces. And today everything is permitted." It goes all the way back to the Bacchanalian and Dionysian stuff. It's some serious Wine God insolence. It's a letting down of inhibitions. That would probably never happen at other public events.

It can be as simple as talking to the person next to you. In a way, we often go through life without hardly ever talking to the person next to us, whether it's somebody on a bus or somebody you live next to, or somebody walking down the street. At Dead shows and Raiders games and other carnivalesque events you can strike up the best friendships with people you may never see again. You might scrawl a number on a piece of paper or something like that, but what really counts is what happens right there, that breaking down of social inhibitions and then that larger sense of self. This doesn't happen to everybody, but in extreme cases it is the breaking down of all inhibitions, and the manifestations of this freedom can be positive or sometimes negative. At Dead shows, sometimes someone would scream out at an inopportune moment, "We're all dying!" Or somebody at a Raiders game just loses it and does some crazy shit. With a sport there's going to be more fights because there is that adrenaline going.

You know, it's amazing what similar crowds we're dealing with here. I'm sure there are lots of people who have gone to both. There's one other thing that unites the two scenes, the concept of trekking, caravanning down the highway and camping out together. That's certainly a link between Deadheads and Raiders fans. How could I forget, "We are everywhere" was a phrase that Deadheads would always use. "We are everywhere, we are everywhere," and that seems the same with Raiders fans. What other fans are so spread out and travel such long distances to go to games the same way Dead fans would go five hundred miles or a thousand miles to see one show? People would look at them like they were nuts: "Why didn't you wait for them to come to your town?" It's the same way with Raiders fans. They are going to travel. I see all those people camped out by the freeway waiting in vans and campers. There is one big difference. The VWs would all be pulled over to the side because they broke down on the way to Dead shows. But the Raiders fans are cruising through. They are going to make sure their vehicle doesn't break down before a game. If you can introduce me to a Raiders fan in a VW, then we'll know that we've found the missing link between to two cultures.

Scott stopped to have a sip of beer and another piece of sushi, and Kelly and I told him about our trip all the way down East 14th Street through Oakland and into San Leandro. He stopped and thought about it and said:

There aren't many people who would take that route the whole way, maybe you guys, but not many. But it's amazing how it is all connected. It's like the center of the various communities. I mean once the street turns into Mission in Hayward, you have Muffler Man, always a sign of definitive culture. I cruise Mission all the time to go to thrift stores and cheaper stores. And it's pretty much Mexican families, a few Anglo housewives, and me. There are a lot of Raiders decals around in the middle of the day there. But there's not as much cross-filtration [between Oakland, San Leandro, and Hayward] as you'd think. People from Oakland tend to stay in Oakland. It's one of those things. And people in San Leandro are afraid to go anywhere else. And people from Hayward, which I happen to be from and I'm going to favor, are a bit more open minded and get around a bit more. And it's not just black and Latino Oakland versus white Hayward. That's a major misconception, that areas like Hayward and Fremont are somehow all white.

At this point Megan, who grew up in Hayward, jumped in and explained how the demographics had changed over the years:

It is more of a middle- and working-class place. The people who moved out of Hayward moved into the valley region. There were a lot of people who did stay, you know. The people who moved out, though, left room for others to come in. So over the years, the city has gotten a lot more multicultural and more diverse in other ways than it originally was. In the fifties the suburban communities like San Leandro, San Lorenzo, and Hayward were built on former ranches, and that is where everybody is moving to. They were living in the big city of Oakland, and now they were moving to these little suburban communities, and after a while people outgrew that, and immigrants moved in, and people who didn't feel comfortable with it—you know, the immigrants and the area, or were looking for something more flashy—moved up to the valley area where they felt like, "Oh, I can build my 'X'-scale home here. It's not this little twelve-hundred-square-foot box."

Scott jumped in:

I happened to have seen the 2000 census for Hayward, and it's unbelievably diverse. It's like 33/33/33: 33 percent white, 33 percent Hispanic or Latino, and 33 percent Asian and black. There are a lot of Pacific Islanders as well, and many of them are into football. A lot of Filipinos are into the Raiders. You've also got big communities of people like Samoans, and there are a lot of Samoan Raiders fans. So Hayward is really diverse, and it surprises people to hear that sometimes.

When I first moved to Hayward, one of the first things I noticed is that people liked to do weird things with their yards. So I started taking walks and trying to actually chart where the various animals were, and that's when I noticed these people had carved the Raiders insignia into their lawn, and then they painted their houses silver and black. Instead of having a couple of flamingoes out there, why not just carve up the lawn and do the Raiders thing? I guess there are crazed sports fans everywhere who might do something like that, but it seems like it fits in a little more in this area because there is something about the lawn decoration thing that is this last clinging to suburbia. I'm not an expert in this area. It takes a while to really immerse yourself in this kind of roadside Americana. But it is something that I have found in Hayward and San Lorenzo, and it is especially strong in San Leandro. And the Raiders thing kind of fits in with that because Raiders insignias are everywhere, but to put it on your house, that takes it much further.

We finished our beer and paid for dinner. It was time to head over to the stage area to see Pharaoh Sanders.

Luckily, Scott found a booth right in front as the quartet took the stage, Pharaoh in a white caftan-like shirt and crisply pressed black pants was sporting a silvery beard with no moustache. The others, sharply dressed as well, elegantly took their places behind the drums, bass, and piano. They opened up with a song I couldn't recognize and, as I watched the master play his first solo, I remembered the way John Krich described Sanders: "At last, he plants like a football tackle, knees locked before the mike. Adjusts clip, adjusts mouthpiece, and is gone." As I followed the journey of the saxophone, my mind's eye wandered back and forth from Pharaoh's stately visage on stage to the image of a Buddhist temple we drove by on Foothill, the grand old abandoned train station to the west of us, the vacant lots out the window of the BART train, and the sunlight dancing on the water of the bay next to Jack London Square. After the first number, they moved into "My Favorite Things" and were joined by a singer who lent the piece an unexpectedly transcendent passion. "No other night like a Saturday night, what a beautiful night, can you feel it?" he sang, as if he were somehow inside the words themselves. His uncontainable exuberance stood in stark contrast to Pharaoh's stern regal presence.[4]

Outside, a train went by as the saxophone seemed to tear through the ceiling and I imagined Oakland during the days when 7th Street was a music mecca and the Brotherhood of Sleeping Car Porters was a proud union. When the band headed into "Nightingale in Berkeley Square," Pharaoh actually cracked a smile and danced a little. "The streets of the town were paved with stars," the vocalist sang. As they finished up, Pharaoh introduced everyone as "the great." "The great" John Farnsworth "from New York City to Oakland" was on drums. "The great" Alex Blake, "from Panama to Oakland" on bass. "The great" Willie Young Henderson, "from Texas to L.A. to Oakland." "The great" Mike Trebel on vocals "from Cincinnati to Oakland." As we walked Scott and Megan to their car after the show, I looked at the train tracks headed west into the lonely night and nursed the sound of Pharaoh's sax still ringing in my ears.

Six

Crying Won't Help

You say you love me, baby
If that's love, I'd rather be a thug.
Lowell Fulson, "Thug"

It was dark in the alley and the evening sun was going down
When I found my little darlin' she was lying on the ground.
Jimmy Wilson, "Blues in the Alley"

"Oakland is Blues City," Ishmael Reed writes in his 2003 book of the same name, "Oakland Blues singers sang, preached, and shouted out the blues." His book takes the reader on a tour of the troubled yet resilient city ending up at Esther's Orbit Room, "the last of the old-time blues clubs located on the legendary Seventh Street." It was in "West Oakland honky-tonks—all a short cab ride from the Southern Pacific train station," Lee Hildebrand explains in *Bay Area Blues*, "where the first generation of Oakland Blues people had disembarked during World War II." Searching for work in the shipyards and other wartime industries, southern migrants brought the blues and created a rich West Oakland music scene. Players like Jimmy McCracklin, Johnny Fuller, Jimmy Wilson, Big

Mama Thornton, Juke Boy Bonner, Sugar Pie De Santo, and Lowell Fulson rocked the juke joints. While some like Lowell Fulson made it, others such as the little-known Lafayette Thomas came to tragic ends. As Albert Vetere Lannon documents, "Thomas faded from the scene, racked by alcohol and working when he could. He died in the 1970s working on a production line at a Brisbane hose manufacturing plant under ILWU Local 6 jurisdiction; the supervisor threw a blanket over Lafayette Thomas's body and took his place coiling hose—the line never stopped."[1]

The whole West Oakland blues scene took a beating, as Gary Rivlin explains: "The final insult was the razing of Seventh Street, a bustling strip that was once home to the likes of Slim Jenkins's place and the Creole Club. A forbidding and uninviting high-rise housing project took its place." In *Bay Area Blues,* Michelle Vignes's beautiful, stark black-and-white photographs of dead blues spots like the Deluxe Inn, the Shalimar, and the Cozy Den give the viewer the sense of a nearly vanished world. If the music is endangered, the blues themselves are still alive and well.

Fifteen years after penning "Living at Ground Zero," a lament about Oakland's crack plague, Reed is once again singing the blues about the killing coming to his neighborhood and the fact that since "many of [Oakland mayor Jerry] Brown's policies have failed . . . [e]viction rates have tripled" because rents have "increased 20 to 30 percent in the last three years." The news leading up to our return trip to Oakland continued to be grim: the homicide rate was rising, the unemployment rate was at 11 percent, and beleaguered city teachers were forced to take a 4 percent pay cut.[2]

Kelly and I drove up on Thursday before the second home preseason game and decided that since Ishmael Reed had covered Esther's Orbit Room we'd go to the newly resurrected Eli's Mile High Club in West Oakland. Earlier in the day we explored West Oakland, driving to the abandoned train station and parking in front of the fading yellow New Bea's Hotel to stop in Sant Sweets and Catering where none of the Indian proprietors spoke English but were friendly enough to let Joe snap a few photographs of them working nonetheless. The neighbor-

Slackenloader rocks the House of Thrills

hood was full of boarded-up buildings, crab grass, and young people hanging out on the desolate corners. Stray dogs roamed the streets. There were "found art" sculptures here and there amid active and abandoned industrial sites. The streets were edgy in West Oakland and, as we cruised past Sweet Jimmie's and a row of apartments before crossing under the freeway on the way to Eli's, I thought of the mournful tale of lost lives that Rivlin tells in *Drive By*, his heartbreaking story of child killers and their child victims whose families had fled the dangers of the West side only to find more tragedy in the East side of town.

Eli's itself is a warm, welcoming space with a low ceiling and red walls covered with old blues posters of Mississippi Johnny Waters, Sonny Rhodes, Cool Papa, and many more. Originally opened by Eli and Alberta Thornton in 1974, the club was "the Home of the West Coast Blues" throughout the seventies until Eli was shot and killed by a jealous lover as he tended bar in 1979. Since then the club has changed ownership a number of times, struggling to stay afloat in a neighborhood where most of the population lives at or near the poverty line. Eli's was shut down and almost razed by developers who wanted to build pricey new loft spaces in 2002 before Frank Klein bought and saved it in 2003. The crowd was thin and after we paid at the door and toured the room, we sat down and ordered jambalaya and hot links. By the time the food came a few more people had filtered in and Alberta Adams, a Detroit blueswoman, took the stage. She was a stout, elderly woman in a bright red dress who sang while sitting on a chair in front of the stage. She belted out "I Paid My Dues to Play the Blues," "Detroit," and "Come and See Me about It" and did a cover of Koko Taylor's "I'd Rather Go Blind." In between songs she chatted with the crowd, "How many of you ladies ever been in love with a married man? We got some dogs in the house?"

In between sets, Kelly walked over to buy a CD and get it autographed by Alberta and struck up a conversation with the saxophone player, Bernard Anderson, who, it turns out, was not from Detroit but lived right here in Oakland and was a big Raiders fan. I joined them and we strolled outside together to get some fresh air and interview Bernard as he stood there smoking a cigarette in his cherry red suit and matching fedora. He told us he was born in Chicago "but moved to Oakland when I was five, so I was raised here. I've played with all sorts of greats: Sonny Rhodes, Maxine Howard, and others. Since 1988, I've played with Queen Ida, who I've made some albums with." Kelly admired what he was wearing, and he replied:

You like this suit? I used to dress Queen Ida's band. One time, when we were in New Orleans, for the first time, I forgot to bring a suit. Queen Ida said, "Bernard, we're going to be filmed!" I felt so bad. On the way to the studio, I saw this suit in a store window and yelled, "Stop!" I bought this cherry red suit right there. I call it my "New Orleans Suit." I play gigs in clubs around here before going to my second job as a security guard. I start at 1 and finish at 6 a.m.

We told him more about our book on Raiders fans and his eyes lit up: "I've been a Raiders fan since the sixties." He continued enthusiastically:

When I was a little kid, I played street ball, and I was either Tatum or Upshaw. I always liked Jack Tatum and Jim Otto, but I loved all the greats. Since the Raiders have been back, I've had season tickets and hang with the Road Trip Crew off of 66th Avenue. You always know where we are in the parking lot because we've got a giant blow-up Pink Panther doll. We have an incredible spread: fried chicken, spaghetti, a leg of lamb every now and then, and lots of drinks. The ladies bring the food for us. It's a great time."

We thanked Bernard and left him to finish his cigarette before he had to go back in for the second set. Inside we stopped to talk with Trinity Klein, the owner's wife, who, when we told her about our project, gleefully told us a joke she'd heard at a comedy club in San Francisco: "Raiders fans will buy everything—hats, shirts, jerseys, jackets, helmets, makeup, costumes, and any other silver-and-black thing they can get their hands on. They'll paint their house

Greetings from the Black Hole

Photo: Joseph A. Blum

black, build a Raiders shrine in the living room, get a Raiders tattoo, and go back and buy out the rest of the store. They're complete maniacs. They'll do just about anything except buy a ticket." We laughed and sat back down for the second set. Alberta was making her way back on stage, slowly, gingerly, but with style.[3]

I'm in a Strange, Strange Land

> I am streets you drive down drunk and crying.
> *John Krich,* Bump City

The next day on the train on the way to the Coliseum, I flipped through the *East Bay Express* and found an interesting Raiders item in the "Take Out" section. It was a list of "what Al Davis could do with all that dough" once he won his "nearly $1 billion" from Oakland:

- Buy a white Raiders jump suit for every California resident.
- Put 7,575 new cops on the Oakland streets.
- Build two football stadiums in downtown Oakland.
- Purchase the Tampa Bay Buccaneers.
- Give an Xbox, PS2, and Game Boy to each of the estimated 1.8 million California kids living in poverty.
- Finance at least ten more gubernatorial recall elections.
- Provide lap dances for every NFL player and coach (except Gruden).
- Subscribe to the *Chronicle* for the next four billion days (Sundays not included).
- Spring for a single jumbo dog, fries, and souvenir cup at the Coliseum.[4]

In the parking lot we passed by a few of the same people we interviewed at the last game and waved hello before spotting the 66th Mob tailgate. Here they were, the most famous of all the all-night tailgaters. It was a big, boisterous group of guys, some very big ones indeed. The first guy we spoke with was a friendly mountain of a man, Tony Pizza (his Mob name), who told us that "the whole thing started in 1996 as a kind of spur-of-the-moment thing." As we were speaking to Tony, his friend Griz (the fan who had been the victim of the hit-and-run accident after the Super Bowl) walked up and we shook hands. Tony got back to manning his grill and Griz hung around for an interview. I asked him how he was, and after telling us that he was much better, he confessed, "The game was more hurtful than the accident. The people, though, the Raiders fans, were just great. A lot of people offered me help and sent me stuff. I work for State Farm, but I'm unemployed now because of the accident." It was clear that Griz was still moved by the generosity of his fellow fans and felt a deep connection to his tailgate family. As for his history as a fan he said:

> I was born into a Raiders family in San Leandro. When they moved back from L.A. I started going to games and camping out with these guys. The 66th Mob is where it all starts. During the Super Bowl I met the ESPN guy, John Anderson, and I asked him, "Do you know of any other fan base in America that tailgates for a day or two before games?" His answer, of course, was, "No." There's nowhere else like this. No better fans.

We asked if we could take a picture of Griz and Tony in front of the 66th Mob sign and they happily agreed. As we walked on, I found myself pondering Griz's sincerity. He didn't have a lot of philosophy to spout about it, but it was clear that the 66th Mob really was a family of sorts to him. All the political intrigue that comes with the Raiders aside, this was something that struck me as incorruptible.

After Griz and the 66th Mob we came upon Chains and Lady Chains. This happy couple was decked out from head to toe in silver chain mail. When I asked Lady Chains what she did for a living, her response was "Raiders." When I said, "No, really," her response was "Raiders." Chains, on the other hand, told me that he had worked for Ghirardelli Chocolate Company for twenty years. Lady Chains stayed home, handcrafted and fixed their chains, and worked on their bookings: they had apparently been on a Coors commercial and a Japanese television show. The entrepreneurial fan was beginning to emerge as a theme. There seemed to be a minor industry at work. How much of a market could there be? Had Raiders fans replaced clowns and magicians at children's birthday parties? After we had been chatting awhile, Chains and Lady Chains caught sight of legendary Raiders center Jim Otto, who had stopped to chat with some fans before heading into the stadium. They made a beeline for Otto and got their picture taken with him. We took one of them ourselves. It was all about the pictures.

Near the site of the Jim Otto sighting we ran into Ed from Sacramento, an assistant manager for a meat company (a good job for a Raiders fan, I thought) who had been following the team since the beginning. His Raidered-out PT Cruiser was an impressive display of silver flames elaborately spreading out across his black car adorned with several skulls, helmets, and Raiders shields. After Ed, we met Jeff. Jeff, it turned out, was on the NFL Hall of Fame fan video. There was a shot of him in the beginning, cruising into the stadium parking lot on his Raiders Harley. We wandered on past the band area and a few other celebrity fans. I saw Howie walking into the stadium and looked around for Darth Raider and the Violator. They were not in the immediate vicinity. No TV cameras, no action.

Down one of the rows of tailgaters we ran into Patty and Pedro, a very sweet couple from Suisun—the Indian name for "windy city." After Kelly admired Patty's "Raiders Girl" hat, she gave it to her, right off her head. After that, they handed me a beer and shared some barbeque. Patty was a dental assistant and Pedro worked construction. Of the Raiders scene Patty said, "Everyone's great, like a family. A lot of my co-workers wish they could come to more games like me. We have two kids, so we come as a family." They were with Tony, from Vacaville, whom they had just met. Tony was a landscaper who had designed his own Raiders tattoo. Pedro told me that he marinates his tri-tip in a pot for two to three days before games. As for the Raiders, "I think the reason why people hate the Raiders and Raiders fans is that these guys are the outcasts, the outlaws, the people who everybody looks down upon and now they're doing good. Now they are getting something for themselves, and people don't like it." We thanked them for the hat, the beer, and the food, and kept strolling through the lot until we came upon a suckling pig roaster, Herbert, who informed us as he sat in a lawn chair turning the pig that he had been pig roasting at games for two years. He let me turn the pig for a moment while Kelly took a picture. It was a hot day and turning the pig over coals laid on metal sheeting on asphalt came perilously close to volunteering to be roasted yourself, but Herbert didn't seem to mind.

In the stall next to the roasting pig we met Nicole Joyner, whose silverand-blackattack.com website we liked. She was a little tentative about talking to us since she felt that reporters had taken her words out of context. We talked a bit about the legal stuff going on with the city, and she said, "I'd like to think it was all about the fans, because the fans are special. Unfortunately, though, business is business. It's all about new stadiums, and the Raiders are one of the few teams that don't have one." Despite all of the legal hassles, "They still have a fan base of 40,000 regulars regardless. If the seats were just $20 they would probably sell out without a problem." I asked her what she thought about the riots after the Super Bowl, and she said, "Were there really riots in Oakland after the Super Bowl? No, just a few kids on the street. Thirteen- and fourteen-year-olds." Nicole wasn't happy with the treatment that Raiders fans got in San Diego: "People got their tires slashed and were treated badly in San Diego." As for her website, "I've had over 200,000 hits on my website. The NFL noticed it, and I had to totally rede-sign parts of it. I had to take out the Raiders image and remove the part about how to smuggle alcohol into the stadium." With that, we thanked Nicole for her time and headed into the stadium.

In the hallways of the Coliseum on the way toward our seats, the "Ray-duz!" chant drowned out the national anthem. It's a shame it didn't wipe out the game as well. A week after blowing a close one to the 49ers in San Francisco, the Raiders were thoroughly dominated by the Vikings in a 21–6 game whose sole highlight was a 62-yard punt by Shane Lechler. The Black Hole seemed more lackluster than it had the previous game, and people started clearing out in the third quarter. People were sarcastically cheering for the third-string quarterback, Rick Mirer. One notable highlight was the woman in a Raiders nightie. "I love your dress," must have been uttered more than she could remember that forget-table evening. Even though the game was a meaningless exercise, the fans seemed edgy. I was edgy. If this game was any indication, the 2003 Raiders sucked. As we left, we saw a woman in a *Flashdance* outfit smoking a cigarette, pounding on the door of the security office. They opened the door, smiled at her, and shut it again in her face. A little farther along, some women asked a pair of cops for their phone numbers and laughed. It was a weird omen.

On the way toward their last humiliating preseason loss, a 52–13 drubbing in Dallas, the Raiders began to turn on each other as Bill Romanowski savagely attacked black fellow-Raider Marcus Williams, hitting him so hard he broke his eye socket, knocked out a tooth, and effectively took him out of contention for a spot on the team. Romanowski, who I had always hated as a Bronco, had a checkered history with black players (in the past he had spat in the face of 49ers receiver J.J. Stokes). For this new low, the Raiders gave him a slap-on-the-wrist fine and a one-day suspension after Romo issued a formal apology. The whole season appeared to be imploding from the word go, and the *Oakland Tribune* headlines told the story, "AFC's Emperor Looks for Clothes," "Raiders Suffer Texas-size Meltdown," "Paranoia of Raiders Keeps the Fans Away." Even glory-years Raiders great Jack "They Call Me Assassin" Tatum was in trouble, strug-gling with medical bills after having his left leg amputated because of a diabetic condition. It was looking as though we might end up documenting a colossal Raiders meltdown from our bird's-eye seats in the Black Hole. The prospect of slogging through a nightmare season was hugely depressing, but as the old Lowell Fulson song put it, "Crying Won't Help."[5]

Ghost of Raiders past—Coulter Steel, Emeryville, California
(note the edge of the door on the right)

Photo: Joseph A. Blum

Seven

At Ricky's

Since good food and drink are often the accompaniments of good schmoozing, trends in the numbers of various sorts of eating and drinking establishments in America are both startling and suggestive. Between 1970 and 1998 the number of full service restaurants per one hundred thousand population fell by one-quarter, and the numbers of bars and luncheonettes were cut in half . . . These cold numbers confirm the gradual disappearance of what social commentator Ray Oldenburg calls "The Great Good Place," those hangouts that "get you through the day." In effect, Americans have chosen to grab a bite and run rather than sit a while and chat. . . . Whether we live alone or not Americans are staying home in the evening and *Cheers* has become a period piece.

Robert Putnam, Bowling Alone

We were always the second-class citizens of the Bay Area—you know, East Bay grease. The Raiders gave us credibility and toughness we're proud of.

Ricky Ricardo, Ricky's co-owner

The Raiders opened on a Sunday night in Tennessee, so Kelly and I figured that Ricky's, *the* Raiders bar, was the perfect place to watch the season opener. We flew into Oakland late and got a room at the Airport Hilton so we could also

check out the other spot where many Raiders fans watch games, the Airport
Hilton bar. The next morning we went for breakfast at the Sports Edition Bar
and Grill. Although there were Raiders banners up and some pieces of Oakland
sports memorabilia here and there, the place was more antiseptic beige than
silver and black. It reminded me a bit of the airport itself, clean and inoffensive
enough for the traveling business class. The walls were covered with generic pictures of sports figures that represented no particular team and a crew shell was
inexplicably hanging from the ceiling. We walked by a table of very large men
sporting Cowboys, Packers, Buccaneers, and Indiana Pacers shirts and caps. The
guy in the Buccaneers gear was harassing a Raiders fan at the next table, "Hey,
where's Barret Robbins? Is he still wandering around San Diego somewhere?
How much money did they pay him to lose the Super Bowl like that?" The little
old man in a well-worn Raiders cap shuffled away quietly. I noticed a bicycle
hanging from the ceiling next to a model hang glider.

As we sat and ordered, we scanned the room and noticed more Raiders fans
coming in as the morning games rolled on. There were TVs strategically placed
around the bar, and I noticed how odd and dissonant the cheering was when
people were rooting for perhaps ten different teams in five different cities at the
same time in the same room. It was a collapse of the time–space continuum.
There was simultaneity without unisonance, a kind of schizophrenic sporadic
and spasmodic cheering. After a while the boisterous chatter gave way to tube-
induced stupor. This place epitomized the sports bar as an affectless, identity-less
site of image consumption where the viewers/consumers could move from team
to team as the impulse struck them. The overall effect was numbing. Despite the
fact that all the waitresses were wearing Raiders shirts, nothing about the place
spoke Oakland or East Bay.

As Lawrence A. Wenner has observed, this one-size-fits-all version of social
space is all by design: "the postmodern sports bar is 'nobody's place.' Beyond
the Bleachers and Sports Garden, names of these postmodern places are Champions, Challenges, The Ballpark, The Bottom of the Ninth, Sports City Café,
The Sporting Club, and All Stars American Sports Bar." Hence, places like the

Sports Edition Bar aim to create a "heterotopia" that "transcends both place and 'authentic' identity with regards to sports." The result of this is that postmodern sports bars are "democratized" in the process of being totally "commodified." In other words, when the social space of the bar is no longer a site of gender, ethnic, class, neighborhood, or even team identity, the only thing that defines the space is that it is a place to consume images, and anyone can do that. The sports memorabilia in such places is there as a kind of nostalgic touchstone that casts a wide net in order to give an "identity hook" to a vast range of customers. The connection the customer has to the memorabilia is a distant one, however, that resembles the relationship a patron in a museum might have to an ancient cultural artifact. As opposed to the old-school local sports bar, these safe, clean, well-lighted sports theme parks cater to no one in particular in an effort to usher in a new era of highly profitable pervasive standardization.[1]

I finished my eggs and watched a waitress wander around aimlessly with a bundle of silver-and-black balloons. We paid the bill and called a cab to take us over to Ricky's. Our driver was Eritrean and was wearing an A's cap. "Go Raiders," he said as he dropped us off. On our way in we strolled past the parking spot reserved for "Stabler 12" and I glanced up at the big Ricky's sign complete with an old-fashioned cocktail glass. A huge satellite dish loomed above it. At the other end of the building there was Ricky's Team Shop, which sells Raiders gear. We nodded to the small group of Raiders fans mingling by the front door and headed inside, where we were greeted by a rush of Raiders imagery. One of the first things that caught my attention was a big Skull Patrol sign with a menacing skull in the middle and the motto "the first line of defense" at the bottom. I looked over at a poster for the Ricky's Raiders Rally featuring Raiderhed next Saturday. It was vaguely reminiscent of an old Haight-Ashbury psychedelic rock poster, except that it was in all silver and black and featured a good number of tough-looking skulls and the tag line "Bash the Bengals." The room space itself was dark and womblike. While there were TVs everywhere, they didn't overwhelm the setting like they did in the Sports Edition Bar. I strolled around and checked out the plethora of Raiders memorabilia—signed jerseys from Jim Otto,

Fred Biletnikoff, and Kenny Stabler as well as entries from Atkinson, Vella, Plunkett, and Bradshaw. As opposed to other generic bars, most of the stuff here was addressed specifically to Ricky. There were photos of former and current Raiders hanging out in the bar. I looked up at a Jersey Shore Raiders Booster Club t-shirt signed by Phil Villapiano that was inscribed "To Ricky's Raider Bar, You kept the spirit alive, 'Stay Wild.'" There may have been a few pennants of other teams here and there, but it was clear that Ricky's was Silver and Black holy ground, a Raiders shrine.

We walked into the other room and were greeted by another row of jerseys signed by Raiders greats: Lamonica, Sistrunk, Dalby, Martin, Tatum, and Hubbard. And in the corner on a table at the intersection of Hubbard and Tatum was a little sign that read, "Reserved for Al Davis." I noted a poster of Ben Davidson and a collage of seventies Raiders under the moniker "The Soul Patrol." As we were surveying the place, I noticed that a lot of people knew each other. As patrons came in they were frequently greeted by name. A guy in a Tim Brown jersey was sitting next to his girlfriend, who was wearing 49ers gear and taking a friendly ribbing from just about everyone who passed by. When former Raider Sam Adams grabbed a fumble for his new team and ran in to score, a woman stood up in front of one of the big screens and yelled, "You go, Sam—you're still our boy!" We noticed an old stained-glass Ricky's sign on the wall that informed us that the bar had been established in 1946. That, I thought, was the central difference between this place and the sterile Hilton bar, its East Bayness. In San Leandro, fairly close to the Oakland city limits, Ricky's drew people from both the suburbs and the city.

Wenner argues that the local sports bar is a throwback to the neighborhood tavern, the archetype of the great good place:

> Its main attraction is a friendly, homogenous, cohesive social culture, often forming along the lines of ascribed characteristics of race, ethnicity, sexual preference, country of origin, language or occupation. However, achieved subcultures, such as those formed around interests in sports, politics, gambling,

or literature, can also bring a cohesiveness to the character of the tavern. . . .
The sports bar is a "retrofit," a remodel, a new coat of paint on the turn of
the century tavern that functioned as a man's "third place," a place where man
visited in part as a response to industrialization.[2]

Wenner goes on to argue that "the cultural logic of sports bars functions at the
nexus of a high holy trinity of alcohol, sports, and hegemonic masculinity . . .
the sports bar is partly modern and partly postmodern, partly the 'great good
place' and partly a commoditized construction of bricolage on the highway strip
or mall."[3]

Although there is plenty of beer flowing at Ricky's, it defies several aspects of
Wenner's analysis of the sports bar. While home to plenty of macho Raiders fans,
the bar is not an exclusive realm of patriarchy, since plenty of women (including
Ricky's wife, Tina) both work at and patronize Ricky's in a nonsubservient capacity. It is also not exclusive in terms of ethnicity, since its proximity to Oakland
combined with the outlying suburbs makes it an open space where a very multiracial crowd happily commingles without sacrificing a sense of local identity.
Indeed, Ricky's reunifies communities that have, in many cases, been separated
as a result of deindustrialization and suburbanization. It is a site of multi-ethnic,
mixed-sex blue-collar schmoozing. As Robert Putnam argues, while organized
community activities (what he calls "maching") have steeply declined, "schmoozing" (or informal social communion) has persisted and is a sign that a hunger
for community still exists. While "watching is not the same as playing," Putnam
observes, fans' "sense of shared enthusiasm for common passion can generate a
certain sense of community."[4]

Thus, Ricky's is a Raiders fan utopia where the real social divisions that separate fans in other areas of their lives are left at the door and for the few hours
that the game is on, the imagined community of Raider Nation is realized.
Importantly, an expensive ticket ($47 at a minimum) is not necessary to watch
the game at Ricky's, the beers are only $2.50 rather than $7.50, and parking is
free rather than $15, so the economic barriers that might exclude many fans at

the Coliseum do not exist at Ricky's. Working-class "East Bay grease," as Ricky put it, is welcome. Hence rather than being an exclusionary bastion of drunken "hegemonic masculinity," Ricky's feels more like a welcoming family.

After we got a table and ordered a "Ken 'the Snake' Stabler" steak sandwich and a "Jim Otto" smoked turkey sandwich, Kelly and I went over to the bar to talk to Ricky Ricardo, the proprietor of Ricky's. Ricky, a very warm man with dark hair and beard, seemed glad to meet us and welcomed our questions. He poured a draft beer for a guy in a Black Hole t-shirt, then explained to us, "The bar moved to this location in 1962." When I asked him what it was like during the glory years, he told me about the days when his father ran the bar:

My father had buses full of fifty to a hundred people going to the games in the seasons before television. The Raiders players were always around in the early sixties. They came here a lot and many of them still do. We've always had a lot of Raiders fans coming here—in the sixties to seventies, even after they moved. The darkest day was when Al took them to L.A. We kept torches burning because we believed they would come back. Ricky's was like a shrine—like they never left. We had satellite, though, so we didn't miss a Raiders game (we had to take that down eventually). People lined up to see the games. They would also get together to go down to L.A. to see them play. I even went to London on August 5, 1990, to see them play. I brought a giant banner that said "Welcome Home Oakland Raiders," because I thought they'd be back soon. Of course, it took another five years before they did return.

We worked really hard on bringing them back to Oakland. The politicians listened to the fans. Ignacio de la Fuente called me before their return was announced and said, "Ricky, it's a done deal." I had a printer make up the *Oakland* Raiders schedule. When the Raiders did come back, it was bedlam around here. Our lots were full of TV trucks because of the schedules. Even L.A. news vans came down here to this place to get the story. It was like a fairy tale. A lot of the fans did fall off, though. Some went to the Niners, but a lot of them stayed true to the Raiders.

So the saga rolls on. Al is a maverick. He's the ultimate chessman in the way he plays other people. You'll never know if they'll leave. For example, they don't print anything with the name "Oakland" on it. So, it's out of our hands as fans.

Ricky had to get back to work, so I thanked him and jotted down a few notes. Sitting a couple of seats over from us was a large African American man in an Oakland Raiders t-shirt leaning forward with both his arms resting on the bar. He had been sipping a Budweiser and listening intently as I talked to Ricky. Malcolm, as he introduced himself, had gentle eyes and a big grin. He volunteered his own story and views:

I grew up in Oakland and I still live there. I went to my first Raiders game in 1963 when I was four years old with my dad at Frank Youell Field. So I loved the Raiders and have always followed them. In my view, Al Davis built the team. He built the stadium. And after that, when he got the Coliseum, he had great successes. To complain about Al is to bite the hand that feeds you. None of this would have happened without him. Al just wants to evolve. But everyone wants to get him—politicians shot him down, the NFL wanted him. He led the effort to build the Coliseum. But the same city doesn't want to respect him. The media harps on the last ten or so years and never wants to give Al credit for what he's done. You can't hate Al, all you can be is an interested observer.

We went back to our table to eat and watched people wearing silver-and-black beads and Raiders medallions arriving. A pretty Asian woman with long black hair strolled by our table in a "Raider Angel" baby-doll t-shirt. I went to the men's room and noticed they had a TV conveniently located inside so that one need not miss a second of the game. Back at our table, we met Lee "The Flea" Phillips, who informed us that he takes photographs at Raiders home games and had worked for Raider insider Al LoCasale. Lee told us that his family had had a chance to buy into the Raiders in 1959, but couldn't come up with the cash.

I went out to his van and he showed me several binders full of amazing shots of Raiders games. (Lee, it turned out, was quite a photographer.)

Back inside, we chatted with Señor Raider Man, a celebrity fan who has his own collector's card. Raised in Upland, California, this maniac moved to Hayward five years ago, works for Airborne Express, and has been a fan "since 1996." A tall, stocky man dressed in a customized number 69 jersey with his moniker on the back, he also sports football pants, pads, a Raiders fanny pack, official "ass-kickin'" rally towel, Mardi Gras beads, silver-and-black face paint around his goatee, dark sunglasses, and a giant silver-and-black sombrero to top it all off. He told us how, when in San Diego for the Super Bowl, he beat up three non-Raiders fans during a brief sojourn down to Tijuana. He seemed to relish telling us about "kicking peoples' asses," detailing every kick and punch. He told us that in Tijuana he went after the Chargers fan first. At another game, he informed us, he drank a bunch of tequila (which, he assured us, he doesn't normally do) and "knocked out a guy in a Cowboys jersey." Disavowing any memory of this event, Señor Raider Man told us that his friends relayed the story to him later. All of this mayhem was done, according to this self-appointed antihero, "to support the team." He seemed immensely pleased by this.

A large group of women sat down next to us all decked out in Raiders gear. It was game time, and the whole bar erupted into a deafening roar for the first kick of the Raiders game, a rematch of the AFC Championship game against the Titans. With each first down the whole bar would chant, "One, Two, Three—First Down!" During the big plays a guy in a Raiders jersey, pants, and pads with a football helmet, an eye patch, and a foam shield just like the one on the Raiders logo would jump up on his table and break into a frenzied cheer. The whole place was cheering like we were at the game itself. When Charlie Garner caught a pass and went 46 yards for a touchdown the place went nuts and the "Ray-duz" chant broke out. There were high-fives and hugs all around. People also had fun chanting "defense," telling the TV announcer to shut up when he said something stupid, cursing the referees, and heckling the players. Although no one could hear them in Tennessee, it turned into an ongoing conversation that the crowd had with itself, full of irony and good humor. After the big Raiders score, though, the Titans went back up 12–10 before halftime.

The first person we talked with at halftime was Andrew the Shieldhead. Andrew told me that he was making Shieldhead t-shirts and was working on "a multimedia project." His vision was "to compete with Nike." Andrew said that he had been at the Super Bowl in San Diego and that he "gets a lot of recognition from people." While he hoped to make something off of his Shieldhead activities, he was not in it for the money: "I do this because I'm a fanatic." While I was at the table with Shieldhead, Kelly went outside to interview Bob, the bar's co-owner and Ricky's brother.

I left Ricky's to chat with Bob out in front while Jim stayed inside. As we talked, Bob kept his eye on things, telling the two rambunctious little kids waiting for their parents not to climb or swing on the skinny trees across from the entrance. When people arrived, Bob would often greet them by name, shaking their hands or slapping them on the back. He gave new customers directions as they walked in. We sat in the two white plastic chairs designated as the smoking area. Bob's manner was thoughtful as he told me about himself, his family, and how he views the Raiders. Since his father was the founder of the bar, Bob literally grew up there. Ricky Senior had died in February 2003, and Bob and his brother Ricky were fixing their father's house up themselves in order to sell it—"we don't hire people to do our work like affluent folks do," he told me wryly. Bob stayed in the East Bay his whole life:

> I went to college at Cal State Hayward and played basketball. I got a bachelor's degree in political science and did a teaching credential in K–6 writing. After that I got accepted to law school, but decided that education is a better thing to do. I don't teach anymore, but I do coach basketball, which is how I am still able to be a teacher. Currently, I own Outbound Travel and am partners with Ricky. We own everything here.

He gestured around the L-shaped setup of Ricky's, its gift shop, a salon, and the travel agency, which fronts the street. A tall black man left the bar and Bob nodded at him as he got into his car. I asked Bob about San Leandro and the East Bay. He continued:

> In my lifetime, the East Bay developed into a bedroom community of San Francisco from the previous generation, who had had local affiliations and grassroots identification with the place. These had been the children of immigrants—working-class people. Before them were the children of the people who came to the Bay Area because of the World War II industry— people from the South, African Americans, children of sharecroppers. So things here have changed a lot.
>
> I remember one summer while I was in college I had a beef with my dad and ended up working in a brass and aluminum foundry near here. This was probably one of the worst jobs in the world. I worked with desperate people: parolees, immigrants, hungry college kids. There were four engines the size of 747s in the place that generated so much heat and noise it was awful. Overhead, sand was pouring into molds and toxic gasses were spewing as molten metal poured out. It was like working in hell. But that was the kind of industrial work there was around here.

We ruminated a bit on the conditions of peoples' lives in the East Bay, and in Oakland in particular, which prompted a few bitter remarks from Bob:

> The politicians will build new Republican-sponsored armaments and aircraft carriers, but they won't support the schools or the people here. They used 9/11 to feather their own caps. It was a terrible thing, but they've used it for their own purposes. Because of my business, I travel a lot—in India on third-class trains, Afghanistan, Iran, Turkey. I've even been shot at. Americans like to think that it's like America all over the world, but it's not. It's not even like America here. The violence in Oakland, for example, is appalling. A black man shoots another black man and no one does anything about it. Nobody

can find the time to make it right. Regular people have nothing—the rich have everything. If you give people a piece of the pie, they won't revolt. But you can't trust the rich to share anything. The answer to all the problems is to balance the wealth in the world. If you take even just 10 percent from the rich you can make things a lot better.

Bob stopped to get up and take one of the boys out of a tree. I switched subjects when he returned by asking him how he became affiliated with Oakland and the Raiders. He told me that the connection for him began with a reaction to the West Bay press's attitude toward the East Bay. As a kid he had liked the 49ers until the *San Francisco Chronicle* ripped East Bay fans. He characterized it like this:

The East Bay is working class and all that. It is not the West Bay, which is chardonnay-drinking intellectuals who believe that they are better than you. It's the upper crust versus you guys who work on our cars and build our homes. So, I liked the 49ers, but then I lost allegiance because I didn't like getting pissed on all the time by Republicans and the affluent. I like working people—regular folks. These are the people who support their team.

I went to my first Raiders game at Kezar Stadium in Golden Gate Park in San Francisco. You could walk down to the field to talk to the players because no one was there. I do think, though, that Al Davis gets too much credit for making the Raiders what they became. In high school, I hustled programs in Frank Youell Field. My friends and I would sneak down to the field to be unofficial ball boys. That was a different era.

I asked Bob what he thinks of fans now. "I don't like it very much and feel like there's been some lost innocence. The combination of sports or professional football and liquor has created this ugly side where people drink too much and swear too much. Fans can take things too far nowadays—too much of a good thing goes too far and people don't police themselves enough." I thought this was interesting from a man who was one of the owners of the most famous Raiders bar. "I actually like watching basketball more now because drunks can't watch it. Football is different—you can watch it when you're drunk." I laughed. He went on:

Raiders fans changed after they came back from L.A. The original Raiders fans were workers with a hometown affiliation. Many even worked for the Raiders organization in some capacity. The new Raiders fans have gotten to the point where they want to be recognized. They have a sense of community, but it comes out of a sense of outward enmity and inward amity. It's gotten to an absurd level in some respects. Many Raiders fans have this notion of constantly being under attack. So, for example, if people were being attacked by Martians, Jews and Christians, Catholics and Protestants would all pull together. That's how Raiders fans can be and it can be great, but people can take it too far. So Raiders fans will throw things at other fans in the stadium. I'm not saying that there aren't plenty of good fans—there are—but the others are definitely there. I would think that the Raiders organization doesn't want bum fans, but that's what's happening. And it just turns me off, peoples' uncouthness, their ignorance. The drunker you get, the stupider you get. I know that football is an emotional game, but if they were placed in their grandmothers' living rooms, they'd change. So I'm not your typical gung-ho Raiders fan. I'm really turned-off by peoples' lack of respect and self-respect. A lot of what people see as scary Raiders fans are people under the influence. My attitude is, "Don't lose respect for yourself, your team, and your community."

As far as the Raiders organization itself, they've lost their affiliation with the community. They're no longer the Oakland Raiders. Al Davis holds a grudge toward Oakland. He's aloof and doesn't try to market the Oakland Raiders, and in some ways he seems to blame the fans. Davis has a totally pompous attitude toward everything, toward his own greatness. I think Jon Gruden left because he stole too much of Al's thunder. Davis has caused a lot of problems with his own marketing. He could have gotten the fans back, but he didn't. A good marketing team, like Green Bay, is oriented toward its community. Instead, the Raiders don't develop community, the stadium is an atrocity, and they sell the seats to the ghetto at the same price as the upper-class neighborhood. The Raiders are truly like pirates who ride their pirate ship from town to town taking plunder as they go. So, Al Davis has really ruined it for me because of leaving Oakland. But, you know, you're always in love with your first love—but they've broken your heart.

I asked Bob what it was like to work at the bar, and how he viewed the customers, a predominantly Raiders bunch. "You mean at Ricky's where the customer is always wrong?" he joked.

Seriously, I've always worked the door and I treat everyone the same across the board. I'm fair. If you have a preconceived notion about anyone, that's bad. And race is just not an issue in this bar, either. People appreciate that and when they come here, they don't always like it when others go too far. So the way we keep people from being over the top is through their own sense of community. They like hanging out here, so they don't want to lose this place or embarrass themselves.

Kelly came back inside and we focused on the game. The third quarter featured only a sputtering Raiders offense and a Titans field goal. In the fourth, with the Titans clinging to a 15–13 lead, the Raiders were the victims of a horrible call that gave Tennessee a touchdown on a play where the receiver never got his feet down in the end zone. This injustice was followed by Gannon going down with what appeared to be a knee injury with 7:11 left to go in the game. I ran to the restroom and the guy behind me was saying to himself, "Rich Gannon cannot be hurt. Repeat: Rich Gannon cannot be hurt." I nodded in agreement and returned to my seat to see Gannon jog back out on the field and run a miraculously efficient 65-yard drive to score a touchdown to make it 22–20 Titans with 3:30 left in the game. But the big comeback was not to be as Tennessee hit another field goal, stopped the Raiders, and left the crowd at Ricky's to cuss and mumble about stupid penalties and bad calls. As usual, we were robbed. Despite the loss, the mood in the bar was subdued but amiable. We got up to leave and thanked Ricky for his hospitality on the way out. An elderly man in a Raiders chef's hat was rolling two big pots of cooking oil outside. Shieldhead walked up to us and the security guard by the door said, "He's crazy, but I like him." Ricky smiled and said, "He's a really nice guy." Shieldhead grinned and replied, "We're family."

Eight

Working-Class Heroes

The promise of the industrial garden . . . was realized, if unevenly, in places like San Leandro and Fremont. Working-class Oakland neighborhoods in Oakland's flatlands, in contrast, faced a steady hollowing out, as the city's small-scale manufacturing economy contracted. Gone were the hundreds of railroad jobs that had sustained an earlier generation of black Oaklanders. Gone, too, after the advent of containerization in the mid-1960s, were many of the longshore and warehouse jobs. . . . The city's massive canning industry had declined by the middle of the decade. Oakland's automobile industry had simply disappeared. Between 1961 and 1966, Oakland lost ten thousand manufacturing jobs.

Robert O. Self, "California's Industrial Garden"

As Kelly, Joe, and I wandered through the crowd at the Raiders rally on the Friday before the home opener, I noticed a good number of people in union hats and t-shirts along with their Raiders gear. The Communications Workers of America, the International Longshoremen's and Warehousemen's Union, the International Brotherhood of Teamsters, the American Federation of State, County, and Municipal Employees, the Service Employees International Union, the Firefighters, and the Ironworkers were all represented here and there in the crowd. I thought about the Raiders' blue-collar image and pondered the irony of the fact that just as the Raiders were beginning to foster their working-class rebel image in the sixties, the real working class in Oakland was being pummeled by deindustrialization and union busting.

We asked Chris Rhomberg, a sociologist and student of Oakland, to comment on the relationship between blue-collar Oakland and the Raiders' rebel image:

> This isn't real rebellion, of course, but a highly stylized and aestheticized fantasy of rebellion. Or, rather, I think the Raiders really symbolized not rebellion so much as a certain image of working-class mobility. That is the idea that work is hard and punishing, that you have to make your breaks and take them, even breaking the rules if necessary (and the Raiders were always famous for collecting penalties), and that success comes abruptly and from out of the sky, as it were. "Commitment to Excellence" is a fine motto, but wasn't the bottom line always "Just Win, Baby," and doesn't that express the dominant value system in a capitalist culture?

The high point of working-class rebellion in Oakland was not when the Raiders brought together fans in the Coliseum parking lot in the sixties, but when, in 1946, twenty thousand workers shut down downtown Oakland to support a retail clerks' strike in one of the most noteworthy general strikes in American history. Defying big business, the city's political elite, and even some of their own conservative union leaders, Oakland's workers took ownership of the city. Singing, dancing, picketing on rollerskates, fighting with police, and marching by City Hall chanting, "Hail, hail, the gang's all here," working-class Oakland residents staged a strike that was part political theater and part revolution. Described as a "carnival-like atmosphere" by many, the strike was called a "holiday" by the local unions.

Strike participant Stan Weir remembers, "Never before or since had Oakland been so alive and happy for the majority of the population." As Rhomberg puts it, "The emergent celebration of working-class identity in the city center defied

John Spinola of Ironworkers Local 378

the cultural definition of downtown as a place of commercial consumption and the regime's political control of urban space." In effect, shoppers became strikers. After the strike, the consciousness of local workers was transformed, and they even brought it into the ballpark. As one contemporary observer noted, "Four months after the General Strike, at the opening of the baseball season in Oakland they had the Oakland motorcycle drill team lead the dignitaries into the ball park. They were not all trade unionists in that ball park, but I never heard anybody get booed so loudly and hard as those cops did that day."[1]

What the Raiders represented today, I thought, as I surveyed the crowd in Frank Ogawa Plaza, was a symbolic site where the partial construction of identity occurred. Many of those workers who in the past might have been strikers have now been transformed into shoppers: they consume, in the case of the Raiders, a commodity that speaks blue-collar grit or street authenticity or whatever else depending on the imagination of the consumer. In tailgating, or coming to a crowd of 10,000 people for a Raiders rally, or cheering as one with 50,000 at the game, or with many more virtually through the far-flung media nexus, people can perhaps recuperate a fragment of the collective identity that events like the Oakland general strike offered years ago. As community in America declines and fragments, in a metropolitan area like Oakland an event like this free rally brings together people from the inner city and the atomized suburbs to share in something that, however loosely, binds them together in some ill-defined way. Even thought of as a transitory, imagined community, Raider Nation itself has seemed at times in danger of disintegrating.

It was a sweltering day and Kelly, Joe, and I were sweating as we weaved through the crowd, taking pictures and doing quick interviews with fans. We got out of the way for a guy on a tall unicycle, strolled by a gaggle of Raiderettes, and watched people lining up to get autographs from Raiders legends. With its mishmash of corporate booths, media cameras, and fans dressed in homemade costumes, the whole gathering struck me as a cross between a mall event and a high school pep rally. We saw Señor Raider Man, Phil and Angel, Gorilla Rilla, the Oaktown Pirates, and a whole range of other fans in elaborate getups. A sexy

Latina walked by in a "Yo Amo Raiders" tank top. There was a booth for organ donations and a totally empty "No Alcohol" zone. I got a beer and Kelly went over to interview an Oakland cop who was guarding the players' tent. He told her (anonymously) that he been born and raised in Oakland, had worked on the force for thirty years, and had season tickets. "It's a little more wild now than in the sixties," he told Kelly. As for the Raiders organization, "It's all about the money. They'll probably move again. Money-wise it will hurt the city. We'll lose jobs." Despite his pessimism about the Raiders' future, he seemed glad to be at the rally. It reminded me of a story one of our interviewees had related to us of seeing a cop stop his car in the middle of the road after the Raiders won the AFC championship, get out, and start dancing with fellow fans on the street, yelling, "We did it! We did it!"

Joe snapped a picture of an older African American woman dressed from head to toe in silver and black holding a beautiful handmade figure of "The Oakland Lady." It was, as usual for Raiders events, a multi-age, multiclass, multiracial crowd that, for the moment, was in a friendly mood. Everyone was happy to chat with us. The Raiders organization had someone running around filming the fans. Somebody tried to get Joe to move off the steps by the VIP tent, claiming that he didn't have an "access pass." We met Gus Cardenas from San Bernardino, who let us get a shot of his "Destiny Angel" Raiders tattoo. Then we ran into George from Inglewood, who had also driven up the several hundred miles for the rally. He was pulling his son Anthony behind him in a little red wagon, both of them wearing Raiders jerseys. After George and Anthony, we met Edwin Brown, a proud retired teamster from Oakland who'd been a fan since the beginning. Standing near Edwin we met "Skull Lady," whose photo would make the first page of the Sunday sports section in the *Oakland Tribune,* as well as "the Radiator," whose costume was a chaotic mix of Raiders symbols that was hard to decipher.

I noted a guy in a Raiders tie-dye t-shirt and we stopped to interview Raider-Gloria who had legally changed her name to fit her game day character. Gloria, who was wearing silver hiking boots, black Capri tights, a number 75 Howie

Long jersey, pads, eye-black, sunglasses with Raiders shields in the center of both lenses, and a silver pom-pom on her head, looked to be in her mid forties. She was born and raised in Oakland and works in customer service for a trucking company. She told us, "I've been dressing up now for seven years. My dad was a season ticket holder before the Coliseum was built and the Raiders played in Frank Youell Field." As for the Raiders' PR problems, Gloria said, "I think the PSLs [personal seat licenses] should have been lifetime. People shouldn't have to renew." She didn't think the Raiders would move again, though, because "Al really loves the team and the fans." Gloria explained to us that she had once made some silver-and-black candy canes at Christmas, sent them to Al, and had gotten a personal response thanking her. Before we moved on she told us, "We are a Raider Nation, a Raider family. It's like your marriage vows—for better or worse—no matter what their record is."

A terrible band in silver-and-black leotards was playing ear-splittingly loud music on stage as we walked over for the beginning of the costume contest. Mercifully they stopped. The organizers seemed to have chosen the B team for the contest, and the fans in the audience playfully booed the whole lot. The KNBR radio announcers who were hosting the event finally awarded first prize to Augusta Raider from Fresno for an Elvira-like getup featuring a top hat. Once the time came for the players to be announced, the volume seemed to get even louder and I began to wonder if the average Raiders fan was partially deaf.

As the various players took to the stage, I gauged the crowd's response to see where they stood in the hearts of Raider Nation. Callahan got moderate applause as he flattered the crowd and made way for the defensive unit. Biggest cheers: Romanowski and Woodson. On special teams, place kicker Sebastian Janikowski got cheers combined with a spattering of boos in memory of missed field goals past. On offense, Gannon got the "MVP" chant going and then mentioned that there were "15,000 tickets left" to the home opener, but Tim Brown and Jerry Rice got the wildest cheers. As for the linemen, Lincoln Kennedy stirred it up when he told the crowd, "We represent well." The whole exercise struck me as a little half-hearted on the players' parts. My ears hurt and I was glad when the hype subsided and the Raiders had been ushered off-stage to their expensive customized cars and SUVs. I interviewed a nice woman behind me named Kim, whose Raider Doberman was named Trotter after William Monroe Trotter, a black antislavery advocate who helped start *The Abolitionist* with William Lloyd Garrison. Kim had been a Raiders fan for twenty years and a dog trainer for thirty.

As we strolled toward Broadway, a fight suddenly broke out between two Raiders fans, one in a black jersey, the other wearing white. The two ceremonially stripped down to their black-and-white tank tops and began dancing artfully, sizing each other up as they bobbed their heads back and forth between raised fists. Almost instantly, the crowd formed a circle around them like an ad hoc boxing ring. Somebody behind them was getting it all on a video camera. But not everyone was happy with the show. A black guy in a Rice jersey shouted futilely, "That's dumb, that's dumb as shit! We're supposed to be on the same team! This is a fucking pep rally!" The two continued to dance in a graceful, almost stylized fashion. The bigger of the two, in white, took a swing and the smaller guy skillfully ducked the punch and hit the big dude with a jab that glanced off his jaw and did little damage. They stopped, hung on each other, and broke as if it were a boxing match. The smaller one smiled while dancing and the big guy nodded as if in response. There were no security guards anywhere, so I ran over to one of the tents near where Joe had been scolded about his "access pass" and the guard said, "I don't have a gun. I'm not going over there."

On the way back over to the fight, I saw a guy with two arms full of gang tattoos ushering his little girls out of harm's way. By the time I returned to the scene of the fight, the police had arrived and had the small guy and another dude who wasn't even involved in the fight in handcuffs. A woman in a Wheatley jersey that she'd converted into a see-through mini-dress with a halter-top was standing behind the cops taunting the dudes in handcuffs. It was time to go. The ugly scene was only made better by meeting Byron and his sweet little girl, Brandi, who was beaming as she twirled around with her Raiders flag waiting for the light to change on Broadway.

On Saturday we went out to see if the Raiders campout would still be going despite the dismal preseason, disappointing opening loss, and intense heat. Not surprisingly, by midday there were already six to eight cars parked on 66th Avenue holding down the fort. We noticed that a couple of the cars were empty, but several SUVs had the engines on to keep the air conditioning going. One of the campers was outside putting up his Jolly Roger flag, so we stopped for a moment to talk. He told us, "The party won't get started until the early evening, but then it will keep going all night and roll on into the parking lot once the gates open at 8:00 a.m. Bloody Marys at 6:00 a.m.!" Across the street, Griz was hanging the "66th Mob" sign on the fence by the closed entrance to the parking lot. They had already pitched a tent with beach chairs, tables, snacks, and a portable TV.

We headed over to the Coliseum entrance closer to the Arena and found two groups already set up. In the first was Jack, whom we had met before the first game, along with Pancho, Bonnie, and Robert. By the second campsite we met Dino and Jersey John, who told us that he flies out from Houston to go to games. "I party late with the guys and then go sleep in the Days Inn with my wife. By 8:00 p.m. this whole street will be packed with cars." I looked over at the cars and semis zooming by on the freeway, turned the other way and glanced at the barren expanse of asphalt in the parking lot, glowing with rising heat. The smell of exhaust was ever present.

Finally we drove over to check out the motor home campers. By now it was 2:15, a little less than twenty-four hours until kickoff, and there were twenty-five motor homes lined up to get into the Coliseum lot, some elaborately decorated with Raiders art and, of course, big flags and banners. The line snaked around a corner and went all the way down a side street full of industrial sites. Mike, the first guy we ran into, had driven over Friday after the rally and camped there overnight. He told us, "The Moose Lodge helps us out sometimes and lets people park in their lot when the cops decide to harass the line. They also let people use their bathrooms and sometimes they have good food." A little farther down the line we met some retired folks sitting around under a rare shade tree outside their rig. Roberto, Joyce, Ron, and Pat were welcoming folks who reminded me of my grandparents. According to Roberto, "Sometimes with five hundred people competing for a hundred and fifty motor home spots, it can get ugly. A lot of people park their motor homes really early and then come back on Saturday night for the big party. It's more about 'How are you?' and catching up on things. Then it's about the Raiders." When we told them that we were staying in a hotel downtown, they looked at us a bit incredulously. "Why would you do that?" Roberto asked. "They're young, honey." Joyce said. "They might want to go out to dinner." By this point my pregnant wife looked as if she was going to pass out, so we thanked them, got back into the car, and drove past the assembly of the motor homes to the freeway.

Early Sunday morning, I sipped on a Bloody Mary in the Fat Lady, a fine bar and restaurant located in an old Victorian in downtown Oakland that had been a brothel in the 1880s. Ornately decadent, the place looked like a cross between a cozy boudoir and an Old West tavern. I looked at the motto on my napkin, "Better to Live Rich Than to Die Rich," and glanced down the bar at a row of Raiders fans eating omelets and sucking down cocktails. Last year, during the Raiders playoff run, we met a group of firefighters here at the Fat Lady, one of whom we interviewed for the book. Kevin, a firefighter from Engine Company 2548, Firefighters Union Local 55, was a genuine blue-collar Raiders fan. Kevin is a stocky, good-natured guy with an easy manner. When we caught up with him in the middle of the 2003 season, he made it clear that he didn't think Raiders fans deserved their thug image:

Most of the fans get a bad rap, but it's the TV's fault because they show all the guys that are dressed up, crazy, yelling at people, but 95 percent of the people in the stands are normal people just out there to watch a game. If you watch the clips [the media creates] after the games, they are always showing crazy guys and all that crap and the media plays that up, but it's not nearly all that bad. Where I sit, they are all firemen and friends of firemen. All these firemen were all scattered about. So the Raiders were cool because some of the guys with PSLs approached them so they put us all together. We've got four rows of about eight people, about thirty-two people. Some of us went to the Super Bowl last year. We took a motor home down. But we didn't get any tickets. We sat in a bar and had a hell of a time.

I was born and raised right down the road in Albany and I've been coming here for a couple of years. My buddy owns the pub around the corner. I grew up a Raiders fan. My dad and all his brothers were Raiders fans. They went to Frank Youell Field years ago. A lot of Raiders fans are like that, they're almost like a family. They're nice. But they're very committed. We used to go to the tailgate in the parking lot, but now you've got to get there too early in the morning. If you don't get there by 8:00, you can't even get in the lot. So that's why [the firefighters] use the BART lot because you can get there at 10:00 and still park. It's East Oakland, toward 73rd Avenue, toward the hills. Usually there are between twenty and forty guys. We usually come here and drink and go eat over there. Sometimes we eat at both places. During the playoffs it was really crazy. Last year I was in East Oakland. We covered the Coliseum (our fire truck did anyway) and on Thursday before Sunday's game there were fans camping outside of 85th Avenue, in Baldwin. By Saturday night it was all the way around the block. For me, it's just a day but for those guys [who camp out], it's a weekend.

When I asked Kevin about Oakland and the East Bay, his response was thoughtful:

The East Bay itself is a very nice place to live. I think Oakland gets a bad rap. There are a few parts of town that are in bad shape like the East Oakland/West Oakland flats. You know there is a lot of crime there. The other 90 percent of Oakland is really, really nice and people don't realize that. I mean, the one time a bad thing happens, [people say] "Oh, God," and it gets blown out of proportion because Oakland gets a bad rap. I work for the city, so I'm biased, but I like it. There are a lot of nice places to live here, but I don't live here because of the price and the schools. The schools are pretty mediocre. So a lot of firemen live in outlying areas because years ago you had to live within ten miles of the city, but they rescinded that because people fought it. But Oakland should be a lot better perceived by the media.

Then he offered some comments on working as a fireman in Oakland:

It's active, it's fun. In a big city like Oakland you get to do a lot more stuff, a lot more fires, a lot more rescues. In the small cities it's all training, training, training, but when stuff happens, they don't know what to do. They've never done it, so they have to call on the big cities to help them out. Oakland is weird, we get a lot of strange stuff—I mean the cops get more strange stuff. Oakland has a good name in the ranks of the fire departments in California. During the Oakland fires, I was brand new. I had about a year on. I was in East Oakland that day, and it was the farthest we could be from the fire, so we ended up there a couple of hours later. It got so bad we had to call people from home to come in. Then everybody and their mother came in. You know that fire only burned for twelve hours, from 4:00 a.m. in the morning to 6:00 p.m. when it was out, but the fires in San Diego were brutal. We only sent fifteen guys down there but we should have sent fifty. Everybody wanted to go. I volunteered, everyone volunteered. One of our units was in that strike team with the guy from Novato [who died fighting the Julian fire]. We all went to his funeral. That was very emotional.

You know, it's funny how much firemen like to go to fires. It's like if there is a big fire at a house or up the hill or whatever, we live to do that. We're like, "Let's go!" So at one point we are very—I shouldn't say happy, but we're glad to be busy doing something. But then, on the other hand, you go, "This poor guy lost his house."

As for the disturbances after the Super Bowl:

We saw it when we got back and went to Station 20 to park the motor home there and drop everybody off. There were lots of broken bottle bits. They were throwing that stuff at them. Since that happened, there is a new policy. If we get involved in something and it is rioting, we have the police escort us in and out. If it gets real bad, like the week before the Super Bowl, they decided that if something got burned bad, they would just let it go. After the Tennessee game we were coming back this way and it was crazy. People were lighting bonfires and stuff. They weren't throwing anything, they were just really excited and I guess, two hours later, it went to hell. Once you start something stupid, there are a bunch of followers. They turned over [fire department] vehicles. You know, the City of Oakland paid for it. The Raiders don't pay for it. The firemen don't pay for it. The taxpayers pay for it.

[The police don't have] a very good relationship with the citizens. The cops are very abrasive all the time. You can't be a nice cop in the bad parts of town because they will run you out, but the cops are kind of pricks anyway. So we see the cops hassling the people all the time. They don't respect the cops and the cops don't respect them. A kid grows up seeing that, his parents are yelling at the cop, and he gets to be twelve, and he does it. It doesn't take long. It's a cycle.

We finally talked about the Raiders' relationship with the city and their fans:

Like I said, they both hate each other and are suing each other in court. Nobody is going to win. It costs the city a lot of money. It costs the Raiders a lot of money. The city is in a financial crisis right now. We're closing firehouses and we're suing the Raiders and they're suing us. The Raiders really gouged us on ticket prices and sometimes they're not that good. If they were good all the time, they'd sell out.

Haven in a Heartless World

> Bay Area metal trade workers have always been affected by forces beyond
> our control, buoyed and buffeted by precious metals bonanzas, wars, depres-
> sions, and the economic cycles of industrial capitalism. But this time is dif-
> ferent! For the last two decades we have been suffering the local effects of a
> profound reconfiguration of global economic and political forces, resulting
> in the transformation of the United States from an industrial to a postindus-
> trial society. This transition has already expelled the vast majority of us from
> our crafts and forces those of us who remain in the trades to labor under
> deteriorating and degraded circumstances. . . . Most hold in contempt the
> low-wage service sector jobs that we fear we might be forced to accept, but
> the emerging postindustrial world offers us few opportunities.
>
> Joe Blum, *"Degradation without Deskilling"*

As we walked over the pedestrian bridge from the BART station the parking
lot looked like a makeshift tent city. The Raiders opener may not have been a
sellout, but the crowd in the lot was massive and far more energetic than it had
been during the preseason. We met Joe at the end of the bridge and made our
way around the Coliseum by row after row of boisterous tailgaters until we ran
into the South Shield party at the far end of the lot where Raiderhed was playing
a set. Joe took a few photographs as people drank beer, ate, and rocked out to the
metal/rap fusion that Raiderhed was dishing out to the tailgate. I laughed at the
customized "Higher 1" and "Stonerdude 420" jerseys on the band and detected
the strong sweet smell of reefer drifting through the air.

We chatted with a guy who showed us his Raiders tattoos and strolled on
along the edge of the parking lot until we found our friends the Mahlers and
stopped in for a bite to eat and an interview. Jim was our union president, and
we had met his brother Jerry and his parents, Hank and Diane, at past games.
They had always been gracious and generous hosts. Like many of the fans we
interviewed, the Mahlers were a "Raiders family." Having spent his work life
as a card-carrying member of the legendary International Longshoremen's and
Warehousemen's Union and his leisure time as a Raiders fan since the sixties,

we immediately thought of Hank as a good person to interview. Hank is a distinguished, silver-haired man who bears a striking resemblance to Raiders great Kenny Stabler. He was happy to oblige us when we asked him about his history as a fan:

I've probably been a fan since 1967. I was aware of them from 1960 when they came into being, but they played in San Francisco for the first three years, and I was a 49ers season ticket holder so I was kind of shocked at this new team coming in to play in our backyard. But when they got the Coliseum built and they played their first game there in '66, I was a season ticket holder, because I had gone to Frank Youell Field, which is a little stadium that holds about 15,000 people and, if you ask now, 800,000 people must have had season tickets there. Anyway, it was a great place to watch football. You're right on the field. You could hear the players talking and I really got intrigued then. I didn't have season tickets at Youell Field, but watched a lot of games, so when the Coliseum opened I made sure we had season tickets right off the bat. We had them from '67 until '82 when they went on their twelve-year road trip, and then when they came back in 1995, we were right there again. So I missed twelve years, but other than that, I've been a Raiders fan.

[Back in the early days] everybody I worked with used to put down the Raiders and even though I was a 49ers fan, I started rooting for the underdog, you know. When [the leagues] finally merged and had interleague games, then I swung 100 percent over to the Raiders and no more 49ers. In fact, the two teams I root for are the Raiders and whoever the 49ers are playing. Well, after every game while the Raiders were at Youell Field, they used to have a buffet at a place called the Cactus Room in downtown Oakland, a very small little bar, but they got food out for the Raiders so the Raiders would come there after every game because it wasn't like today, you know. There wasn't a lot of money to throw around. So the buffet was there for the Raiders. So naturally, you could come down there and have a couple of beers and rub elbows with the Raiders, and it was great. I mean it felt like they were part of the city, and you were right there with them, but now, I mean everybody lives all over the place and you never see anybody off the field. At [another bar] Clancy's, he used to have buses going to the games from his place every week they were in town. Then we'd go back to his place after the game. It was great. He was a good, good fan. He's been around for a long time.

I think that now the fans get a bad rap throughout the league because when you see them on television, you see three or four of those guys with the spiked hair and shoulder pads, and they portray these guys as bullies, but they're not. Mostly, they're the nicest guys in the world. The guys who cause the trouble are the guys that drink beer out in the lot for four hours, go in there and raise hell. Those aren't the real Raiders fans. Those guys are looking for trouble. Everybody always talks to the fans with the costumes on who make a big deal of themselves. When you talk to them, a lot of them will say, "I've been a hardcore fan since 2001!" But there are a lot more of us who were here before all of that. I'm not sure if it happened when they went to L.A. or if it's the culture. It's hard for me to deal with. I still want to go back. It was really more family-oriented down here. Everybody bought four tickets, the wife, and the two kids, and you. In our section, we knew everybody and they knew everybody else. It was a family. But now, you don't see too many families at all.

When I asked Hank what he thought of the Raiders organization and the court decision in the Raiders case against Oakland, he said:

[The Raiders organization] leaves a little bit to be desired. They have a circle-the-wagons, us-against-the-world attitude. Do whatever Al says. I mean everybody marches in lockstep with him, so there's no individual opinion in a one-man organization. As for the court case, I think there were some lies told on both sides there, but I can't believe a man of Al Davis's intelligence and stature would be hornswoggled into believing something that wasn't true. It's just hard to believe. Will they stay? The court says they are going to stay until 2010, we'll see after that.

Finally, we asked Hank about his career and what he thought about Oakland:

I worked on the waterfront. I belonged to the Longshoremen's Union, was a clerk, and spent forty-two years doing that. I retired in '99. I did the planning for the container ships, a lot of computer work and inputting all the vital information about what was on the ship, the hazardous materials, the lifts, et cetera. Well, we went from three-by-five carbon paper to printers and fax machines, you know. The whole technology thing just turned everything around, reduced the workforce by 60 percent maybe. Containerization. We used to bring the ship in, and to discharge it and reload it would take, like, nine days. Now, they can do it in a day and a half. And with maybe twenty people where before they had two hundred people. Obviously, there's a big savings for the employer there. Our union though, was a strong one, a great one. I mean, I never went out on strike for anything I disagreed with. Every move we made, I was in agreement. It was a solid union. There was very, very little dissent. I was a good soldier, not an officer, though.

I grew up in Oakland, went to high school there and worked there for forty-two years. I lived on Telegraph Avenue in North Oakland and I never really had any problems there. I guess now the homicide rate there, it's like a shooting gallery. There are a few sections that you don't go to at night, just like any other city. [The media] makes it seem like it's rampant throughout Oakland. It isn't. And of course that part has changed since I grew up here. I don't even know how you would have gone about getting drugs in those days. I mean, people smoked marijuana, but they would be, "Man, I can't get it." Now I guess you can buy it at recess. Anyway, I always wanted to live on the other side of the [Caldecott] tunnel because the weather was better. It's like forty degrees difference. Now I live in Walnut Creek.

Oaktown Devils

Honey, I cannot afford the ticket, the parking fee, eats, or drinks. I mean, four dollars for a watered down sixteen-ounce glass of beer is ridiculous. See, the owners, most of whom never played a lick of sports in their life, pay athletes millions of dollars for bragging rights to say their team is the best. Then, in order to make money, jack the price onto the consumer, us, the fans. . . . Understand this, TV makes people think sports is important when in actuality, it's just a game. Now three blocks from here you can find homeless, dope fiends, kids who can't read . . . nobody gives a damn about that 'cause some sorry owner wants to say my team is best. Plus, now there is no loyalty. . . . What I mean is when I was a boy, your superstar played for your team until his career was damn near over, today with free agency, one guy will play for a different team six straight years, there's no consistency. It's like every year you root for a different team without having loyalty to any of them. The players go where the money's at and I don't blame them, it's the nature of the beast.

Rainbow Jordan in Renay Jackson's Oaktown Devil

Throughout the season we continued on our quest for authentic blue-collar Raiders fans. We spoke with Joe and John Spinola, two ironworkers from Crockett, a former C & H Sugar company town northwest of Oakland. Our photographer, Joe, had shown me a photo of them working on one of the local bridges wearing construction hats decorated with Oakland Ironworkers Local 378 stickers that had the Raiders shield fused with the union logo. When we talked with them over beers at the Pacific Coast Brewing Company, they had just completed work on the Al Zampa Memorial Bridge project. Both men are robust and clearly have a zest for life. With his cropped salt-and-pepper hair and dark moustache, Joe was casually attired in a gray-collared shirt and black jeans. John, who has a stocky build like his brother, has a full beard and was wearing blue jeans, a blue shirt, and a black cap.

On the subject of working-class Raiders fans, Joe explained, "Stereotypical ironworkers are likely to be a Raiders fan more than anything else." His brother John added, "It kind of fits the mold. In general, most ironworkers are not 49ers fans." Joe continued, "Our local is Ironworkers Local 378 out of Oakland. So

Photo: Joseph A. Blum

John and Joe Spinola on the Zampa Bridge

naturally we're not going to support the 49ers. Maybe it's just the image, the Raiders image. They just follow them. I was working at a Volkswagen plant and one of the main mechanics was a big-time Raiders fan and had season tickets. That was when I went to my first Raiders game, around 1977, and it was wild back then." John added, "Actually some of the best times I've had were in the parking lot before the games. Sometimes you get so involved in that you're late for the game." As for what makes ironworkers natural Raiders fans John pointed out that "ironworkers, a lot of them, are just kind of belligerent fans." Joe added:

Ironworkers are of the same nature as Raiders fans. They are fanatical about anything. They don't take crap from anybody. They just tell you how it's going to be. We're not popular with the management-style people on the job. We don't always see eye to eye, but at the end of it all we get our work done, and we're productive, very safe at what we do, considering the scope and the danger that we're exposed to. It's kind of fun. It gives everybody a little bit of an attitude, and yeah, sometimes, a chip on your shoulder when you do this kind of work, but it goes with the territory. You know, it wouldn't be worth doing if you didn't have a little bit of moxie in you, a little backbone. On a platform four hundred feet in the air and there is nothing around you, you might have some nerves but you've got to shake them off, and you never know what's going to happen. So it's all interesting and fun—kind of hairy work really. A lot of guys being put in the air like that. It's not for everybody.

John continued on talking about the nature of ironworkers and their fraternity. It was clear the two were having a good time discussing it:

It's in our nature to drink beer and like to eat and just have friends around and party when we're off work and everything. We work with guys sometimes on a project, we'll work with [a guy] for six months or a year, maybe less, and maybe you won't see him for ten, fifteen years, and then you wind up on another job together somewhere. It's all like a little family reunion when you see those kind of guys, especially the guys you've worked with over the years, you know, and sometimes you remember a guy from when you were twenty years old or something and then you grow up, and you're thirty-five or forty years old and now he's retired. It's great how the whole thing works.

When I asked them about unions and the state of labor, John replied by talking about their father:

Me and Joe, we used to come down to the port when I was young. My father was a longshoreman for thirty years, a working-class guy. That was in the old days of Oakland. He worked through the containerization before he retired. They have a very strong union, but even they have lost ground. They move thirty or forty times more than they ever did with maybe a tenth of the people they used to have. It's unbelievable.

Back in the eighties, [the ironworkers] did a couple of things. At the steel mills that were retrofitted by nonunion help from out of state and everything. There were probably four ironworkers to every other craft on the picket lines. The most belligerent were the ironworkers. They had to call the police all the time. Organized labor, though, is having a tough time. The company seems to have the ball on their side more and more. They do all these conniving little things. It's tougher to strike or to do anything to try to stop it now.

Like Kevin and Hank, the Spinola brothers worked in Oakland much of the time but didn't live in the city itself, a trend that was true for much of the Bay Area white working class in the skilled trades from the sixties onward. As Robert Self notes, this happened as "the promise that home ownership could be made available to ever larger numbers of workers—through a combination of mass-produced tract developments and the conversion of inexpensive peripheral agricultural land—produced a more stable class order." Hence, many workers who might once have lived in the city were able to relocate to an affordable suburban "garden-like home."

The hope was that a "metropolitan Oakland" could support the economy while defusing the combustible industrial working class centralized in Oakland. While suburbanization may have helped accomplish the former, it did little to keep the economy of the city of Oakland running smoothly as what Self terms "homeowner populism" created working-class suburbs with middle-class amenities while ringing Oakland with what Donald McCullum, president of the Oakland NAACP, called in 1967 a "white noose of suburbia."

Yet this image of Oakland as "a chocolate city with vanilla suburbs," as Chris Rhomberg explains, "was never wholly true and is becoming even less so" as gentrification has taken hold in recent years. What *has* happened, within Oakland, its immediate suburbs, and the country at large is economic stratification. With the movement toward a two-tier economy, however, the affordable housing and the solid working-class jobs that sustained working-class suburbs have become rarer and the future is less bright for the working class (white, black, brown, and yellow) as the movement toward a service-sector working class makes the blue-collar American Dream a thing of the past.[2]

Blue-collar Raiders fan Renay Jackson, the godfather of "gangster lit," lives in East Oakland, where he is raising his three children as a single father while working as a custodian for the Oakland Police Department. We first saw Renay on the *News Hour with Jim Leherer* on PBS where he talked about his writing while sporting large wire-rimmed glasses under a Raiders hat. He was also wearing a natty suede black-and-white Raiders jacket. With his moustache, goatee, black jeans, and trim build, Jackson cut quite a figure. This, of course, piqued our interest, so we got in contact with him to discuss the Raiders as well as the state of the Oakland flatlands and how his life there has informed his writing.

When we met at the Pacific Coast Brewing Company he was wearing the same gear. We started with the Raiders:

> I've been a Raiders fan since 1972. The Raiders was always my team, man. Lamonica was throwing the bomb, the Snake. Shit, the man threw the bomb in Oakland. We had outlaws on the team. So it's kind of identified with the gangster mentality, you know. It was like the Raiders were the gangsters of football, that was the feeling to us. You know the 49ers fans, they drink wine, eat cheese and sliced salami, watching the games with their kids. Raiders fans drink beer and have a hot dog or something, cursing, and you wouldn't want to bring your wife and children there. You might get into a fight there and you have a totally different atmosphere. And blind loyalty, basically, is what it is. So when they become a Raiders fan, it was like becoming a fan for life. The Raiders probably have the rowdiest fans. You're taking a chance if you're

going to a Raiders game wearing the other team's colors. You know, because they are stupid, man. They will deck you for that. So that makes it a bad environment for a lot of people because you should be able to wear the other team's stuff—but not in Oakland, Jack.

The Raiders had a reputation that it was "us against the NFL," and it seemed like we always get the short end of the stick with a close game or close call. We get cheated all the time. I mean it happens every year, the most penalties and stuff, and most Raiders fans I know, we kind of feel like, well, that this is kind of questionable. It's basically the league against Al Davis. It's not only Al Davis who believes this about the Raiders, it's the fans. We lose, you know. But sometimes, the Raiders are messed up. You know, when Romanowski hit Williams in the face, nothing happened to him for that. It was like, too soft, something was supposed to happen to him.

Back in the day, man, when the Raiders lost, that made Sunday a bad day. I was miserable the rest of the day. Now with everybody after the money, and no team loyalty and stuff, I don't really care too much anyway. I like football for football and the Raiders are my team, but it's like sports in general. It's different from when I was little. Too much money, because they jack it onto the fans. They make it too expensive to go. Two beers, for $15 and $61 for a lousy seat. For me to go to the game, I'm going to be bringing some peanuts with me. For two tickets and something to eat, it's maybe over $200. It's like a day and a half's pay at work. So man, it's too expensive for me. The price is too high. Al Davis fools everybody. I think he's probably trying to move now. But on Sundays, man, everybody puts on their Raiders outfits and there we are. It is like now we already know that when Sunday comes, you're going to see the Raiders on TV and stay home. [If they are blacked out] I have the TV on during the [other] games and the radio on the Raiders game, and I'm barbecuing.

On the subject of the post–Super Bowl disturbances, Renay took a hard line:

After the Super Bowl, as a black man, you know, you look at the news and say, "Don't let it be none of the brothers," and you see all the Mexicans breaking all the Mexican businesses, I mean, it was like Jingletown. As a race we do a lot of damage, but that was Latinos. After the Super Bowl, if there is anything about the Raiders that relates to Oakland, it's that Oakland has a reputation as a gangster city. It is the people from Oakland, like those people [that got] on the news all around the country. People all over the United States think Oakland is the dirtiest team in football, and the fans, the image they project across the country is like the rowdiest fans. So they tie in together like that.

As for blaming the disturbances on tension with the police:

That's full of shit, man. People just want to get out there and do wrong. It doesn't have anything to do with the game. This has nothing to do with the police. This is a mob scene. I mean like with the Rodney King verdict thing and people burning down their own neighborhood, but there was a lot of people stealing and this thing here, that's all they were doing. Everybody hit the streets and they were doing wrong, turning over trashcans on the corners, breaking into businesses. They broke into the bank, spattered paint all over East 14th and International Boulevard. That didn't have anything to do with football. The folks were getting out there and all of them weren't youngsters, either. They get that liquor in them. One thing I've noticed about Raiders fans, they just get sloppy drunk when they watch the game, and the mentality is stuck on stupid. That's why I told you, they are still in that Raider gear and I'm a Raider die-hard, but, man, I'll tell you that [even when the Raiders are getting] their asses kicked, my homeboys were still up there hollering "Raiders." It's like they were still talking at you, and most Raiders fans, that's the mentality they have. It's beyond loyal.

When we moved to the subject of Oakland, Renay explained:

Oakland is broken down into sections, man. You have the "haves" and you have the "have-nots." And you have those little wealthy pockets, and you have the poor. It is kind of systematic that they get the Latinos and blacks out of Oakland. I mean projects like Acorn. They pull those things down. They move people. They rebuild those things for different people. For the working-class and middle-class blacks and Latinos, places like Antioch and Stockton are getting more desirable and they are moving out there. The white folks are coming back. They got tired of driving two or three hours to work every day and they are moving back to Oakland, building all this stuff. I mean, housing has gotten ridiculous. Oakland, man, you used to be able to buy (six or seven years ago) a three- or four-bedroom house for $150,000. Now they've got like two bedrooms and they're asking like $300,000.

But you still have these pockets of ghetto, and a whole lot of young black men, maybe in their twenties, who look at selling drugs as a profession. They go to jail, get out, keep selling drugs, and kill each other—80 percent of the murders are drugs. They're down there and life is miserable, basically, and they can't see no way out. And Jerry Brown is the mayor and, you know what I'm talking about, he's bringing 10,000 new residents downtown. They're building all this shit downtown and all of a sudden, people can't afford it. It gets all messed up. You know, haves and have-nots, and the folks that can afford it are the white capital set.

I live in East Oakland, right up 38th Avenue, and they have, like a Raider block, man. Right across the street, my neighbor Art, he's a Mexican guy and he used to be a little gangster. But he's really cool. On Sundays, him and about six friends of his, all dudes, they are standing on the porch. He has twelve steps leading up to the sidewalk, and they come, standing on the porch with black-ass glasses on, Raiders black, from top to bottom, man. They are standing there like gangsters ready to go into the ghetto, and everybody on the block is down with the Raiders. I mean they save year round, like some people might save to go on vacation, to get season tickets. I'm not down with that. I will stand over there with them with my Raiders stuff on, but I'm going back to my house.

I grew up in North Richmond, and that's probably one of the poorest communities in California. The average income for a family of four is like $9,000 a year for the mother on welfare and the daddy, whose profession is selling dope. That's where I was born and that made me leave for Oakland, to the east side, in my early teens. I lived in poverty neighborhoods my entire life, that's why Oakland is my city, man. When you read my books, you read what these eyes have seen. It's all make-believe, but I saw similar stuff.

Renay told us about his day job:

I am a custodian. Right now it's for the police station. I never wanted to work there for my whole career, because, you know, the young African American mentality, I didn't want to be anywhere near the police. [But] I've been at the police station for the last five or six years. A lot of [the police] were assholes. Many of them were cool. They were just regular folks. If I was in my twenties (I'm forty-four now) and down in the police station, I'd go to the Academy. When I was in City Hall, I saw the politicians work. They get free tickets to every Warriors home game, and they get free tickets to every A's home game, and every Raiders home game and, many times, I'd see those tickets in the garbage. When I worked at City Hall, I got a lot of tickets to go to games. When the teams were sorry, the tickets were plentiful. When the team is good, they don't give them away. But I don't like people tripping. They think they're so important, you know, it goes to their heads, man.

Renay was a lot more enthusiastic as we discussed his writing and the amazing story of how he went from helping his daughter with her writing homework to the front page of the *San Francisco Chronicle* and the *Oakland Tribune*, appearances on the *News Hour*, and a book contract:

My writing? Well, everybody knows that I started helping my daughter with her school writing. She was in the seventh grade and she wrote about "What I did this summer" [and wrote about a sentence]. And so, I'm like, "Baby, you cannot do that in the seventh grade. You've got to write more. Write it all, baby. Get descriptive." So it was like that. After she left, I kept writing. And before I knew it, I knew I could write a book, and I started telling everybody, but nobody thought I could.

I got the determination from when I was a rapper. Rap music came out in '79. By 1982, I had a rap song on a record and I was selling it in City Hall and all over the city of Oakland, with a little bit of airplay. The title of my record was *The Job Is a Mother*. One of my partners I met watching a Raiders game, and I played that music and I told him, "Man, I could do that shit." He bet me that I couldn't, so I became a rapper because of a bet. I did three rap albums. Back in the eighties, in my community, I showed quite a few people how to make a record. A lot of them went on to making a whole lot of money. People are always trying to charge everybody for information. I didn't. I'm not into that.

Renay then explained how he runs writing and publishing workshops for free.

Nobody told me nothing. So why would I charge them? I've got my own little style, my own little niche. I've met a lot of East Coast writers that do the gangster lit, too, but I think theirs is weaker than mine. [Once my story hit the media] all of a sudden I have all of these offers [from presses that had previously rejected my work] and people putting pressure on me from all different directions, and I was thinking that this must be like it is with them recruiters trying to get kids to play football, or maybe worse because I was talking to four or five agencies. Do I pick the one with the big publisher where I'll be well known, with my picture all over *Black Expressions* and *Infinity* magazines, or do I go with the small little mom-and-pop type publishing house? I had people cuss me out. I was telling them [I was going to go with a small Bay Area publisher] North Atlantic.

I don't expect everybody to like what I do. But there is a market for what I do. I sold 40,000 [self-published] books and that shocked some people. I had this little army of people selling books. That same rap mentality, [people sold them] in barbershops, beauty parlors, restaurants, corner stores, any place of business that would sell them. I had them all over. And they were going home and selling books to people in their neighborhood. I think that corporate America don't want folks to know this information. They don't want those kind of books out there.

On the morning of the Raiders' home opener, the *Oakland Tribune* featured an article entitled "Wild in Oakland" about the Raiders' prowess in going 7–1 in home openers since returning to Oakland in 1995. "Home is where the hole is. . . . We're talking Black Hole," the Bill Soliday piece crowed. In the article, Mo Collins discounted the lack of sellouts and said, "I'll take our 20 to 30,000 against anybody's 80 to 100,000 any day. Our fans are unique. They follow us around. They go to hostile environments. They don't care. They're going to support their team, and that's all you can ask as a player." Tim Brown said of the 50,000-plus crowd that the paper anticipated, "Hey man, people need to work, kids need new shoes . . . all that stuff. You don't worry. Whoever is there, we know we are going to get their best. Knowing you can raise or lower your hands and the crowd is going to do whatever you ask them to do . . . that is what makes it so special." And it did feel a little special before the kickoff as the crowd in the Black Hole flipped off the Bengals when they came on the field and went nuts as the Raiders were introduced. Still, there were a surprising amount of empty seats in this, the most legendary, fanatical site of Raiders fan zeal. At times, the music was louder than the fans were, and I couldn't help but notice the guy a couple of rows in front of us who slept through most of the first half. At one point, some dude got up on his seat, turned around and screamed his guts out, "C'mon Raiders fans, they need our help!" "Shut up!" somebody yelled back.[3]

The Raiders were outgained by 180 yards, and the feeble Bengals had ball possession over two-thirds of the game. The crowd was frequently cranky with shouts of "C'mon, you morons!" "Goddamn it, Gannon!" and "Make the tackle, fuckhead!" filling the air. When the team left the field at halftime, there were scattered boos. It was a long way from the magic evening of the AFC championship game after which my ears rang for a day and my voice was left hoarse from shouting for joy. The team just felt off, out of sync, and the crowd kept waiting for the party to start. It wasn't really until the fourth quarter, with the game tied at 13, that the spark was lit when Phillip Buchanon picked off a John Kitna pass and ran it back 83 yards for a touchdown and the ecstasy flowed as the crowd jumped and danced and swayed to the music. But it was a shallow high as the Raiders squeaked by one of the worst teams in football to win the game 23–20. The cops didn't even let the Black Hole enjoy the afterglow as they gruffly announced, "Start packing it up! We can't go home until you go home!" A couple days later, Raiders' longtime executive assistant Al LoCasale retired, two games into the season. It was another bad omen as the Raiders headed into Denver on shaky legs.[4]

Nine

Raiders Rage

Most people are confined to lives of monotony. Year in and year out, workers in offices, factories, and large and small companies follow the same daily routine. They catch the same bus or train; they drive along the same route. . . . They endure hours of boredom, often doing a job which offers them little or no satisfaction. They come home to face the predictable problems of family life or the loneliness of a flat in some dreary location. What greater contrast could there be with a life of piracy. The pirates escaped from the laws and regulations that govern most of us. They were rebels against authority, free spirits who made up their own rules.

David Cordingly, Under the Black Flag

As David Cordingly points out in his study of piracy, the romance of the pirate persists despite the fact that "most men and women who were attacked by pirates found it a terrifying and deeply shocking experience." Indeed pirates were "tough and brutal young men armed with knives and cutlasses" who "deliberately knocked down or slashed anyone who showed resistance," the result of which was that "often the attack ended with some of the victims lying dead on the deck or with their bleeding bodies being thrown over the side to the sharks." Thus, it is not surprising that the Raiders' image appeals to a lot of people with a chip on their shoulder. Perhaps this more than anything else is what unites Al Davis with his fans even as *his* corporate piracy frequently succeeds at their expense. Raiders fans have attitude, whether it be their renegade capitalist owner, his lumpenproletarian fan base, or just the average smart-ass Raiders fan who enjoys watching rival teams lose and hates losing to them more than anything else. When the Raiders lose, give them a wide berth.[1]

The news going into the Raiders' devastating Monday night pummeling in Denver was that Sebastian Janikowski, the team's renegade Polish field-goal kicker, had been arrested for a bar fight in Walnut Creek, adding to his list of off-field indiscretions and helping to build his Raiders rebel legend. In Raider Nation, a stay in jail is no shame when compared with missing a big field goal. In this case, the field goals wouldn't matter as I sat with my Raiders fan buddy Brad in the Rock Bottom Brewery in downtown San Diego and watched the Silver and Black endure a royal beating at the hands of the hated Denver Broncos. I had gone to the Rock Bottom because it was the 2003 season home to the San Diego Raiders fan club, but the crowd was grim-faced soon after the helmeted skull banner of the "Original Raiders Fan Club, San Diego" was hung over the railing of the upstairs balcony. I got a quick interview with a kid in rockabilly gear and a retro Raiders cap who told me he liked the Raiders, "'Cause everyone in San Diego hates them," but I didn't have the heart to pester the rest of this grumpy bunch. Brad left after a burger, two beers, and 24 unanswered Bronco points by halftime.

I stayed to the bitter end and watched a guy in a Garner jersey walk by glaring, a guy in a Gannon jersey snap at a waitress, and another guy yell "cheap old bastard" at the TV when Al Davis came on. It was getting ugly. Somebody yelled "punk ass bitch!" as a Raider missed a tackle and the pride-and-poise boys sank even further behind. "Why are the Raiders fans still here?" I overheard one of the busboys wonder to a co-worker. "I wish they'd go sink into a Black Hole." The manager was going over a "customer complaint" with one of the waiters, who said, "These guys get up in my face and get all macho with me." At one point, after it was 31–0, Gannon jogged over to the sideline and started screaming at the coaches, getting in their faces to the cheers of some of the Raiders fans in the

Raiders rally, downtown Oakland

Photo: Joseph A. Blum

bar. The wheels were falling off, and anybody with any sense could see that the 2003 Raiders were not on track to go back to the Super Bowl.

I interviewed a waitress named Beth who had worked a lot of Raiders games. "These guys are really loud and a bit touchy-feely. The guy at the third table slapped me on the ass because his friend bet him to do it," she said, glancing behind her. "No tip is worth that. 'Gannon' over there by the bar was really rude to me, and then he walks up to me and says, 'I'm sorry, honey, it's the Raiders, not you.'" She looked at my Raiders hat and said, "Some of them are really nice . . . and some of them are really *weird*." I thanked her for her time and started walking the long mile home to my flat. Seeing a lone depressed Raiders fan after a brutal loss inspired a number of courageous Chargers fans sitting in chi-chi bar patios to flip me off. This was followed by a "fuck your Raiders" from a drunk in a three-piece suit. I walked on into the heart of the mean American night.

Panthers and Pirates

> Among the wage earners, sailors were by far the most militant. They included men of all colors and a few women who went to sea disguised as men. They displayed a legendary contempt for wielders of arbitrary authority, from constables to kings. Several thousand of them became pirates, whose declared purpose was to "plunder the rich."
>
> *Priscilla Murolo and A.B. Chitty,*
> From the Folks Who Brought You the Weekend

The next week in Oakland Kelly and I met Michele Clark at the Pacific Coast Brewing Company, which was rapidly becoming our home away from home. Michele is a pretty, dark-haired, and down-to-earth director of a nonprofit in East Oakland, and was referred to us by one of our Raiders e-mail contacts, Bobby Davis. She is decidedly *not* a Raiders fan, which is why we were curious about her. Having worked for nonprofits in Oakland for seventeen years, she had a critical view of the Raiders organization and the impact support for the team—both governmental and fan—have had on the city. Michele, who lives in the hills above Lake Merritt, currently directs the Youth Employment Partnership center, which is located on East 14th Street, right in the heart of Oakland's Raider Nation:

> We are in the ground zero of the area that the riots were in, so I'm very familiar with the neighborhood. It's extremely diverse culturally there. I think [Oakland] is the most diverse city in the country, and that neighborhood is the most culturally intense area in Oakland. My building happened to be part of the riot. We lost fifteen ten-foot-by-six-foot windows, $15,000 worth of damage. There was no insurance on them because you can't get insurance for the plate glass in buildings in that neighborhood. It was interesting to think: "Would it have been any different if [the Raiders] had won [the Super Bowl]?"

It was quiet at first. I think the police called us around 3:30 a.m. because they couldn't assure us that the neighborhood would be all right. They called me back to meet them at 5:00, and they told me that [people] had smashed all the windows but still it wasn't calm enough at that point to get in.

I was raised in Baltimore and the Al Davis deal [with the city of Oakland] and the Colts deal [the Colts owner moved the team to Indianapolis literally in the middle of the night] have a lot of similarities. But the end of the stories are very different, as I watched people I knew who were raised as Colts fans negotiate the trail and get another football team. They kind of changed football culture there, where with the Raiders they were here and then they left, but not *really*, and then they came back, which was pretty shocking to me at the time, but, as my friends pointed out, not that shocking. So the whole Raiders thing seems somewhat alienating to me.

Michele's background and relationship with Oakland is compelling. Having moved to the city with her former husband so he could go to graduate school, she "loved Oakland so much I never went back. I just had no desire to go anywhere else." We couldn't help but think about the movement of the white working class out of the city. Michele, interestingly, did the opposite.

Because she'd had experience working in nonprofits, she was appointed by the county Board of Supervisors to bail out the Oakland food bank, which was in the heart of West Oakland.

The Panthers, five years prior, had been highjacking trucks off the freeway to open their own food bank. It was that intense. I had no idea what I was getting into. And it was pretty interesting and that's how I learned Oakland. I went in the churches, and food was distributed through the pantries and the community agencies. Once I got to know it, I loved it. I know Oakland has a pretty notorious reputation. But to me that is a very compelling argument as to why it needs to have funding, support, change, and all of those kinds of things.

Currently, I run a large job-training program for high-risk teens and young adults. It was founded by a bunch of high school teachers who were tired of their kids going backward every summer, so they all got together and formed the Youth Employment Partnership. It's comprehensive because it has a lot of different parts to it. For example, we've built houses with high school dropouts; we work with the community college system; we have GED programs for some of our clients; and much more—we have about eleven different programs. Eventually, we'll be offering a charter school to children who have been dropped out of high school for more than two years, not pulling from the high school system. I'm a die-hard public school supporter.

Michele took a sip of her Diet Coke and told us about the kids she serves. "Well," she said thoughtfully, "they're certainly not constructively directed. Many of them are idle. They are hanging out waiting for whatever is coming, and there is nothing coming." Because of this, Michele thought, the kids she serves are vulnerable to the unconstructive impulses that Raider fandom can bring:

There is a significant community voice that says, "We must stop hurting ourselves." That voice is very deep, and that is why in all these idle circumstances there are enough community people saying, "Okay, let's not beat ourselves up over this. We'll just end up worse." The Raiders stuff was too big and that voice couldn't be heard. The Raiders stuff is too provoking. They are provoking to the teens and to the adults. The way the Raiders reach the community is about rage. I'm sure you saw the [Rich] Gannon incident and interview [where Gannon exploded at his coaches and then was unapologetic in the media right afterward], right? The day after all that, we had kids who were doing the postures, who were imitating Gannon. They were role-playing exactly what happened in the Gannon interview less than twelve hours later. I was trying to think of what analogy I could draw from this, and it was handed to me in an editorial in the newspaper where it talked about the whole thing as the equivalent to road rage—they called it "Rich rage."

And the kids were talking about it, but they weren't talking about it, like,

"Look at this bad behavior." They were saying, "Did you see how Gannon was telling the coach off? He got right back in his face." They were proud of this. And I have to say the exception is Jerry Rice. You know, they adore him, and when they imitate Rice, we don't get that same behavior. So I watch the counselors scramble for the redirect—you know, "Look at Jerry Rice. He's not doing that stuff."

But these kids are such a small part of the population. Look at what's happening. Did the Raiders sell out again? No. It's funny, none of the kids I work with have ever been to a game, could ever afford to go to a game. Ninety-five percent of them live in poverty, so how could they ever even buy a ticket? The kids and some of the people in my office don't care so much that [the city of Oakland] is losing [because of the Raiders lawsuit]. All they care about is whether or not the 49ers have lost one more game than the Raiders. It's amazing.

Most of the middle- to upper-middle-class blacks in Oakland are 49ers fans. They don't care about the Raiders. It's the poor people who are Raiders fans. The Raiders are street. I know a lot of people who scramble to get 49ers tickets, but they are not interested in entering the Raiders culture. The kids don't know about the institutional contributions that Al Davis has made to football, their main connection to the Raiders is the rage. The [Raiders] culture doesn't operate on an intellectual level. It's the rage—that in-your-face, don't-be-pushed-around, walking-away-like-you're-spitting-on-somebody thing. After a wicked game, they come in to the Center and they're body banging.

After we interviewed Michele, I pondered her point about rage and wondered if the phenomenon was limited to the Raiders. A week before, a Giants fan had shot a Dodgers fan after a baseball game in L.A. and, during the course of the 2003 season, there were two football riots involving mostly white, middle-class college kids. In Mankato, Minnesota, three thousand kids went on a rampage that led to forty arrests after they lost the homecoming game to North Dakota State. Later that fall, in West Virginia, Mountaineers fans took over the streets, overturned cars, fought with police, and set ninety fires after an upset victory over Virginia Tech. Even the American heartland seemed to be afflicted with this sports related mania.

The Autumn Wind

> The Autumn Wind is a Raider
> Pillaging just for fun
> He'll knock you 'round and upside down
> And laugh when he's conquered and won.
> *Steve Sabol, "The Autumn Wind"*

Later in the season we caught up with one of the co-workers Michele had mentioned. Mark Henderson, a genial family man who came to meet us in Raiders gear, had a distinctly different take on the Raiders from Michele's:

I've been a Raiders fan since 1977. My family moved to the Bay Area around that time and, being a young boy, I was really interested in football. My real interest came after their last Super Bowl victory in Oakland, I remember coming downtown, people going crazy and jumping on top of cars and going wild, but it was a different type of crowd back then than it is now. I think people evolved and, as a society, we seem to be a little more to the extreme. Now you have a couple of different mixes of Raiders fans. You have your older fans who know about the Kenny Stablers and Lester Hayeses and all the greats, and these fans know about football. Then you have the younger generation who represent more the Generation X, and a lot of their tendencies are more toward violent confrontation. So they embrace the Raiders image, the Raiders mystique, the bad boy image. It's more like [these younger fans] are adopting an image whereas the older fans know more about football. The fans who know football are into the intricacies of the game and the other fans are like, "Oh, did you see that hit?" They go for the violence of the contact.

I think being in L.A. had a lot to do with it, because when they were in

L.A., more than any other place in the world, you are more likely to be viewed because of all the TV and movies, so anything that happens in that media epicenter gets out there. That was when a lot of rap groups came out. So a lot of the hip-hop generation back in the day were creating a rebel image, a public image of being tough, and a lot of it centered on the Raiders.

I have a daughter, and I don't think I would take my daughter to a Raiders game. The fans that go to Raiders games or even a lot of football fans in general go to release a lot of tension, release a lot of aggression, you know, in a nondamaging way, but it's still loud and boisterous, and with the alcohol, some people get loaded on liquor, dope, or whatever. All of this is experienced at Raiders games. The bottom line is that a lot of people have different reasons for following the Raiders. The whole Raiders mystique may be a fallacy. It may just be a reasoning or justification to release a certain amount of animosity caused by societal pressures. But I think in a way it's good because it gives people a proper release and I think that's one thing sports has done in America overall. It gives people something on Sunday to think about other than the pressures of their jobs, their family, whatever may be going on in their lives. For three hours or so they can get caught up in something that is bigger than themselves, is bigger than a game, but is more like a way of life. You know, some of the youngsters follow the Raiders more than they do religion.

As a fan from way back, for me it has to do with being from Oakland and having pride in where I live, "Commitment to Excellence," you know. The Raiders are always the team of misfits who come together, come out there and play tough. I associate that with Oakland, the old shipyard town, a lot of military ties, an industrial town, you know. Although I would say that Oakland is in the midst of a change. Oakland is rebuilding projects, redeveloping, redesigning itself, redefining itself, and I think that because of the way the economy is going, the high cost of living, that Oakland is fast becoming a higher end place. But at the same time, Oakland is still a tough city. Oakland has a very high crime rate, high death rate, mainly among the African American and Latino populations. Jerry Brown has brought in a lot of businesses. Some people would argue that that has made it more expensive, but I think that would have happened anyways.

I work for an organization associated with the Youth Employment Partnership, and basically what we do there is run a regional job-training program. [We serve people with a] low income in an enterprise zone, and the youth we serve are very diverse in ethnicity. A lot of them are for the Raiders. But they get frustrated sometimes. A lot of the problems probably have to do with the fact that they are on the lower economic level. They don't have any way to get their feelings out or don't know how to express themselves. With the economy in California and around the Bay Area the way it is, people that are true fans don't have the $80, $90, or $100 to pay for one Raiders ticket. [But] again, some of the younger people aren't into the sport or the team itself. A lot of them are just into the image of the bad boy that they put out there associated with the toughness of "I'm a Raider."

As for Al Davis, Mark was critical but philosophical, "[Al Davis] pays the cost to be the boss. A lot of the decisions he makes, I don't agree with, but the Raiders are more than just a football team, they're a business, and his main thing is to make money, and I could see how and why he would rather be in L.A., even though I wouldn't like it myself."

Dennis, one of Mark and Michele's colleagues, is another longtime Oakland resident and a Raiders fan. A trim, handsome man with a quick wit and endearing smile, Dennis was enthusiastic about sharing his thoughts with us over a couple of beers:

I grew up in the Lake Shore area, and that area had a bar called Art's with a pretty solid Raiders connection. They had post–Raiders game parties there. Art's was one of the places where [the players] would go and hang out. The owner would take you out to the Coliseum to watch the game and take you back to Art's. I mean, we would party until midnight after the game. The tailgate parties were with nice guys; there was a big Raiders fan thing. That bar isn't around anymore.

Why I'm a Raiders fan has a lot to do with me growing up here. I mean the bottom line is that Oakland was a tough city to grow up in and the social world in which you were raised, the tough environment, the schools. If you go to public schools it's tough, and then the economic situation, the types of jobs available to you. Everything was just kind of hard in Oakland. And when you grow up here, you tend to be tougher because you feel like the tougher you are, the easier it is to survive in this kind of environment. And the Raiders represented the ultimate in tough, you know? When I was growing up, Jack Tatum was the hardest-hitting cat in football. And so in coming up, that toughness is the thing that gets you respect, you know: "I will back this up." The Raiders were the manifestation of that whole philosophy. I admired it. Not just the defensive guys, but the offense with Ken Stabler, Lamonica. When you throw the bomb, you are in somebody's face. Those cats invented the bomb.

So that was a way that you never had to participate in anything violent in your life because the Raiders took care of that. It's a feeling of revenge that you may feel. All that kind of stuff, it was taken care of. It was kind of an outlet. If you believe in something like the Raiders, it translates over to you as a person. If you believe you can walk into any type of situation and know you're going to win and have that attitude you can approach all kinds of situations that way. School was always very easy for me because I had the attitude of, "Bring it on. I can handle anything." And it was part and parcel of the fact that I like the Raiders, not just the Raiders, but the Raiders were definitely supportive of that philosophy. It was about overcoming adversity.

When they played the Redskins in the Super Bowl, I just called a [random] number in the [D.C.] area code, and it was like two o'clock in the morning there, and I woke this cat up, and I started talking shit, and he says, "Who is this?" [I told him.] "I'm from Oakland, but it don't matter who I am. We're going to win." And then the guy wakes up and says, "Oh man, you're crazy. We're going to kill you guys." So I called him back the day of the Super Bowl and said, "Man, remember me? I called you at two in the morning a couple of nights ago and told you this would happen." The guy couldn't believe it. It was stuff like that, that outrageous attitude, with no harm intended. I didn't have any malice. It was the excitement of, "Hey, here we are!" [The Raiders] were heroes in a lot of ways.

In the pre-L.A. days there was a lot more loyalty because people knew [the players] as individuals. Nowadays they are just images on a TV set. People don't get to see them anymore. The only thing we have now are sound bites or misquotes in the paper. The media is playing this role of divide and conquer. It goes in and takes the players apart and isolates somebody and tries to get them to give somebody up. They never used to do that kind of thing. The press was more in line with the fans back in the day. Now everybody is looking for an angle to exploit.

[Back in the sixties and seventies] football wasn't big money to the players. And some of them had businesses in Oakland—a laundry place, a bar. It was stuff to supplement their incomes. Lamonica had a restaurant where he would come and mix drinks. Jim Otto had a restaurant. Other players had liquor stores. They were part of the community. [Now] they've isolated themselves to the point where they are images to us. There is no connection. There needs to be some type of breaking down of that. They could go to schools. Why can't the Raiders talk to schools in East Oakland? Why can't they go to a high school football practice? They don't have to do anything special.

Dennis also spoke passionately about the community and the kids he serves as a lawyer helping out the Youth Employment Partnership with federal compliance issues, and then explained that his other career was as a jazz musician who has played with the Jerry Garcia Band and with other jazz and world music groups. The Grateful Dead/Raiders connection had come full circle, I thought to myself. We ended speaking a bit more about the nature of Raiders fans:

Raiders fans get more outrageous than any other fans on the planet. You know, there are Raiders fans in Paris. There are Raiders fans all over the place.

It is amazing. I would like stock in the merchandising of their stuff because you can get Raiders stuff anywhere on this planet. Wow! What is the image of the Raiders to a French person, you know?

[Other teams don't like to play here in Oakland] because they have to come and deal with the Raider Nation people. They come out of the locker room, people spit on them, throw beer on them. It is a tough place to play. It is because Oakland has that reputation for being tough. [The fans] are letting all that craziness out. It is like, here is a chance, you know, "On Sundays I can be crazy, people expect it. The more crazy I am, the better." Do I get it out of my system? No. We might get into checking each other out. You gotta outdo the guys. It's almost a competition: who can do more. And people let all their frustrations out. People go crazy. You can't walk down the middle of the street stripping, you know, but you feel like you can do that at a Raiders game. As long as you're a Raiders fan, you're cool. It doesn't matter what your thing is—your color, your sex, any of that kind of stuff goes out the window, man. If you're a Raiders fan, the main thing is about being in the Black Hole.

In terms of community spirit, this place came alive last year [during the Super Bowl run]. You walked around and if you had any kind of Raiders thing on, people would honk and wave, no matter where you were. People would honk and yell, "Go Raiders!" It was all over town. It was a good thing. I will tell you the truth, it's like you marry your first love. You realize you can't live without each other, but you've got to figure out how you're going to live with each other, and there's a certain amount of that here. I think this community wants to have a Raiders team. Of course [Al Davis] is going to burn you if you set yourself up, so you have to go in with that kind of understanding.

The morning of the Raiders game against the San Diego Chargers, Kelly and I woke up in the hotel room and watched "Rush's Challenge" on ESPN's *Monday Morning Countdown* with horror and loathing. After Limbaugh had finished arguing that Donovan McNabb was the beneficiary of liberal media largess because "they have been very desirous that a black quarterback can do well," I glanced at the paper and saw that things were going badly in Iraq and that the number of people living in poverty in the United States had increased for the second straight year. Oakland itself was thinking of privatizing sixty acres of public land, a move that harkens back to the days of Horace Carpentier, the city's first brazen entrepreneurial pirate, who granted himself ownership of Oakland's waterfront in the mid nineteenth century and made himself enormously rich. It was only 9:30 in the morning, and I needed a drink.[2]

After breakfast and a Bloody Mary or two at the Fat Lady, we hit the BART and laughed as the driver announced "Raider Nation Station" when our train pulled into the Coliseum stop. The "Join Arnold" crew was passing out campaign flyers on the pedestrian bridge on the way into the Coliseum, and I tore mine up and dropped it in front of an angry Arnoldista. Inside, our Black Hole neighbors greeted us and inquired about Kelly's pregnancy, which, we told them, was going well. On a football note, we learned that Barret Robbins was back after his long journey through shame and injury. Good, I thought, he deserved a chance. The game was preceded by the usual profanity and heavy metal hoopla. Once it started, the Chargers' LaDainian Tomlinson sliced through the Raiders' defense like a hot knife through butter. Racking up 143 yards in the first half alone, he was off to a record-breaking pace. The Raiders "D" was Swiss cheese. It was 21–14 at halftime and the crowd booed the team off the field. The Raiderettes' sad "Funky World" routine did little to change our grim mood. "Frisbee dogs!" called out one desperate fan, "Bring out the Frisbee dogs!" Mercifully, the halftime ended, but the game brought little solace. With the season on the verge of total implosion, the feeling in the Black Hole was somber. No matter how many people flipped off the Chargers, the Bolts just kept scoring. Losing to the hated Broncos in Denver was pretty bad, but getting whipped by the pathetic Chargers at home was enough to drive a steady trickle of my fellow fans out to the parking lot.

Then, just when it seemed that all was lost with the Raiders down 31–17 and 5:59 remaining to play in the game, they came back. Gannon went six out of seven passing for 110 yards in the last five minutes, scoring first by hitting Alvis Whitted with a 36-yard touchdown pass. Finally, the Raiders' defense held, and the Silver and Black roared down the field again with Tim Brown and Jerry Rice catching pass after pass and Charlie Garner tying it up with a 24-yard touchdown run. In overtime, the Chargers won the toss and it seemed our hopes would be cruelly dashed despite the heroic comeback, but the defense held and Sebastian Janikowski won the game with a 46-yard field goal, transforming the remaining crowd into a sea of jubilation. We hugged, high-fived our neighbors, and headed home, joyfully convinced that the Raiders had turned the corner. We were back.[3]

In the heaven of the spectacle

Ten

Monday Night Lights

Carnival in its widest, most general sense embraced ritual spectacles such
as fairs, popular feasts and wakes, processions and competitions . . . open
air amusement with costumes and masks. . . . [I]t included comic verbal
compositions (oral and written) such as parodies, travesties and vulgar farce
. . . [which for Bakhtin included] curses, oaths, slang, humor, popular tricks
and jokes, scatological, in fact all the "low" and "dirty" sorts of folk humor.
Carnival is presented by Bakhtin as a world of topsy-turvy, heteroglot exuberance, of ceaseless overrunning and excess where all is mixed, hybrid, ritu-
ally degraded and defiled.

Peter Stallybrass and Allon White,
"From Carnival to Transgression"

The party at the AM/PM mini-mart across the street from the Coliseum was in
full swing at 3:00 p.m., well before the 6:00 p.m. kickoff for the Raiders Monday
Night Football game against the AFC West–leading Kansas City Chiefs, an old-
time blood foe. It had been a dismal three weeks in Raider Nation with two
straight road losses to the Chicago Bears and the Cleveland Browns, the loss of
linebacker Bill Romanowski for the season with a concussion, and the news that
former Raiders great Marv Hubbard had killed a man in an auto accident—but

you'd never know it from the buzz around the sold-out stadium. Darth Vader and friends rolled by on their Harleys in black leather jackets and hollered "Raiders!" to a group of fans in jerseys who were splitting a joint on the sidewalk. They blew out their smoke and yelled back "Raiders!" in response. A customized silver-and-black lowrider cruised by with "The Autumn Wind" blaring on the stereo, and the crowd that spilled out the door of the mini-mart was in a jolly, rowdy mood.

The parking lot was rocking with energy as people danced to soul and hip-hop, head-banging rock and heavy metal, downed tequila, wrote up signs, pranced about in elaborate costumes, and greeted each other happily. The Raiders season was on the brink of total disaster, but the atmosphere had a playoff-like intensity. We saw a couple making out in front of their motor home and watched a man chug half a bottle of vodka. A larger number of people were in costumes tonight, and the outfits covered a wide range, from a squad of Raiders army men and the Grim Reaper to a Raiders Playboy bunny and a silver-and-black Rasta man. A throaty "Fuck K.C.!" chant broke out in a corner of the lot and would continue sporadically for the rest of the evening inside and outside of the stadium. I saw a Dia de los Muertos Raiders skeleton, a Raiders football head, and a Raiders shield tattoo that took up a man's entire upper torso.

Inside, the hallways were mobbed and echoing and the "Ray-duz! Ray-duz!" chant was deafening. The cops looked a little edgy, and we saw a few people being carted away in handcuffs before the game even started.

"We got another K.C. idiot over there," I overheard a cop say to his partner.

"That's what they're paying you for," his partner said.

"Yeah, I'll go watch him get his ass kicked and then take a report," he replied smugly as he slowly made his way through the crowd. In the Black Hole, the mood was festive as people mugged for the cameras and gave the Chiefs a creatively menacing welcome. The twelfth man was present and accounted for, yelling, screaming, and insulting the Chiefs with gusto, one fan consciously upping the next in volume, wit, and vulgarity. There were a couple of Hells Angels in our section, but they were pussy cats compared to the "regular" fans, who were in fine form booing and heckling the Chiefs persistently and the Raiders when their offense sputtered on the way to a 10–0 Chiefs lead at halftime. As I watched a very drunk guy in striped silver-and-black face paint get taken away in hand-cuffs for some unknown offense, I pondered the meaning of extreme fandom. How did the public space of a football stadium, where spectators are supposed to passively consume the commodity spectacle that is a football game (a sport chockfull of the Taylorist ideology of managerial control and worker efficiency, not to mention martial spirit and jingoism) become a contested space where a good number of fans constantly test the limits of acceptable behavior?

Along with my friend Scott, I have always been a social libertarian and a fan of the carnivalesque. For Mikhail Bakhtin, "Carnival celebrates temporary liberation from the prevailing truth of the established order" and suspends "all hierarchical rank, privileges, norms, and prohibitions." Thus, there is something subversive about events that mock "high culture" and official prohibitions and celebrate the vulgar, Dionysian excess, and deriding iconoclastic laughter. Some adherents of Bakhtinian theory emphasize its utopian populism and go so far as to argue that the excesses of carnival represent an embryonic form of political resistance. Others dismiss this and argue that carnival is a "licensed release" that lets people blow off steam and consequently functions as a mechanism of social control. Critics also point out that during carnival, the weaker members of soci-ety (women or gays, for instance) are as likely as the powerful to be abused and demonized, and thus carnival may not be a liberating occasion for all.[1]

Clearly there was a bit of all of this going on in the Black Hole: the scatologi-cal humor; the populist leveling of the fussy and pretentious by a "creative disre-spect" that exalts the weird and makes a prince of the pirate; extreme drunkenness and drug use; ecstatic collectivity (sometimes channeled into super patriotism); persistent homophobia; and occasionally, violent sexism like that exhibited by the drunken lout who came up to my pregnant wife when I was in the restroom and proclaimed, "If I don't watch myself, I'll rape you." While I should confess that I have frequently given myself license to drink, swear, and act like a nut at games, this transgression seemed to me to be far from utopian. That, of course is the problem with any event where people get a sense that the usual prohibitions may be ignored—one person's happy anarchy is another person's fascist free-for-all. That said, the goodly number of arrests and fights we saw at games does not negate the fact that it is only a tiny minority of people who get crazy and abusive or violent. For most people, it's a good crazy, a healthy disavowal of the prison of everyday life. Risk is the price of admission.

Not everyone thinks the price is worth it. *Oakland Tribune* sports reporter Dave Newhouse has become a sharp critic of Raiders fans. The title of a 2002 article proclaimed, "Black Hole Hits Bottom," and he went on to explain, "I've visited numerous stadiums and arenas in my 40-plus years of sportswriting, and I haven't yet seen anything that matches the crazed atmosphere at the Net. I've observed plenty of lewd behavior, but what goes on in Oakland, believe me, is worse." While being careful to exclude up to 80 percent of fans, Newhouse does decry the "monsters in makeup" who make up "Oakland's second zoo." When we emailed Newhouse in 2003 he cited a number of violent assaults and noted that "fans have been urinated on and slugged in restrooms." As for our section, "In the Black Hole, fans scream gutter language, give the finger, and grab their crotch to opposing players." Interestingly, his *Oakland Tribune* piece argues that the "out of control atmosphere" at the Net has no impact on the games: "If Raiders fans believe their zealousness is helping their team, then they've really lost their minds. . . . Read my lips: It doesn't make any difference."[2]

In *Stiffed: The Betrayal of the American Man*, Susan Faludi argues that the impotence that Newhouse is intent on shoving in Raiders fans' faces is itself the source of the extreme fan's transgressions. As Faludi observes in her chapter on Cleveland Browns fans, corporate sports has led to the "ultimate marginalization" of working-class sports fans since the focus on TV revenue as the main source of income has "revealed just how passive and insignificant a force he [is] to his team's fortunes." Thus, while many media pundits have blamed fan violence on alcohol and a loss in civility in the culture, they have ignored the fact that "the reduction of fans to props could induce rage, that the *show* of violence might itself be the flip side of a compulsory display of glamour. . . . In the show

Oaktown pirates

Photo: Joseph A. Blum

business realm the fans now lived in, rage, even if kept off camera, served to draw attention, to gain recognition, and to express horror that fame would never be forthcoming." Hence, Faludi sharply notes, "Rabid fans increasingly became focused not on helping the players perform, but on cultivating their own performances. The show in the stands began to conflict with, even undermine, the drama on the gridiron." What everybody wants, by this logic, is to ascend to the heaven of the spectacle, to become part of the show.[3]

No Other Life Seems Real

> For every Raiders game for the last several years, I have worn the "stadium pal." The stadium pal is a urine disposal system, which consists of an external catheter, tubing, and a bag which attaches to your ankle. It allows me to drink as much as I want without worrying about missing a play to urinate.
>
> *Mikie Valium, Raiders fan*

In *The Society of the Spectacle,* Guy Debord argues, "In societies where modern conditions of production prevail, all of life presents itself as an immense accumulation of spectacles. Everything that was directly lived has moved away into a representation." Thus, as critic Greil Marcus explains:

> A never ending accumulation of spectacles—advertisements, entertainments, traffic, skyscrapers, political campaigns, department stores, sports events, newscasts, art tours, foreign wars, space launchings—made a modern world, a world in which all communication flowed in one direction, from the powerful to the powerless. One could not respond, or talk back, or intervene, but one did not want to. In spectacle, passivity was simultaneously the means and end for a great hidden project, a project of social control.[4]

In a world where the spectacle comprised not just one event but "a social relationship among people mediated by images," there was "no real life, yet no other life seemed real." The consequence of this, according to Marcus, is that "nothing seemed real until it had appeared in the spectacle, even if in the moment of its appearance it would lose whatever reality it had." It was, as Debord put it, "the material reconstruction of the religious illusion" as people sought authenticity, identity, and a whole other range of subjective emotions by consuming a product. To ascend to the heaven of the spectacle was to enter the image yourself, surrender yourself to the "something bigger than oneself" that was the commodified image writ large across the social landscape. I thought about the celebrity fans all vying for their three-second TV shot, the stadium jumbo screen, the newspaper photo, the website, collector's card, or business card. What mattered here was not a football game, but elevating oneself to the godlike realm of the televised image, penetrating the aura, and attaining the illusory sense that you were part of the show. The spectacle seduced people by selling them the idea that their passivity was an enactment of their freedom and individuality rather than a surrender to a democracy of "false desires."[5]

Another, less dystopian way to think about the Black Hole experience comes from John Fiske, who has argued that "one reason for the popularity of sport as a spectator activity is its ability to slip the disciplinary mechanism of the workday world into reverse gear." According to Fiske, fans who are "monitored" at work become monitors at the game, and the players become objects upon which "fans can punch away their frustration." The whole experience can be incredibly intense and, for Fiske, "This intensity is often experienced by fans as a sense of release, of loss of control. Fans often use metaphors of madness to describe it . . . and madness is what lies just outside the boundary of civilization and control." Thus, I thought, as the fans booed Gannon's weak performance and cheered when backup quarterback Marques Tuiasosopo ran on the field to replace him after his injury in the second half, the Black Hole turns workers into managers for a few hours, and they exercise their imaginative control with an angry passion driven by the revenge of the average Joe or Jill over their shitty boss. "Serve *me!*" say the angry curses at players, "Recognize *my* power!"[6]

Yet another view of the meaning of fandom comes from Michael Oriard, the preeminent scholar of the culture of football, who agrees with Susan Faludi about the NFL's "abandonment of its working-class fans." As he points out, "Without television, professional football paid poorly and had no national audience; the coming of television transformed it into the number-one American spectator sport but at the same time began the inevitable estrangement of the fans from the players." The result of this transformation, according to Oriard, is that expensive tickets, public subsidies, merchandizing, and TV contracts have "created opportunities for merely rich owners to become filthy rich from football" and rendered fans "less necessary." While "ordinary fans remain important for TV ratings and the revenue they determine" a single "corporate luxury box is worth hundreds of ordinary tickets." Thus, while he argues that Faludi "romanticizes" a golden era when fans really *did* have a kinship with the players, Oriard does see the average fan as more marginalized today than in the past.[7]

In an e-mail interview Oriard further explained his view of fans:

I resist both the reductive "subversion" and "containment" extremes in cultural analysis. . . . I thus view football fans' experience in the same "messy" way that I view other aspects of sport. Despite the terribly negative impact of corporatization on football fans, I assume that fans continue to find in football and their own teams something meaningful for themselves. At the same time, I assume that the meanings they find contain elements of delusion and self-delusion. My own predilection would be to not force the messiness of the ethnographic data into a too-tidy resolution of any kind. That would be truer to the world as I see it.

Father of the Nation

There are a large number of imposters out there that do misrepresent the Nation. Ashamed of some of the acts that they may commit, I am thankful for the support that they give. I think everyone has done something in their time that others felt was not quite civilized. There isn't a game gone by that I have not seen a fight at the NET. There isn't a game gone by that I have not drank to get drunk, talked as much shit as possible and ate till I couldn't eat any more. Tailgates are the reason for the season. I go to socialize with other die-hard fans, harass other fans and have the best time possible. An occasional photo op or autograph is likely.

Paul, Raiders fan

As I looked out over the silver-and-black sea before me I wondered about Oriard's observation about delusion, self-delusion, and the messy nature of determining what it "means" to be a fan. As the Raiders tried to storm back in the second half, people's responses were earnest, angry, ironic, humorous, and just plain crazy. Clearly not all fans (myself included) are dupes, but there is definitely a suspension of disbelief necessary to gear oneself up enough to care passionately about an essentially meaningless game. And sometimes the magic spell loses its power.

The spell of the spectacle did lose its power this year for Jimbo, the father and onetime owner of the term "Raider Nation." In late August 2003, before the regular season even began, Jimbo shut down his Raider Empire Listserv with the following explanation:

I have made a tough decision to shut down the list as I no longer have a passion for the Raiders. Don't get me wrong, I will still go to the games and pull for the team but my involvement will stop there. I will enjoy the games for what they are—a sporting event, not a way of life.

I have found it increasingly difficult to agree with the Raiders outside the game antics. In fact, I disagree with everything the Raiders have come to represent outside the Coliseum. That means I no longer wish to push the Raiders' propaganda regarding fan misbehavior, the lawsuits, etc. My experience with Raiders fans has been, on the whole, very good but there were those who fit the description of "ugly, ignorant, dumb fuck Raiders fans." Unfortunately, there are enough of the dumb fuck variety to make being lumped into the category of "Raider fan" a less than desirable attribute. I established and pushed Raider Nation . . . [and it] became bigger than anything they could ever hope to achieve. I sold it to the NFL and now am bowing out with nothing more to prove. The joke's on the rest of the fuckers who are, at best, the bottom dwellers—I toast your ineptitude.

When we interviewed Jimbo via e-mail after he renounced his Raider Nation citizenship we were surprised to learn that even the storied fan nickname was a trademarked commodity: "I conceived of Raider Nation in 1995 after the return of the Raiders to Oakland. If you look at the fan wall at the Coliseum you will see Raider Nation listed—that is how my PSL was registered." As for the legal history of the term, he explained that, "Raider Nation was a servicemark and trademark which I owned. For two years there were negotiations with NFL properties which culminated in a settlement to transfer ownership of the name and logos to the NFL." He started his Listserv "to offer an alternative to Raiders fans from the other mediocre and 'Nazi'-driven mailing lists that existed at the time. You were a Raider fan as defined by some small group of pinheads." But Jimbo became disenchanted because:

The Raiders outside of football suck, period, end. They have no concept of how to build community support and, in fact, have done a good job of eroding the fan base in the Bay Area. Their incessant lawsuits, which fostered the "us versus them" image, now come across as nothing more than someone (Big Al) with enough money to make people miserable and/or get what he wants by twisting the law. The positive spin the organization tries to weave around these lawsuits would only deceive the diehard Raiders fans and/or someone who is brain dead. . . . Big Al exists to sue people who get in his way, including Raider fans.

The bad side of Raiders fans existed in what I would describe as the "hard core diehards." They have no life outside of the Silver and Black. They exist to glorify the punk/thug image of the team. I would classify them as wannabes who live out this fantasy through the team's image. It is sad that some would rather attend a Raider game than find work to put food on the table. Take the Violator, for example, a PR coup for the Raiders when they flew him in because he could not afford the airfare. Did anyone think they maybe should encourage him to get a life?? Same for most of the denizens of the Black Hole—they live vicariously through the team's "bad boy" image. It is unfortunate that many do not know when the game ends and reality begins.

The good side of Raiders fans is in the unbridled enthusiasm they bring to the games. The experience at the House of Thrills is second to none. If you sit in the stands and cheer for your team respectfully and let the opposing team's fans do the same there is great positive energy generated. The camaraderie and feeling of community is also positive. It is rare these days to find a common bond amongst large groups of people, which breaks down artificial barriers of race, education, and class. When channeled correctly all these things are very positive—when not, they cut like a two-edge sword.

I thought about Jimbo's disavowal of Raider Nation as I watched the Silver and Black, down 17–10, start what would have been a thrilling comeback drive at their own 6-yard line. As Tuiasosopo marched the team down the field, a guy in a white Raiders jersey and a Bill Clinton mask walked up the stairs holding a cigar, and I saw a whole band of guys dressed like KISS in silver and black strolling behind our seats. Three more "regular guys" got arrested while the Hell's Angels just down the row watched the game peacefully while eating ice-cream cones. The game ended with Tim Brown catching a pass by the goal line and getting wrestled down inside the 1-yard line as the clock hit 0:00. As the *Oakland Tribune* headline put it the next day, "Time Runs Out on the Raiders."[8]

Skull Lady

Eleven

Real Women Wear Black

Football in our period, as before and after, was an arena in which masculinity was at issue, not a settled matter.

Michael Oriard, King Football

What's happening is that women are discovering how deeply satisfying the sanctioned conflict of football can be.

Sally Jenkins, Men Will Be Boys

[T]o be a football fan as a woman is empowering. I feel so empowered.

Carrie Donnelly, Raiders fan

Jim and I arrived at our seats, a bit out of breath from hurrying down the stairs to our section. "Gotta little Raider brewin' in there?" asked the African American guy in a number 24 Charles Woodson jersey as he observed my growing belly and grabbed my hand.

"Hey, he's already got a Raiders binky waiting for him when he gets out!" I laughed as I was helped over the seat from the row behind me, marveling at the care with which my fellow Black Hole denizens handled my increasing bulk. It was another dismal game, and while the chivalrous souls around me could find it in them to aid a pregnant woman, ugliness was brewing elsewhere. Charles Woodson had spent the intervening week after the loss to the terrible Detroit Lions criticizing his coach, and Callahan was in turn probably wondering if he'd have a job with the Raiders the next season (he wouldn't). The Raiders had also lost second-string quarterback Marques Tuiasosopo to a knee injury. Yet early in the game, the fans were not acting like this was the 2-and-6 Raiders who were falling apart. We heard the usual boisterous chants of "Ray-duz" on the way in, and things seemed to be looking up with Buchanon's 79-yard run at 11:53 into the first quarter. But, as with everything this season, the Raiders had given it right back one minute later, and would go on to lose in overtime 24 to 27 after blowing the lead in the last few seconds of regulation time. It didn't matter that Callahan had listened to the critics' complaints and had gone with the running game, because the Raiders' defense just couldn't stop the big plays. The only positive things this week happened off the football field. Prosecutors announced that they wouldn't pursue felony manslaughter charges against former Raiders great Marv Hubbard, thus taking him off the hook for a fatal car crash, and Oakland was rated the United States' "eighth funnest city" according to the makers of the board game Cranium.[1]

By the middle of the game, Oakland didn't seem to be very fun, though.

"Get that girl with the Jets shirt on! Shit! Get her!" screamed a tiny brown-haired woman in a Raiders jersey as she went after an equally diminutive blonde in a Jets jersey.

"Take your bitch home!" yelled the silver-and-black clad hellion as her male companion held her back, her arms outstretched and clawing at the air. The woman in the Jets jersey backed up against her six-foot-four-inch boyfriend, who, ironically, was dressed head to toe in Raiders gear. After the angry Raiders woman had been carted up the stairs, we saw the Jets woman shake her head, marveling after nearly getting jumped by someone of her own sex. I couldn't help but think about Jerry Porter's comments earlier that season regarding one of his foes on the Titans: "He's a girl. I don't like playing football against girls." After the game, our friend Jim told us that he had seen a group of women decked out in Raiders gear attack a couple of female Jets fans. "I was surprised to see how aggressive those girls were," he said.[2]

On the face of it, "chick fights" among women fans seem somewhat surprising given the history of women's involvement in football. We are used to seeing women as cheerleaders, beautiful feminine baubles emphasizing the tough maleness of the football players on the gridiron. Football, among all the other contact sports, with the possible exception of prize fighting, enshrines masculinity and uses femininity as a foil. In fact, football's history parallels fears in the United States that society was becoming "feminized." In *Power at Play: Sports and the Problem of Masculinity,* Michael Messner points out, "That the modern institution of sport was shaped during the time when women were challenging existing gender relations helps to explain the particular forms that sport eventually took."[3] It is interesting to note that football's early history coincides with women's suffrage, a moment in U.S. history when women really were contesting the established order. Michael Oriard also documents other events that challenged the taken-for-grantedness of masculinity:

> With industrialization, the closing of the frontier, and the migration to cities, the American male was cut off from the physical demands of everyday outdoor life, through which his manhood had once been routinely confirmed. Thrust into a new world where traditional masculine traits were no longer meaningful, he found in vigorous outdoor sports such as football a compensating validation of his manhood. The outcry against football brutality was great, but concern over the possibility of an emasculated American manhood greater.[4]

Oriard goes on to discuss how middle-class men, in particular, were fearful of feminization, since their work generally involved no physical labor at all. For working-class men, such anxieties would come later. Football, which was initially played by elite college men and soon after by working-class professionals, was the perfect sport to allay such fears. Its brutality and aggressiveness—its sheer physicality—bespeaks a power through might. When one is successful on the football

Raiderettes and company

field, one is successful because of one's physical prowess. Even the strategists on the field (the quarterback, for example) have to be in the peak of physical health to withstand the continual body blows. "Girls" can't take the abuse. Football is thus a potent vehicle through which masculinity is made manifest.

Obviously not all men are cut out to be football players. Nor do all men define masculinity through violence and physical dominance. For a wide swath of men in the United States, however, that is exactly how masculinity is defined. Hence, if you can't *be* a football player—or even a player in your work life—you can watch the game as a fan and identify with the guys on the field. As Susan Faludi notes in her chapter on Cleveland Browns fans in *Stiffed*, one of the powerful venues which many working-class men in Cleveland have had for shoring up their masculinity and their sense of self in the face of deindustrialization, the resulting job losses, and marginalization has been football fandom. This identification can prove treacherous, however: "The sort of 'team' in which a man could lose himself while finding himself as a man no longer seemed to exist. Not in the workplace. Not on the battlefront. Not even on the playing fields."[5]

Nevertheless, in many ways a football game is indeed masculinity writ large: twenty-two beefy guys battling each other for possession of the ball and the field. The allure of the game for men is its lack of apparent ambiguity. This explains the rampant homophobia permeating the stands and the Internet as men attempt to police the boundaries of acceptable masculinity and keep the game as unambiguous as possible. When male fans call each other or players "fags" or "homos" or hurl any other number of homophobic insults, they are making sure that the identity they've defined as "male" remains pure. Which is why women are used in very specific ways to prop up male identities.

Cheerleaders serve as feminine counterpoints to the sweating, grunting players. In the middle of one's field of vision or TV screen the stars perform the central show; on the sidelines, serving as a kind of frame, are the hypersexualized and generally silent kootchy dancers. The huge squad of Raiderettes (note the diminutive), in their ultra-feminine low-cut pirate tops, black miniskirts, and white go-go boots with a rainbow of flowing locks serve as a kind of gender commentary on the players. Like Las Vegas showgirls, the Raiderettes, along with their sisters throughout the NFL, shake their booties and their boobies and all but strip for the slavering mass of male fandom. The Raiderette whom we spoke with on condition of anonymity at the Raiders rally before the home opener might not see herself this way, especially since she thinks that she and her colleagues "represent women fans and that we set a standard for women. I believe that this is how women fans should represent the Raiders—as the Raiderettes do." Nevertheless, while the players tackle, hit, and grab each other, the scantily clad cheerleaders wave their pom-poms and smile for the camera. As Sally Jenkins puts it in *Men Will Be Boys*: "With its emphasis on the extreme possibilities of the male body and psyche, coupled with the emphasis on relatively naked, voluptuous women as cheerleaders, football has reinforced traditional notions of male–female relations like no other public ritual." In this arena, the football player acts while the cheerleader is a passive bit of eye candy. It's the old male gaze at work, an exercise of patriarchal power. Or is it? In the realm of the spectacle, both the men and women on the field are targets of the gaze. Which is where female fans of football come in.[6]

Why do women watch sports? What could possibly be interesting for the woman fan? Jenkins documents that "a full 40 percent of the [NFL's] television audience is female," and "[a]ccording to various surveys, including Nielsen research, anywhere from 28 to 40 million women watch the NFL on TV each week, and as many as 60 million watch the Super Bowl. League figures show that women make up 40 percent of game day attendance. Forty-six percent of all NFL Licensing purchases are made by women." Jenkins' conclusion is that "women are discovering how deeply satisfying the sanctioned conflict of football can be." Judging by the lines to the women's restrooms and the rows of female faces in the stands in the Oakland Coliseum, the Raiders attract their share of the fairer sex. When we spoke with Tish, Michelle, and Kristie, three women fans at the Raiders rally, and asked them why they liked the team and football in general, Tish answered, "I've always loved football. It's an aggressive sport and fun to watch." "I like to watch contact sports," Michelle added, "they're physical and action-packed where every play is different." Impulses similar to the ones that lead men to watch football entice women as well. It's also important to note women's increasing participation in the world of work. If men watch sports to escape from their lives, if football, for example, offers a release from tension and a venue for displaced aggression, it should not be surprising that women might find some of the same kinds of satisfactions in viewing sports. In the wake of not only the Women's Liberation Movement of the late sixties and early seventies, but also the passage of Title IX, which has enabled girls and women to participate in sports in school, women's positive attitudes toward sports make sense. For even though there have always been women spectators at sporting events, the ways that women watch sports—and watch men play sports—are changing.[7]

The women fans in the Black Hole are a case in point. From Raider-Gloria and Skull Lady to your average Jane in a Jerry Rice jersey, the end zone is filled with rabid women, as stat-savvy and vehement as their male companions. For some, like ESPN reporter Alyssa Minkoff, the Black Hole represents a place where she can "satisfy and even nurture [her] desperately underutilized reprobate streak." In her article "Sweetheart of the Hole," Minkoff describes her weekend in "The Black Hole in Raider Nation" and says that she went to the game in order to "get back in touch with [her] 'Inner Bad Girl.'" While the article mostly details a novice's journey through the parking lot and the stands, it is interesting that Minkoff characterizes her impulse to experience Raider Nation as being "bad." What this depiction makes apparent are the ways in which gender crossing can be titillating—as long as it's crossing from the world of women to that of men. Being in the male realm where physical might clearly rules can be a welcome respite from the female realm of sticky emotion. "Bad girls" not only choose to hang out with men instead of women, they also often act like men in the way they approach relationships and life. Football games in general and Raiders games in particular offer the female fan the opportunity not only to vacation in the land of men, but to dress up in the most outrageous ways possible.[8]

Skull Lady, whom we met at the Raiders rally earlier in the season and whose antics in the Black Hole (including several cameos on the jumbo screen during games) we noted with amusement, would not agree with our anonymous Raiderette that the cheerleaders should set the tone for women fans. With her skull-encrusted construction helmet, silver-and-black face paint, black jersey, black lycra leggings, skeleton epaulets, shin guards, elbow-length gloves, and long blonde hair, Skull Lady cuts quite a figure. She told us she'd been dressing up for games for four years after her five-year-old niece picked out her outfit and told her that she "had to come to all the games dressed this way." Just two rows from the field, Skull Lady sits right in front of one of the squads of Raiderettes. "Don't get me wrong, I *like* the Raiderettes," she explained without disavowing her own brand of costuming. While a large part of Skull Lady's impetus is her occasional big screen appearance, this does not negate her genuine enthusiasm for the game and the team. The Raiderettes may be the official promulgators of female sports fandom, but the women in the stands who roll up their sleeves and throw themselves into the games right alongside the male fans are redefining the strict gender dichotomization of sports. Interestingly, no men we spoke with seemed to mind rooting with the girls. Sitting side by side with women fans, men ogled the cheerleaders, or made fun of them, and discussed the game with their female companions. In fact, the group of friends and family surrounding us in our seats in the Black Hole included equal numbers of women and men. And throughout our research, many a man told us that he became a Raiders fan through his mother or grandmother rather than through his male relatives.

A parallel to men growing up in a Raiders matriarchy is the large number of women who were brought up in the Silver and Black by their fathers. Amanda and Carrie Donnelly are two such women. Both in their early twenties, the Donnelly sisters are warm and gregarious. Carrie, the older of the two, has long, curly brown hair and an infectious laugh. Amanda, who is quieter than her sister, smiles a lot and has shorter, blondish hair. While their mother is a huge Raiders fan, it was their father who raised them to gravitate toward all things silver and black. A former blue-collar worker in the aluminum industry who became a social worker after a back injury, their father grew up in Alameda and went to Raiders games from an early age. Just about every member of Amanda and Carrie's family has season tickets, including their mother, who grew up in the East Bay community of Castro Valley. As Amanda puts it, "[The Raiders] are not just a team, but something that we believe in—something holy—that we are very passionate about." The Donnellys' father, however, is the biggest "fanatic," according to Carrie. "When we were kids, we were given no other choice. Any presents we were given had to be silver and black. For example, we had to have silver-and-black NFL jackets."

"We wanted pink jackets," added Amanda, "but it had to be silver and black."

"My father even painted our house silver and black when we were kids," Carrie added with a laugh. And it didn't stop there; Amanda smiled and explained, "We had the Raiders flag out on Memorial Day, and my parents had to have a black car." When the Raiders played a game, it was stressful in the Donnelly household, in part because of their father's superstition. As Amanda remembers it:

> When we were growing up—like the second through fourth grade—all of us would be watching the game, and one of us would have to go to the bathroom. We would come back into the room, and the Raiders would have done something, so my dad would pay attention to what everyone was doing, like where they were sitting, for example. He would say, "You need to move over a little bit. You need to go over there. You need to hold a soda. You need to go back to the bathroom." And then, when the play was over or the penalty call was resolved, he would say, "Okay, you can come back now." He would blame one of us if something bad happened because we had moved or held a soda in the wrong way. It was intense.

Carrie told us about the time they were at a game a couple of years ago and she lost her ticket on the way in. Not wanting to upset her father even more than he already was, Carrie ended up sneaking past the ticket-takers and jumping over the turnstile. After being chased by the Coliseum police, she was eventually apprehended, but because her father confronted the cops, he was the one who got taken off in handcuffs. He managed to finagle his release when he mentioned his family's connections in the police department. Once everyone finally got to the seats, Carrie told us: "My father said, 'It's all right.' He was so happy and proud of me because I had big balls."

One might be tempted to think that Amanda and Carrie could not possibly be genuine Raiders fans in their own right because they were coerced into it by their father. On the contrary, both label themselves die-hard fans, who "always seem to date men who aren't football fans at all. We have to explain football to them and they end up becoming fans, too." As Carrie puts it, "To be a football fan [as a woman] is something different. At Raiders games there are always tons of women. The Raiders are known to be rebellious and masculine to a certain degree. So it's fun as a woman to be a fan. I can act sexy, and guys get really into it when you tell them 'I love football.'"

"Yeah," Amanda added, "and look at the clothes. The Raiders have great t-shirts that are cut for a woman."

"I have this shirt that says, 'Real Women Wear Black,' which I love. We got really lucky with the color." Carrie smiled hugely, clearly pleased to flaunt her "inner bad girl."

Thus, in Raider Nation, "real women" wear black, not feminine pastels. It is interesting to note that Carrie's t-shirt is a spin-off from the older "Real *Men* Wear Black." It is also one of the most popular designs in Raider Nation, judging by the numbers of chests we saw adorned with it. Even though this is a commercial product, brought to you by the Raiders and the NFL, women have nevertheless appropriated the spirit behind the shirt—and in some cases have gone beyond it in their own ways. Whether it's Raider-Gloria, who legally changed her name to emphasize her allegiance to the Silver and Black, or Skull Lady and her elaborate costume, or the woman wearing a black thong emblazoned with the Raiders shield under her jeans, or the myriad other women fans wearing jerseys, waving black pom-poms, or watching their husbands cook extensive spreads for their tailgate parties in the parking lot, women have embraced the spirit that motivates many men to support their football team. The impulse on the part of women to support a football team wholeheartedly, and to root, dress up, and raise their children to be Raiders fans may seem puzzling on the face of it. Football is a fierce sport, masculine through and through. Yet it is precisely *because* football in general and the Raiders in particular embody such an aggressive ethos that these women are die-hard fans.

When women embrace Raiders fandom, though, they give it a unique spin. In the introduction to her collection of essays *The Pirate's Fiancée: Feminism, Reading, Postmodernism,* Meaghan Morris discusses how Nelly Kaplan's film *The Pirate's Fiancée* uses as its inspiration the song "Pirate Jenny" from Brecht and Weill's *Three Penny Opera* by transforming it into a feminist fable. Kaplan, according to Morris, performs a kind of piracy on the men's text by creating a character who ultimately acts as and for herself rather than simply playacting something different. It's not too much of a stretch to claim a similar agency for female Raiders fans. In pirating the pirate, women fans embody the cathartic aggression that is so alluring to male fans at the same time as they enter the community of Raider Nation with all of its conviviality.[9]

"Don't Fuck With Us"

Photo: Joseph A. Blum

Twelve

Los Malosos

Daddy, I like the Raiders, too, but you shouldn't have robbed a bank to
see them.

Six-year-old daughter of the Raiders Bandit, 1991

I have tattooed the Raider logo on my arm and my wedding was in silver
and black. . . . I am extremely proud to be a Raider fan and will die
buried in my full Raider attire. My will states this and my wife has agreed
to honor these wishes.

Chris Eaton, police officer and president of the
Imperial Valley Raiders Booster Club

Los maschingones, Aztlan Raiders, Malosos de Aztlan: No chinges con
nosotros o te chingamos!

Los Malosos de Aztlan bootleg t-shirt

The news just kept getting worse in Raider Nation as fans learned that Rich
Gannon was gone for the season along with a host of other players. If that was
not bad enough, news came that Raiders Bill Romanowski, Barret Robbins,
Dana Stubblefield, and Chris Cooper were reported to be linked to the BALCO
steroids scandal. When Tyrone Wheatley came to testify before the grand jury

investigating the nutritional supplements lab, he cursed and threatened a group of photographers before slapping one of them on the wrist. The sniping continued in the locker room as well, and speculation about head coach Bill Callahan's job security kicked into high gear. After the loss to the Jets, the man in charge concluded, "We didn't close the book when we had a chance to put a nail in the coffin." The same could have been said about the whole season.[1]

Elsewhere soldiers continued to die in Iraq and California's brand-new celebrity governor was rolling back the car registration tax, leaving the already resource-strapped city of Oakland pondering layoffs and cuts in services. News in the private sector was also bad for workers, with the Southern California grocery strike dragging on as employers insisted on cutting health care benefits and imposing a two-tier wage system that would mean poverty-level jobs for all future workers. East Bay workers picketed local Safeway stores urging customers to shop at other markets.[2] Kelly and I had been on sympathy pickets with local strikers in San Diego, and we spotted a few Raiders fans on the line. In the midst of the strike, we interviewed Raiders fan Carlos Canal, a picket captain at an Albertson's in Coronado, a pricey suburb across the bay from downtown San Diego. Carlos, who lives in Murrieta, a blue-collar suburb northeast of the city, grew up in Skyline Hills in the eastern part of San Diego with ex-Raider David Dunn. We asked him why he was a Raiders fan:

> I liked the colors, I think. I was always a Silver and Black–type person. I know they bug a lot of people, like the San Diego Chargers fans, they always think we're the bad guys, that we're all these gang members and thugs. That's the sort of thing they have been projected as, like with NWA or up in L.A., but there are a lot of good Raiders fans out there. I never grew up listening to a whole lot of rap. I never got involved with gangs. Basically, I kept to myself. My friends were Caucasian. And I'm riding around in a hot rod, and I'm Hispanic, so I was really an oddball there. And [David Dunn], he was pretty cool. I remember he got beat up one day. He turned out to be a Raider. That is what surprises me.

Right now I'm a grocery clerk. We're [locked out] and there's no end in sight. It just brings you closer to your co-workers. It's got its ups and downs. Sometimes you think, "Oh my God, they're going to break us." That gets you pretty down. It's been long. A lot of people thought it would be like a vacation, a week. A lot of people thought it would be three days [rather than months], you know? I didn't think it was like that. I just hoped it would end soon, and fourteen weeks later, here we still are. I am a picket captain for $100 a week. That has been pretty tough. For $100 a week you can't do anything. I live up in Murrieta and I'm doing the drive to Coronado to be with my guys, you know, my crew and we're spending fourteen hours sometimes. Luckily, we had a real strong union come over and picket with us last week. And we had a lot of different people from San Diego when we did a rally last week. That was great. The rally really helped morale.

[Because we're locked out] we can't even cross if we wanted to. But there are people working for Vons who've crossed, and we've already heard horror stories. They're being terminated. They were people they wanted to get rid of for years, and now they don't have to pay them pensions or whatever, and that's the way they want to get rid of them. [The central issue is] health care. Health care and people's pensions. I believe in [the company] making a profit because a successful company gives you hours. It gives you a job—but not to the degree that they are trying to take this. They just want cheap health care. [What the company is offering] is not going to help you get by. Not if you have a mortgage. Working people should be able to keep up. We made the company successful. We haven't had a big raise in years. It's like 25 cents here, 35 cents there. With the economy here in San Diego—the high price of housing, the price of gas—it's not enough to get by. A lot of people think that a lot of grocery store workers are making $17 an hour. They're not. Let's say there are a hundred people in the store. Maybe fifteen would be full time. Most of us are part-time, hoping to get over thirty hours to be able to make it. That's what has been so hard about it. A lot of people are not getting the facts. Sometimes the union hasn't done a good job, but I still believe in them.

It has changed the way people see their employer. A lot of people are going to end up leaving. I gave them my 110 percent. Now [when this is over], I'm going to come in and do my time. I'll get done when I'm done. That is how much loyalty they'll get from me. The bottom line is greed, you know? Walk into a Wal-Mart and you'll see what you're going to get. It will take ten years to make $15 an hour. How many people are going to stick around for that? You know, fifteen years? All those years, for what?

When we made our way back to football, I asked Carlos where he had watched the Super Bowl. He replied, "I couldn't watch the Super Bowl. I mean, I'd rather work." As the strike dragged on, we frequently thought of Carlos holding the line in his Tim Brown jersey, representing the beleaguered UFCW and the hated Raiders in ultraconservative Coronado. Long after the end of football season, the union settled, saving the benefits of the current employees in exchange for a two-tier wage scale. The race to the bottom was on in California's service sector.

The Saturday before the Minnesota Vikings game Kelly and I went to the grand opening of Vella's Locker Room in downtown Oakland, the latest expansion of the chain formerly known as Raiders Locker Room before legal wrangling forced a name change and removed the pirate's face from the shield that accompanies the store's moniker. As we walked down Broadway, we could see the silver-and-black balloons tied to the trees and lampposts outside the store along with the unmistakable visages of Señor Raider Man and Gorilla Rilla, who at one point was prancing about on the median for the amusement of passing motorists. Unlike the huge event at the Universal City Walk in L.A., this midseason affair had drawn a small crowd of about twenty people. We noticed a third celebrity fan whose spikes and makeup were undercut by his librarian-like glasses. He just didn't measure up to Señor Raider Man's psycho aura or Gorilla Rilla's surreal absurdity. All three superfans were hawking signed cards for $1. Also present and signing 8-by-10-inch color glossies for fans for $10 was Raiders tight end Teyo Johnson. Kelly got us a couple of signed pictures and as we were heading into the store Gorilla Rilla led a homeless man in a Dodgers cap up to Teyo Johnson who, upon being hit up for change, searched his pockets. He sheepishly came up empty, then gave the man a free autographed picture instead. The homeless man shook Teyo's hand gratefully and wandered off with a gorilla escort for about ten yards. Teyo looked like he wished he'd had a pocket full of quarters.

The next morning at the Fat Lady, a nice old man in his Sunday best came up to us at the bar after seeing our Raiders gear and told us he'd been at the famous Heidi game when the networks cut off their coverage before the Raiders' dramatic comeback win in order to air the musical *Heidi*:

> I was at that Heidi game, the one they show the highlights of all the time. It was great. I was there back when they almost ended up being named the Señors. The colors were black and gold. I saw them at Youell Field. We'd walk down in those days. They used to sell tickets out of a garage painted blue and white. The guys in the stands in those days were like tree trunks, standing all game. We'd laugh and yell, "Sit down!" Fans in the old days were different. Now, I just don't go to games, I watch them on TV. I went to L.A. a couple of times and have gone since they came back here, but it's not the same. People get so drunk, what's the point? It's not like it was.

We shook hands and he headed out the door. I ordered another Bloody Mary and Kelly went over to talk with a pair of old-time fans sitting farther down the bar. Rocky had a Rollie Fingers moustache and was wearing a seventies-style Raiders jacket, as was his friend Don, who looked a bit like Ted Hendricks. Rocky had not missed a kickoff in thirty-two years, including the Raiders' L.A. stay. Don flies in from Las Vegas for the games. When I got up to go to the restroom, I met a guy who told me that he played golf with Barry Sims and that Sims had told him that Gannon had been seeing a sports psychologist since the Super Bowl and had never gotten over the debacle. With that bit of Raiders gossip, we left to experience a slice of the Rick Mirer era.

On the way into the stadium, we walked past a guy whose t-shirt proclaimed "Win or Lose, Raiders Fans Know How to Booze: Just Get Hammered, Baby" and featured an angry, red-eyed, cigar-smoking skull. We made our way through a small cloud of pot smoke in the tunnel and weaved through the crowd to our seats, where the people around us all happily commented on Kelly's expanding girth and wished her luck with the baby after this, her last game before late-pregnancy lockdown. It was a good-sized crowd of 56,653 marred only by the presence of a small gang of Vikings fanatics in purple jerseys and goofy horned helmets right in the middle of the Black Hole. Fortunately for them, Phillip Buchanon started everything off right for the Raiders by picking off a Daunte Culpepper pass and taking it 64 yards for a touchdown just 49 seconds into the game, and their Silver and Black counterparts were satisfied merely to pelt them with pistachio nuts and hot dog wrappers. The Vikings fans tested their luck by cheering "One, Two, Three, First Down!" to mark every Minnesota advance and were answered with a resounding "One, Two, Three, Fuck You!" by the Hole.[3]

At one point the invaders were greeted by a crazy drunk in a Raiders poncho who stood on his chair in front of them and proceeded to flip them off and give them lip for about half a quarter. Still, peace endured. This was helped, of course, by the Raiders, who led 14–3 at halftime and held on to win 28–18, aided by a masterful performance by Charles Woodson covering Vikings superstar Randy Moss, a 100-yard running game by Tyrone Wheatley, a gritty performance by third-string quarterback Rick Mirer, and a key interception by Rod Woodson. The massive police escort that the Vikings fans received once the game was over didn't hurt either. Nonetheless, it was a happy crowd that left the stadium that day with the verses of "Oaktown" still ringing in their heads. It had not been "the blah hole," as one media wag had dubbed it earlier that week. As Raiders wide receiver Jerry Porter put it, "We're not really out of it. Kansas City lost. The moon is aligned right. If Jupiter is full, we might make the playoffs." On the BART on the way back to our hotel, Kelly sat next to a sweet woman and her little girl who asked about her due date and then said about the game, "We picked a good one. I hate it when they lose and those 49ers people get after you. We picked a good one, honey." The little girl smiled and buried her head in her mother's side as the train rolled on toward downtown.[4]

Later that night, the airport was jammed with Raiders fans waiting for the late flights back to Los Angeles and San Diego. While we were waiting in the bar, a call-and-response broke out as a big jolly guy in a Marcus Allen jersey and several strings of Mardi Gras beads shouted, "Who'd we come to see?"

"Ray-duz!" the bar answered.

"Who won tonight?" our man continued.

"Ray-duz!" came the reply.

"Who's always in the house?" came the question as the guy in the Allen jersey put his hand to his ear in a playfully dramatic fashion.

"Ray-duz!" said the bar once again.

"Who's three and seven?" asked the big guy, breaking into a funny little dance.

"Ray-duz!" yelled the crowd.

"Who sucks this year?" the cheerleader continued as he hopped on top of his barstool preening and clowning.

"Ray-duz!" yelled the bar, laughing and clowning along. A handful of business travelers in the corner exchanged astounded looks. It was as if they had walked into some surreal postmodern mead hall. You had to love it.

The Raider Bandit and Other Sad and Sordid Tales

Later that week we read in the paper that a couple from Clovis had been viciously assaulted in the Coliseum parking lot before the Vikings game. The man had been inside one of the portable toilets when he heard someone push over the neighboring one. When he stepped outside, he glanced at one of the men who had upended the adjacent toilet that a woman had been using. The assailant asked the Clovis man what he was looking at. He replied that he wasn't looking at anything and was punched in the face several times. As he tried to fight back, five more men jumped in and he was struck in the head several times with Corona bottles. His girlfriend tried to help him and was beaten as well with fists and bottles and had her sweater partially ripped off. After this brutal assault, Nash Rodriguez of Union City, Jorge Perales of Newark, and their buddies went to the game, only to be apprehended afterward once the police had found the battered, bleeding, and weeping couple by the roadway and staked out the attackers' cars. Only Rodriguez and Perales could be identified: they pleaded guilty to felony assault and received six months in jail and five months' probation with orders to stay away from both the couple and the Coliseum. The couple from Clovis had apparently done nothing to provoke the attack.[5]

The thought of having been at the same game while Kelly was pregnant with our son did indeed send a chill down our spines, even though we knew that these six thugs were a minute portion of the more than 56,000 people there that day. Truth be told, there has always been a violent subculture at Raiders games, which, as the assault at the Vikings game shows, is not just an "L.A. gang thing" as many like to characterize it. In fact, some of the most notorious incidents at Raiders games spring not from the bowels of the Crips and Bloods but from regular guys who lose it. Shane Geringer, the nineteen-year-old Los Angeles Raiders fan from suburban Agoura who put a Pittsburgh Steelers fan in the hospital and inspired a stern response from the Los Angeles County Board of Supervisors, didn't hail from a rough 'hood. Both "the Raiders gang," who held up banks in the San Gabriel Valley and Gardena, and "the Raider Bandit" from Norwalk, who held up Los Angeles and Orange County banks, were given their nicknames by the FBI and police because of their black clothing, aggressive style, and, in the case of the Norwalk bandit, a Raiders hat. None of them, however, were self-proclaimed "fans."[6]

The real Raider Bandit, Claude Dawson Jones, was not from Los Angeles at all, but from Sacramento. Clawson, who had once worked for Bank of America, netted $25,253 in twenty-four bank robberies that took him through the tail end of the 1990 Raiders season and into the beginning of the 1991 season before police arrested him in a motel room that he had converted into a shrine to the Silver and Black. "There was Raider paraphernalia all around. It was safe to say he was an avid fan," said the FBI spokesman. Before he was caught, Jones had used his plunder to buy Raiders tickets, toast them with rounds for the house at local bars, and go on an expensive road trip to Detroit to see the pride-and-poise boys beat the Lions on Monday Night Football. Jones had tickets to the Raiders AFC Championship game as well as airline fare when he was apprehended. Why did he do it? According to Jones, "All that Raidermania hit me. I've got to go see the boys play." And that's how it started with Jones (who wore a 49ers cap during the heists); he hit his first bank on the way to see the Raiders play Green Bay in Los Angeles because he was out of gas money. After that, he was on a roll. "Sometimes people like the bad guy," Jones said in true Raiders spirit. "I was brash, cocky. It's kind of like, as long as you can get away with it, there are no rules." Behind the bravado, however, Jones was an unhappy man who drank and drugged too much. He hated his job at the bank, which had asked him to take a 25 percent pay cut, and his later job at the Franchise Tax Board. Worst of all, his wife had become a 49ers fan. So, too, were the majority of the prison guards, who refused to give Jones updates as his beloved Raiders were roundly pummeled by the Bills in the AFC Championship game for which Jones had sacrificed ten years of freedom, as well as his marriage and contact with his two young daughters. The former high school football star and air force veteran wrote Al Davis a letter of apology, but had the consolation of knowing that, as he told reporters, "There are a lot of Raiders fans in jail."[7]

Next to the Raiders Bandits, perhaps the most notorious figure in the Raiders hall of shame is Luis Fernando Uribe from Norwalk, who got five years in jail for stabbing a Chargers fan with a pocketknife in 2000. Uribe has been universally held up as the poster boy for Raiders fan thugdom, and his assault on Daniel Napier is usually presented in lurid terms—for example, in this 2003 *Seattle Times* article:

He turned his back, so he never saw it coming. By then, Daniel Napier was lying on the concrete aisle, two Raiders fans pinning him to the ground. One pounding away with his fist, cracking the bones above Napier's eye. The other pulled out a knife, sliding the blade deep into Napier's side until a crimson pool formed on the concrete steps at Qualcomm Stadium. As the ambulance sped away, whisking him past the parking lot tailgates and out onto the highway, Napier watched the medics scramble around him and wondered if he was about to die.

The article goes on to detail how Uribe and his accomplice Dan Garcia called Napier "fat" and "began to curse him" and make "obscene gestures." For his part, Napier "shouted back," the article says, and his girlfriend and another woman "blew a kiss at the men." Since the stabbing, we are told, Napier has suffered from "a scar far deeper than the one above his abdomen" and has undergone extensive counseling and left his La Mesa home. The article then goes on to claim that "the Raiders were the team of L.A.'s gangs," whose fans are a "lawless," class-less bunch who are "the poster children for thuggery."[8]

Many Raiders fans we have spoken with agree with this assessment of the "L.A. gang" influence on the team's fan base. Chris Eaton, president of the Imperial Valley Raiders Booster Club and a cop himself, told us, "With the tough, aggressive mindset that most L.A. residents have and probably need to exist in that cesspool, Raider fans became angry and lost sight of what they really were. Instead of Raiders fans joining gangs, gangs joined Raiders fans." Eaton went to cite several examples of "Silver and Black thugs" harassing families and "a hard-core gang member with his teardrop eye tattoo threatening to 'fuck up' a thirty-something-year-old housewife who was cheering on the Cardinals" at a game in Phoenix. His theory was that it is "primarily the L.A. or Southern California Raiders fan" that is "giving the Raiders a black eye (no pun intended)." Indeed some of our own Raiders fan friends have the same theory; but is it true?

In the case of Luis Fernando Uribe, I had a chance to investigate the question. Lizet Gonzales, a social worker from Norwalk, grew up down the street from the Uribes and knew Luis well. Would she describe a brutal thug who terrorized the neighborhood and had murder in his heart, as most reports have indicated, or is there more to the story? One evening Lizet, her cousin Hector Martinez, and I sat down at a café in Whittier to talk about Luis. Lizet, a pretty, articulate woman in her mid-twenties, told us about her experience with the Uribes:

I grew up with [the Uribe family]. [Their kids and I] were all in the same class together. Luis joined the army and fought in Vietnam, and was a good husband, too. And he worked at Northrop, so he was a mechanic. He was middle class, you know, a hardworking Hispanic. He was seriously Mexican, not like all the other Hispanics living on the street. So he was born in Mexico and immigrated here when he was young. I called him Dad. He was a very loving guy. He loved his kids. And he loved to party. There was a party at their house every weekend, and during the Raiders season, there would be a Raiders party at their house every single game. There were people over barbequing, the usual. I have a lot of Anglo friends, and it is strange to hear for people who aren't familiar with the culture that you just get together every weekend and barbeque and party. That was the house. It was never out of control. The police never had to come to any of these parties. There were never any fights. It was totally family. It was totally quiet. It was Raider Nation all the time.

I couldn't really tell you what the Raiders meant to [Luis]. I think he was just a fan. It is cultural. If you are Hispanic, you're a Raiders fan, and if you're not, it's kind of weird. It's like you think you're better than the others. But I am not a Raiders fan. A lot of people say [being a fan] has to do with Commitment to Excellence. It is wanting to be better and, you know, being an immigrant and working hard and working for your family and working to get your family better than you were. All of the Raiders fans that I know are Hispanics. I think a lot of Hispanics, a lot of Latinos are Raiders fans, but a lot of Latinos are hardworking immigrants, and when they really want to identify with the culture, they want to be a Raiders fan so they belong. It's to be something. You know, what are gangs about? [When you are a Raiders fan] you aren't doing anything illegal. They just need to belong. It is something to belong to. And when you do identify with the Raiders, people like to party. You become a Raiders fan if you want to party a lot. If Los Angeles had a football team would Raiders fans be for that team? I really don't think so and I don't understand why.

Luis was always outside on the block. He looked after the kids. He looked after us. I guess I always saw him as a father figure. He united people, introduced people. People would talk to him on the street. When people moved in, he would introduce them to the neighborhood. He was kind of like the Dad that I never had. He was not violent. I never knew him to be violent. I've heard the story about what happened at the game. I'm sure there was drinking involved. Well, of course, we didn't hear his side of the story, but my friend was there. That guy he stabbed was egging him on. He gave them dirty looks and said things. Not about the Raiders, but specifically to him, actually. So he finally got fed up and went up to him. The guy started the fight, and he was really big, and I don't think that anybody ever mentioned that. If you've seen the video, he was a lot bigger than Luis. So he took the knife out of his pocket and stabbed him. That's what I heard. There was racial stuff being said. And Raiders stuff, but mostly racial stuff. Yeah like, "wetback Raiders," and stuff like that. People thought they were gangsters, and they weren't. I guess they appeared to be because they were wearing Raiders clothes. And I guess if you're wearing Raiders clothes, then you're associated with being a gangster and that's accepted. Schools don't allow Raiders gear. Luis was just a hardworking guy. He didn't look like a gangster. He looked like a regular guy.

[Luis's family] feels they used him as an example. They're not angry about it because they know that what he did was wrong, which is a surprise to me, but they are really good about it. They're not at all resentful for the fact that he's [in jail] because they feel he did something wrong, but they are resentful of the way he got treated. He had no hope. He never had a chance of being put on probation. I would not make excuses for them, either, because I don't think it's right that they went down [to San Diego] in the first place. They know how they are and they continue to do it. That's your hard-core Raiders fans, but it's not right. They are going down there to get trouble, but they keep going. I'm not saying that it's right for the San Diego fans to overreact, but it's not right for them to go down looking for trouble, either. They love to go. My friends still go to the San Diego game.

Luis has three sons, two daughters, and a wife that he totally left behind. He was the breadwinner and they were living comfortably. I'm not saying that they were well off at all, but now they are seriously struggling, and [his wife] is trying to keep her head up with all her kids. My friend Anthony (he's the oldest) finds himself being the man of the house. Now he is finding himself having to work to help his mom. He's very responsible now. (He's still a Raiders fan.) I guess, in a sense, this has been a good experience for him, but I'm sure he's having a really hard time. The little girl, Luis's daughter, she's the youngest one, and she really misses her dad. She's very bright, but she goes to see him and says, "Yes, my daddy's at work and I want to see him." And I find a little bit of the Raiders in her. She's nine now, and she does have a little resentment of the Raiders because she misses her dad. They all miss their dad.

So if Luis was not a hard-core gang member, but rather a mechanic, and if the Raiders Bandit and the thugs who assaulted the couple after the Vikings game were neither gang members nor dreaded Los Angeles fans, what gives? While it is clear that gang members may have attended Raiders games, their numbers would not be large enough to create the mythic portrait of the Raiders fan/thug. In fact, as we have already noted, other sports fans, like those in Philadelphia, Detroit, New York, New England, and even some small college towns, have filled jails in the bowels of stadiums, brawled, fought police, stolen other fans' wheelchairs, thrown bottles and chunks of ice at coaches, referees, and each other, and prompted the fear of opposing fans. Still, without denying some of the grim realities behind the negative image of Raiders fans, they inspire a particular dread that frequently verges on hysteria. The Los Angeles gangster myth is central here because the Raiders fans gained this reputation at the peak of the gang hysteria of the late eighties and early nineties, years when inner-city Los Angeles came to represent all that troubled the suburban mind and inflamed the media's imagination. As Mike Davis has noted in his seminal book on Los Angeles, *City of Quartz*:

Like the Tramp scares in the nineteenth century, or the Red scares in the twentieth, the contemporary Gang scare has become an imaginary class relationship, a terrain of pseudo-knowledge and fantasy projection. But as long as the actual violence was more or less contained to the ghetto, the gang wars were voyeuristic titillation to white suburbanites devouring lurid imagery in their newspapers or on television.[9]

What happened in the case of Raiders fans is that the presence of a small number of gang members at games has inflamed this fantasy and every incidence of violence is held up as evidence of the accuracy of the "pseudo-knowledge" that sees a gang member behind every Raiders jersey, when, in fact, it may actually be "regular guys" crossing the line rather than the dreaded criminals from South Central Los Angeles. The fact that "normal" folks might lose it and commit violent acts just does not fit into the dominant narrative about American society. Our experience at more than a decade of Raiders games in San Diego is that the gang fantasy is based on the presence of a tiny group of fans who are then overdetermined to represent half the stadium. This exaggerated fear, in turn, becomes a source of conflict as suburban San Diegans see "inner-city" hooligans everywhere, and the average Raiders fan is made to feel like one of America's Most Wanted.

What is also frequently at play in the stands in San Diego is the crossing of borders of class and race. Because the Raiders still have a far more urban, blue-collar, and multi-ethnic fan base than most other teams, the annual Raiders invasion of San Diego seems like a black and brown invasion to many Anglo fans, or an unwelcome infusion of "street" for mild-mannered suburban Chargers fans of all races. The result is an annual festival of hysteria and ugliness that is far less one-sided than the media portrays. Like the gang panic, the Raiders fan panic is a yearly display of largely white suburban anxiety writ large. The annual Raiders–Chargers game is then both a literal and symbolic battle between the imagined communities of America's Finest City (San Diego with its bland suburban hegemony) and Raider Nation (Oakland and L.A. with all their rough urban flair). In the national imagination, Raider Nation is the loathed "other," the "bad side of town," and it just doesn't matter if reality is a bit more complex.

Even the Raiders themselves have gotten into the "blame Los Angeles" game, with Al Davis saying after the team moved back to Oakland, "One of the [other team] owners said to me, 'I'm scared to get off the bus.' Howie [Long, a Raiders star] would always make a big issue out of it, how he wouldn't bring his wife and kids to the game. And other guys would say, 'I'm not bringing my wife.'" Raiders star Tim Brown also pointed to Los Angeles as the source of all the trouble at Raiders games as he commented on the controversy of the Raiders' yearly visit to San Diego: "I tell people—especially the guys who weren't in L.A.—when we go to San Diego, this is basically how the fans were in L.A., all the fights and all the turmoil that's up in the stands. That's basically how it was in every L.A. game we had."

Interestingly, however, a 1993 study showed that there were fewer crimes around the Los Angeles Coliseum during Raiders games than there were at Lakers or Kings games and the crimes that did occur there were largely nonviolent crimes. The point here is not to deny that there were and are a good number of fights at games or to excuse the violence, but to point out that something about Raiders fan violence captures the imagination more than other fan violence, and that Los Angeles Raiders fans, even more than Oakland fans, are the favorite boogiemen.[10]

I explored this topic with Mychal Odom, an African American graduate student at the University of San Diego who is completing a master's thesis on urban history, and who is also a former college player and a huge Raiders fan from L.A. He argued that this image has to do with the way people have come to see the urban working class:

The people in the eighties that are Raiders fans are the children of working-class people, but there are no more jobs and gangs have come in and crack cocaine, and all this stuff that essentially changes the community, which essentially changed the image of Raiders fans. The image of a hard worker is a lot different than the image of an unemployed person, an unemployed criminal. Where I'm from in Long Beach we had shipyards. The shipyards finally left in the mid nineties, but they had been sliding for quite some time and so had the aerospace industry. At the same time aerospace is losing jobs and factories are closing. Gangs are on the rise. And NWA [the rap group Niggers With Attitude] comes out and popularizes this picture of street gangs who were wearing Raiders clothes. I think that's when the two images [Raiders fan and gang member] collided. So what people are really talking about when they talk about Raiders fans is a change in urban America.

Mike Davis supports Mychal's observation by noting that, during the eighties, "Most tragically the unionized branch-plant economy toward which working-class blacks (and Chicanos) had looked for decent jobs collapsed." Thus, the Coliseum neighborhood and other troubled parts of urban Los Angeles in the heart of the media capital of America became a nationally broadcast ad for urban blight in movies and the media at large. The contrast between Oakland and Los Angeles, then, is not a contrast between cities (Oakland's flatlands suffered problems similar to those of inner-city L.A. during the period that the Raiders were in Southern California) but a contrast between an idealized memory of a noble, hardworking (and whiter) working class in 1970s and before and the criminalized and demonized blacker and browner working class of Los Angeles in the eighties and nineties. Thus observers can nostalgically valorize the mythic Raiders fans of old while heaping scorn on the debased lumpenproletarians who have tainted the image of the lovable rebels of the golden era.[11]

And as Mychal explained, the myth of "South Central" spread with urban problems:

Places that are South Central Los Angeles now weren't South Central Los Angeles before crack cocaine and the whole crack epidemic and sprawl of gangs. I've seen parts of Long Beach referred to as South Central. Now everywhere is "South Central." It's like there are two Los Angeles's. We have the south of [Interstate] 10 people and north of the 10 people and now all those people west of the 405 [freeway] want to separate off from the City of Los Angeles. That's interesting.

The Raiders for me always represented the people that at least live in Los Angeles County, the people who haven't moved out of the core. You know eastward or to Orange County or to the north. The Rams were always a suburbs team once they moved to Anaheim. I remember growing up back home in the eighties the Raiders became synonymous with gangs and crime. In Long Beach, the Silver and Black was associated with, locally, the toughest street gangs. So Long Beach has a gang called the Insanes—Insane Crips. They're probably the largest gang in Long Beach and the most criminally active. So they donned Raiders clothes. And up in Los Angeles, I think the Eight Treys (the 83rd Street Crips) wear Raiders clothes also. Monster Cody was an Eight Trey. So black and silver and the Raiders is closely associated with toughness in the streets and that's one thing we picked off was the toughness of the Raiders. Gang members happened to like the Raiders, and I think that's an interesting dynamic whether it's sports or not. Back home, if something becomes synonymous with what gangs wear, you couldn't wear it anymore.

When people talk to me they say, "Well you're not the typical Raiders fan, you're not a thug." The Oakland fans I've talked to said that that whole correlation comes out of the L.A. Raiders image. They're located right in downtown Los Angeles, in the heart of L.A. and around the corner from South Central, where the fans fight other fans. But that image is not always accurate. What people don't know is that Crips have other colors associated with them as well. Where I grew up gangs were associated with the Ducks and Cowboys. Snoop Dogg wears a lot of Steelers clothes because his gang, which is the Rolling 20s, wears black and gold. I can't even wear a Raiders jersey in my neighborhood because my neighborhood is a Cowboys neighborhood. I have friends who are Raiders fans but they're not going to wear Raiders jerseys. North Carolina is big, you know, baby blue for the neighborhood Crips. They wear North Carolina down in San Diego. The Crips wear Dodgers colors all the time, too. But it's the Raiders image that got associated with the toughness of street gangs and the media ran with the idea.

Why am I a Raider fan? To me the Raiders embodied professional football. And it was so cool because Art Shell became the first black coach and he had played for the Raiders. My uncle and dad remembered him from the seventies. To me the Raiders are solid and steadfast. I don't buy throwbacks because the Raiders have had the same jersey for forty years. They were the one team that reached across to a bunch of people. You know working class, middle class. I have Cambodian friends who are Raiders fans, Vietnamese and Laotian. So across a lot of ethnic groups, they are all Raiders fans. One thing about the Raiders is that you either liked them or you didn't like them. It's just not one of those teams that you don't care about. In L.A. you were either happy because the Raiders won or because they lost. The Raiders are the team of urban L.A. The logo alone is the toughest thing to me—the pirate, the eye patch, the knives. What I really noticed is upper-class Los Angeles fans, if they were Raiders fans, didn't openly associate with being a Raiders fans because of what they looked like. Obviously not all of the people who bought tickets were from the ghettos of Los Angeles. The people who were proud of being a Raiders fan were proud of being from Los Angeles. Because you had to not be afraid to simply go to the Coliseum right in the middle of it. And really it meant you had to be comfortable with going into the inner city. [The fear of the Coliseum] was almost a self-fulfilling prophecy. If you act like you know what you are doing, then you don't get picked on. You don't insult people by acting like you think they are going to do something to you. That's one thing. Raiders fans weren't all Latinos or all African American. There were Asian American Raiders fans, white fans. Outside of race, there were a lot of commonalities.

What I always thought was cool is being proud to be a Raider fan because that means you can be proud of being from the ghetto, you know? That's what it means to me, whether you are from South Central, East Oakland, or wherever. You can be proud of where you're at. That's what the Raiders are.

Now working-class people of the eastern cities have been heralded by the conservatives in America as their heroes, but not Raiders fans. It's a mask for white working-class conservatism. The Republicans' working class is still less working class. I have yet to meet a person who is a staunch conservative and a Raiders fan. I'm pretty sure they're out there, but I've never met one.

I'm proud I'm not from San Diego. I'm from Los Angeles and I'm a Raiders fan, so you can't beat me on much, no matter how much you want to try. I know when I don't want to be messed with [here in San Diego] I put on my Raiders jersey, put on some baggy pants, and put on a do-rag and walk around town and people stay out of my way because I'm a Raiders fan. I just like to see people cower, because some people's anti-Raiders sentiment is a mask for other stuff. That's why I get mad sometimes because it's not just football to them. It's more class and race issues to the people who are anti-Raiders. When someone disses the Raiders and they're one of those people who are really trying to step on where you come from, I take that sort of thing to heart. But I am proud of where I come from.

One time I went to a Raiders–Chargers game and there were these religious fanatic people with bullhorns. And they had a little message for me, "Hey, eighty-one." I was wearing my Tim Brown jersey and he says, "Hey, eighty-one, you're a loser. How does it feel to be a loser?" I am like, "Hey man, apparently you don't understand the stereotypes of the folks with the Raiders because if you think we are crazy, then why are you yelling at Raiders fans after they just lost?" So we were pretty mad. I think this is just because the Raiders are kind of the anti–San Diego team. These people make all these crazy comments and then try to hide behind, "Hey dude, it's just football." No, it's not just football. It's more than football, you know? You can insult me all this time, and I know you don't insult other people this way. So that's one thing. And with the Mexican Raiders fans, to some of these [San Diego] people it's the Mexican invasion, like the Mexican killer bee or something. So it's not just blacks. It's blacks and Mexicans. Even though it's close to the border, it's such a conservative culture here in San Diego. That's the biggest fear of conservatives in California—that blacks and Mexicans unite. So that's how they look at it. Oh, it's Raiders weekend, right? And it's almost an invasion of San Diego.

The Dumbest Team in America

After the Raiders lost a heartbreaker 27–24 to the Chiefs in Kansas City and fell to 3–8, even the most optimistic adherents of the Silver and Black knew that the boys were finished. There would be no miracle run to squeak into the playoffs at 9–7 and shock the league by gritting it out all the way to the Super Bowl. Rick Mirer was no Jim Plunkett. Safety Rod Woodson was done for the season, joining defensive end Trace Armstrong, running back Justin Fargas, and linebacker Taravian Smith on the injured reserve list, and the only good news was that the misdemeanor vandalism and public drunkenness charges against kicker Sebastian Janikowski had been dropped and the league was delaying the penalties for the players who reportedly tested positive for THG, allowing center Barret Robbins as well as defensive tackles Chris Cooper and Dana Stubblefield to finish the season. When the best news in Raider Nation is that punter Shane Lechler's 45.67-yard average leads the NFL's all-time list, things are looking grim. Nonetheless, as our Nigerian cab driver sped my friend Hector and me from the airport to our hotel, there were still six cars and trucks already lined up to spend the night outside the Coliseum gates in inclement weather nearly twenty-four hours before the kickoff in the Raiders–Broncos game.[12]

That night Hector and I went searching for the ghosts of Raiders past, stopping in for a beer at Clancy's, one of the old Raiders hangouts. It had been transformed into Clancy's taqueria and was empty except for two cops sitting in the corner working on enchilada plates. There was still Raiders stuff on the walls along with Raiders pint glasses and a Budweiser Raiders dummy, but the place was dead and the woman was sweeping up, getting ready to close at nine o'clock on a Saturday night. Back out on Broadway, we passed a homeless family heading toward the freeway underpass. The mother was wearing a Raiders AFC Champions t-shirt. We stopped for dinner at Everett and Jones Barbeque, outside of which was still a huge banner that read "Mayor Jerry Brown Bets Everett and Jones and Brothers Beer that the Raiders Beat the Bucs: Join us for the OFFICIAL SUPER BOWL PARTY. GO RAIDERS! JUST WIN, BABY!" Well, at least everyone had a good meal that night, I thought, as we sat down in the packed restaurant surrounded by roadhouse Americana and Raiders pennants to survey a menu that featured a host of fine dishes and a picture of the owner with Charles Woodson. As opposed to Clancy's, this lively, black-owned business was humming with activity as the wait-staff delivered huge platters of brisket, ribs, and chicken and the sound of blues blared out of the lounge.

After dinner, Hector and I walked by a wiry old guy in a sharp black suit and a stylish hat. It was Birdlegg of the Tight Fit Blues Band, who had stepped out to get some fresh air between sets. Hector and I made our way through Jack London Square passing by a bronze statue of the famed author of *Iron Heel* standing by the harbor and ended up in Heinold's First and Last Chance Saloon, one of Jack's old hangouts, and whose bar was permanently tilted due to the great earthquake of 1906. We both teach at the same community college in San Diego and both grew up in Los Angeles as big Raiders fans. Hector, a stocky, red-headed, green-eyed Mexicano from El Monte, nursed a vodka and soda as we chased the ghosts of L.A. Raiders past:

> Growing up in a Mexican family, nobody in my family was into football. My dad was into baseball and boxing, and that's what I grew up watching. He didn't understand football too much. I remember watching the 1980 Super Bowl when the Raiders won it. I was ten years old, and I started to root for them after that. Then in 1982 they moved to L.A. and it was like my favorite team coming to L.A., and I loved it. I remember the *Herald Examiner* had a special feature, "Meet Your Los Angeles Raiders." They had pictures of Cliff Branch and Jim Plunkett and I remember putting them up in my room. I really liked Cliff Branch—he was my favorite. Then Marcus Allen got drafted. He was an SC guy [USC Trojans]. Marcus Allen was big. So my friends in the schoolyard started rooting for the Raiders. You started seeing a lot of Raiders

gear all over when they went to the Super Bowl.

After the Super Bowl, especially, everybody became a Raiders fan. The Raiders homogenized a group of fans where everybody liked them. I think it was the toughness. By that time I think I was in junior high. The whole mystique and toughness of the team became associated with a lot of kids in the neighborhood. We had gang problems and stuff like that, so everybody wanted to be a little bit of a tough guy, and the Raiders were an easy fit for those kids. El Monte is definitely blue collar, definitely working class. I ended up going back there [after graduating from USC] and teaching high school. There was a certain drive that I would take (when I was staying with my parents) from my parent's house to the high school where I was teaching, and it could have been [like driving through] a Midwestern blue-collar town. It kind of looked like the rust belt, you know, a rust belt kind of look. [El Monte] is a blue-collar town, about 85 percent Mexican. And it's still run by Anglos, with 15 percent of the population. They have one major gang that they call El Monte Flores, which dates back to like the nineteenth century. It's the name of a family and they were kind of like renegades. There were two or three gangs, but the Flores ended up defeating the other gangs in a gang war. Actually, the kids are a lot safer now that there is only one gang. Once everybody became unified, the Flores reestablished itself as the top gang and it kind of mellowed things out.

In some ways it was a common experience among Latinos in L.A. for football to be part of the experience of becoming American. I think it is a generational thing, too. My parents, having immigrated from Mexico, really had no knowledge of the sport. If they had come from a bigger city perhaps they would have, but they came from a rural part of Mexico. It was like something they couldn't understand. It was complicated trying to learn a new language; it was too uncomfortable for my dad, so he never got into it. As I got older, eventually football surpassed baseball as my favorite sport, and as we went to college, it was really interesting. I went to USC and became a big fan and I started to get my father into it and now my father watches every

USC game. He also watches the Raiders games. He's a big football fan now. He also speaks English a lot better, and he also became an American citizen. So it kind of corresponded.

My dad really learned about football as he assimilated. You know he always brings up sports. He says he has a big memory of football—a Mexican coach [Tom Flores] went to the Super Bowl. My dad doesn't know much about the history of California or anything like that, but he knows that [Flores] came from around Fresno, from a working family.

I asked Hector what he made of the appropriation of the Raiders logo on the "Los Malosos de Aztlan" t-shirts and other hybrids of this sort:

I think the Raiders shield and the Raiders emblem is something that a lot of people associate with the working class. I also think a lot of the Chicanos feel they are outside of the mainstream. They don't feel like they are part of middle America, mainstream America. They feel like they are on the outskirts. I think it's very easy to have the football tie-in with the Aztec symbols, which are very non-American. The Aztec calendar [which is on one popular shirt] is tied to the Raiders shield [in the case of this t-shirt the Raiders helmet is on the Aztec warrior at the center of the calendar], which is also something people see as outside of the mainstream. It's the same way some people might feel about the rebel flag. You know in the South, the stars and bars have become a white working-class symbol. It's a white working-class symbol, right? It's like they feel they are being shit on by the mainstream, being marginalized, so they have to have a symbol of marginalization. A lot of Chicanos and Latinos are very much into the Raiders. That's what they do.

The term "Chicano" itself, was once seen as a derogatory term, one some older Mexicans still see as derogatory, but now people have taken it and feel a sense of ownership of it. So it's easy for people to make the connection between the Raiders logo and the Aztec symbol. They both represent marginalized people and embody pride in identity. There is a commonality there. What does Al Davis stand for? Al Davis is the Raiders way. He's not about doing it the way the other NFL teams do it. That's the myth—we're going to win, and we are going to do it our way.

I think the Raiders have always been associated with gangs and tougher kids. A lot of it has to do with the colors, the black and silver, the whole bad-guys-wear-black type of phenomenon. And look at the logo [the pirate]—it's a symbol of marginalization. So a lot of people like the image, like my friend Frank's dad, who is a businessman, a former vice president of Tele Mundo, and was a season ticket holder. On the weekends he was being bad, kind of letting his hair down. He'd go to the Raiders game, watch the fights and get a lot out of it. It's like the doctors and lawyers who ride Harleys. It's a symbolism and a phenomenon that people connect with on a very different level than any other football team. It's a connection with something wilder. It's the wild west. It's very American in that sense. There were a lot of fights [at the L.A. Coliseum] and people were saying, "I'm not going to take my kids to see people get their asses kicked" and stuff like that. And there were all these other factors in Exposition Park—the working-class presence, the drinking and violence. It all did scare off a lot of upper- and middle-class folks, but the ones that stuck around were looking for some adventure on the weekend. They'd ride down the street on a Harley and live a more exciting life and it made them a little eccentric to the people back in the office to say, "Hey, I went to a Raiders game." And the people in the office would say, "Oh my God, you did what?"

If you are a Raiders fan, it's like a code. Whenever people are wearing Raiders gear and you identify another Raiders fan, it's more of a connection. It is more of a college-type thing. I've been wearing Raiders gear before, at a random event, and somebody else with Raiders gear yells out, "Raiders!" as a way of acknowledging me. I've done that to people, too. It's not something that happens with other teams' fans.

Game day was cold and rainy and the prospect of standing in a damp, windy stadium for three hours was tempered only by the thought of beating the Broncos. As our waitress at breakfast said, "I just hope they beat the Broncos. If they beat the Broncos that would really make me happy. It would make the season okay."

On BART I looked over an *Oakland Tribune* article entitled, "Is Arnold Losing His Superhero Status? Planned Cuts Will Hit Hardest at Lower End of Economic Spectrum." In the sports section, Broncos quarterback Jake Plummer talked about his experience with Raiders fans: "An older lady, a grandmotherly type was walking down with Raiders stuff on. I kind of waved at her and I got the bird back. I was trying to be nice, but I learned my lesson. Those guys around there—whether it's men, women, or children—are in it to get after you." What else was left? I wondered. As the *East Bay Express* put it, "With Oakland's season long ago spoiled by lethargy, player vs. coach infighting, and a designer steroids scandal, the only things that Raider Nation have to look forward to the rest of the year besides five more chances to spackle on hypoallergenic silver and black death masks and trot out their spike-encrusted hard hats are a few prime opportunities to drag the other teams' postseason dreams into the mud with them." Enter the Broncos, my personal nemesis and bringer of more bitter Mondays than any other hated foe. I was just starting to work up a serious fit of loathing when it was ruined by turning the page and seeing the "Queer Eye for the East Bay" take on Al Davis. Apparently Al needs to lose the sweatsuits and the pinkie ring, "And get a new pair of sunglasses immediately. These look like they were given to you in 1962, when you first became coach of the Raiders. The mini-pompadour thing in front of your hair is also about four decades behind the times and harks back to the days of Vitalis." This, I was sure, was yet another bad omen in a season of bad omens.[13]

At the Coliseum stop the driver announced, "Raider Nation stop. The Coliseum, where the Raiders are going to crush the Denver Broncos! The AFC Champion Oakland Raiders will crush the Denver Broncos! Raider Nation stop." We headed into the stadium in our silver-and-black rain ponchos, and I spotted a guy wearing an old-fashioned striped prisoner's outfit chatting with a very wet silver-and-black Uncle Sam. At the seats, our Black Hole neighbors checked on the status of Kelly's pregnancy and said hello to Hector. The game started with baseball-like scores as the Raiders went up 2–0 with a safety and built the lead to 5–0 by way of a Janikowski field goal. After this, a costly penalty led to a Broncos touchdown, but the Raiders took the lead back briefly with another field goal. That was the last time they would score as the Broncos took a 14–8 lead into halftime after another Raiders penalty led to Denver's second touchdown. They were giving it away. In the stands, there was some action as a handful of Broncos fans were roundly booed and heckled, with one losing his orange beanie to a hostile takeover and another Donkey fan requesting a police escort out of the stands. In the second half, the Raiders stayed with Denver through a scoreless third quarter before more penalties and turnovers finally cost them the game, 22–8. It was a dismally frustrating debacle that sent the Black Hole trudging home wet and cranky. After the game, Callahan exploded at a press conference saying, "We've got to be the dumbest team in America." The Raiders were falling apart at the seams. It was like a bad dream that just would not end.[14]

Nevermore

After losing a pathetic, forgettable game to the Steelers in Pittsburgh, there were rumblings that the Raiders had given up. And as I headed into Oakland once again with fellow Raiders fan Danny Widener, I must admit I was looking forward to the Holiday Beer Tasting at the Pacific Coast Brewing Company more than watching the Raiders further unravel against the Ravens. Like the bird in the famous Edgar Allan Poe poem after which Baltimore's gridiron heroes are named, many Raiders fans were saying, "Nevermore." For the first time all season, I saw no cars lined up to get into the Coliseum as we passed by the front gate in our cab. Nonetheless, here we were, just in time for the tasting. After about ten or more samples of holiday cheer apiece, Danny and I ambled down to the produce market on 2nd Street to visit Oaklandish, a gallery and store run by the Nonchalance Collective that features pop culture nods to Oakland's subterranean history with posters, t-shirts, and a variety of other kitsch devoted to the

Black Panthers, the Hell's Angels, the Symbionese Liberation Army, graffiti artists, Julia Morgan, Bruce Lee, and more. When I told a woman there about our project, she showed me an "Aztlan Raiders" t-shirt. After milling around amid the eclectic array of hip-pop cultural artifacts, we went downstairs and found another bar, where Danny and I talked about the Raiders.

Danny is a tall, handsome, light-skinned African American man with long dreads and a compelling presence. Currently an assistant professor of history at University of California at San Diego, Danny grew up in Echo Park and Venice and went to school at UC Berkeley while living in East Oakland, making him a rarity in Raider Nation, an L.A. fan with East Bay credibility. Danny's take on Raiders fans is both academic and personal:

> Football is intensely conformist. It's the only major sport where all the players are always masked, essentially, so people are always anonymous, and even the management ethos of football makes players much more interchangeable. It's like the combine, the way they measure things. There is nothing like that in baseball or basketball. So the Raiders offer people a way to be connected to institutions and also be anti-establishment. And I think that's another kind of thread that defines what it means to be a Raiders fan. What could be more conformist than having sixty thousand people [in a stadium] and you're all dressed the same and yet somehow you are expressing your individuality?
>
> So these white guys from San Leandro and these black guys from East Oakland bonded with the Raiders, not the A's. Oakland is an industrial city. It is a working-class city, and there is class mobility for some of the whites but even those whites don't have mobility to the upper class. And so the Raiders fans, you see them come in from BART. They come from Walnut Creek, San Leandro, over the hills. They are insurance salesmen. They are contractors. They're heavyset—they're Schwarzenegger voters essentially, right? And the African American population, the black population that comes to those games is still relatively young or it is multigenerational, and it is a central-city, Oakland crowd. And it does allow this bond. It allows that kind of interracial

bonding about Oakland, but I don't think it's so much about a progressive antiracism as it is about Oakland's deep insecurity, which is transformed into this collective thing. But it's interesting, the political thing about it. You have these working-class black people who are really lumpen [or underclass] and these petty bourgeois whites. I mean there is a substantial Latino population in Oakland but it's relatively new. [Raiders fans] are a fractured and threatened group. It is the social basis for fascism. It's the culmination of the ideology of action movies—the class anxiety and the masculinist culture—it's an amalgamation of a lot of things. Something about this is really about insecurity and fear and projection.

In terms of masculinity and being a Raiders fan, it's not as aggressively proletarian as the Steelers. People have accessed edginess in a way that they hadn't before, you know? The other thing is that the Raiders have always been, I think, conceptualized as a black team. And part of the popularity of the Raiders with fans has to do with the fact that Americans are now willing to accept—for the same reason that gangster rap is popular with white teens—something that gives them access to "the other." So the Raiders are an urban team, unlike the Rams or the Chargers or the Cowboys. They have always had bad asses. And I think the Raiders allow you to access that same thing you do when you see a gangster movie. It's the gangster theory of life. So there is something about the Raiders that's simultaneously urban, but also fast-paced and modern. They don't just run the ball. So it's interesting because when you think about why you like a team, the style of play along with simply the colors and all that stuff is part of it. There is an aesthetic dimension to it. There is a moment where all the kind of imagery, the style of play, the uniform, the aesthetic—the form and function is all there with the Raiders. And the Raiders used to win. We like that—we're Americans, after all. But the Raiders really seized on that gangster mentality, that flashiness, all of those things in a way that's unique if you think about them in comparison to other teams.

My uncle would take me to games [in Los Angeles] and certainly the attendance in the stands was much more heavily people of color than you would be likely to see in any football stadium today. [Other teams' audiences] at one point would have been predominantly working-class families, but now they are suburbanized, relatively affluent. The Raiders, I guess, managed to deal with the loss of this fan base by moving geographically and by picking up this kind of gangster community. The Raiders also probably would have been a different team if they hadn't moved to L.A., because when they moved they acquired this Chicano and black fan base at the same time gangs became a part of those communities and entered the whole American imagination. I think you could separate football teams into different categories. There are the suburban teams like San Diego and Seattle. Then there are middle-American teams like Dallas and Denver. The Miami Dolphins are *Miami Vice*, kind of flashy. They're legitimate Raiders rivals stylistically. Except for their goddamn flipper.

The Raiders have a leader, a Godfather. The guy who is ultimately in charge. The only person who comes close to Al Davis is Steinbrenner [who is] equally loathed and equally meddlesome. But unlike Steinbrenner, Davis has actually made a lot of innovations in the game. [He is a] hated figure, but somebody who really has revolutionized the game. What is Raider football? It's Al Davis, the Godfather. Anytime you have a glorification of the gangster worldview and that community, you automatically have to have a discussion of authenticity, you have to have a discussion about history. So there are all these narratives about class, so that's one thing. But a core element, the essence of being a Raiders fan is being the real thing. The gangster image just replaced the lunch bucket image [in that regard]. I mean, the spectacle of Raiders fans, the way the commentators talk about it is one thing, but there is actually very little real social violence in American professional sports among American fans, nothing compared with other countries. We are extremely well behaved. Some of that is because they don't let them get as drunk as they used to, and of course we make everybody sit in their seat and follow all these fucking rules in the United States. And we're free: "Love your freedom and sit down." So other teams besides the Raiders just don't allow you to maintain your sense that you're not conforming, not taking any shit off of anybody.

Trying to place people ideologically in America [gets you] into this populist stew. You could construct a scenario that says Raiders fans have always been a working-class team. They are a working-class team in Oakland. When they got to L.A., this was still the working class. It was South L.A. But I think politically it's probably much more to the right because it's essentially about the glorification of violence. It's also about nostalgia. Since they have moved back to Oakland it has much more of this cast of nostalgia. Nostalgia is key.

On game day, the Black Hole was abuzz with the news that Saddam Hussein had been captured in Iraq and, for today at least, the hope was that the end of the fighting was near. Some of the patriots in the crowd had duly adorned the usual black-and-silver signs and outfits with little American flags. Sadly, they couldn't have been more wrong. Danny and I had noted how surreal it had been to see the TV footage of the Iraqi Communist Party celebrating by waving red flags as Wolf Blitzer and company steadfastly ignored the irony. Several rows in front of us, I noticed a guy in black-striped silver facepaint holding up a UFCW picket sign for the TV cameras. Holding the line in the Black Hole, I thought: beautiful. He posed for a picture and afterward, Jack, one of my Black Hole neighbors, said, "It's hard being out there all day and all night. People need something to pick up their spirits. You should get out that picture so people can see it. That would be great. It's not like those CEOs are not making enough money. Shit." I nodded in agreement and we talked a bit about strike tactics, the old sitdown strategy, and how hard it was for unions to get their message out in the media. How long would they be out? Until January? March? It was a hard bargain, we agreed.

Only 45,398 fans showed up that day, but the Raiders rewarded the smallest crowd since 1998 for their loyalty by stunning the AFC North–leading Ravens 20–12 in a gritty, well-played game. There weren't any Ravens fans in the stands and there weren't any hassles with the cops, although I did hear a rumor that a narcotics officer was cruising the restrooms dressed in Raiders gear and a dog mask. I thought of Danny's musing about the incipient fascism in a football crowd. While I had to admit that there is always an element of Raider totalitarianism when it comes to greeting fans brave enough to come and root for the other team in the Black Hole, I just couldn't write off the whole phenomenon as right-wing groupthink. It's love and war at the same time, I thought, not one *or* the other exclusively. As for the nostalgia, yes, it was there. But nostalgia for what? Maybe it was just my hangover, but the whole Raiders fan story was shaping up as a bittersweet tale of loss and unnamed yearning. Danny was having a good time hamming it up in his silver Mexican wrestler's mask. The Raiders played tough defense and sent the crowd home happy. It was the last good day of the season. As we crossed over the bridge to BART, Danny saw a guy selling five-dollar gear and quipped, "Nothing says Christmas like a 'Fuck All Raider Haters' t-shirt!"

Busted

Thirteen

Just Lose, Baby

This team needs help. Serious help. They could be in this dark hole forever. They need some damage control. . . . I know how to get rid of the
psychic virus.
                    Dr. Richard Crowley, sports psychologist, on the 2003 Raiders

For the Raiders, it was Super Bowl or nothing. As a result, their fan base
will take the deeper hit. There will always be hard-core Raiders fans—
those guys in spiked shoulder pads you see in the Visa commercials—but
for those who only recently started affiliating with the team, this year
probably destroyed their interest.
                            Christian End, Sports Fan Research Group,
                    on the toll the 2003 season was taking on Raider Nation

It sure does hurt. It's definitely difficult and frustrating, but we're hanging in there.
                    Leroy Zine, President of the Oakland Raiders Internet Boosters

The Raiders' last home game was another Monday Night Football affair, and
despite the Baltimore win, the rumors were flying about dissension in the locker
room and there was speculation about whether this would be Charles Woodson's
last game in Oakland. A far better result, most Raiders fans thought, would be

to fire Coach Bill Callahan and do whatever it took to keep Woodson. Such was the tenor of the conversation Chuck and I were having as we walked through the airport in Oakland before spotting a bomb-sniffing dog outfitted with a Raiders shield. The country was on Orange Alert, and Reno the Raider dog, which we learned was the dog's name, was keeping us safe from terrorists. "Isn't that animal cruelty?" said one smart aleck passing by with a rolling suitcase. "Only if it was the 49ers," the cop with Reno shot back. The cab driver saw our Raiders gear and said as he dropped us off at the hotel downtown, "I'm right behind you. I've got the world's biggest rib eye waiting for me. After this stop, it's tailgate heaven. Forget the game."

Chuck and I went out to get a few beers and a burger before the game and talked about how he came into the Silver and Black family. Chuck, whose house has been San Diego Raiders central for our whole gang of Raiders fans, runs his own business and has followed the team religiously for years, despite the fact that he has never lived in Oakland or Los Angeles. A tall, lanky, brown-haired Anglo in his mid forties, Chuck has a relaxed, easy manner. We started by discussing how he came to be a fan as a kid:

I started watching the Raiders in 1971. My dad was a General Motors executive, so I was living overseas in Singapore. Having never lived in the US, always living overseas with my folks, I was going to the Singapore American School, and, once a week during football season, they would get a game. There was no football on local TV in Singapore, so the only way I knew about football was that once a week NFL Films would send down film on reels, and we would watch the highlights in the auditorium. I have a memory of not even knowing who the Raiders were—I just liked the uniforms, the logo on the side of the helmet, their style of play. They weren't clean-cut. They had long hair. They seemed to have more of an image of being outlaws. So I was a renegade just by the fact that I liked the Raiders. Any time you're a Raiders fan, whether it be in Singapore or San Diego, you're a renegade. There is something wrong with you. You seemed to be a nice guy, but what's happened?

All I could do for years was follow them by the newspaper until I moved to the States in 1976 and was exposed to the Raiders on a daily basis. So it really has almost nothing to do with place at this point. You don't think of Oakland as a place. I couldn't have told you where Oakland was on a map, to be honest with you. I knew it was near San Francisco, and I had been to San Francisco a few times for visits while traveling in the States [because my brother lived there]. [By the 1980s] we were living overseas again in New Zealand, and my dad and I [traveled back to the United States] looking at some schools for me in the L.A. area. We [went to] a preseason game against the Rams at the Coliseum. This was my first ever exposure to pro football, and I already knew I liked the Raiders.

[Once I was living in San Diego as an adult] there was no Direct TV at that time, so if you wanted to see a game you had to go to a bar unless you were lucky enough to have [the Raiders game] as one of the games on the network that day. This was almost, to me, as good as going to a game because you were with fellow fans and you had that feeling that goes along with being with fellow fans—united in your love for the Raiders. Being in the bar in San Diego was strange because [the one I went to] was a Philadelphia Eagles bar in the morning and a Raiders bar in the afternoon. But every week, you were with your friends for three hours on a Sunday afternoon. There were people— you may not even have known their names—but you were high-fiving them and hugging them during big touchdowns and you looked forward to seeing them on a Sunday afternoon. Everyone there was a personality.

When I asked Chuck what one of his best experiences as a Raiders fans was, he told me the story of heading up to Oakland for the AFC Championship game in 2003:

Being a diehard fan, I obviously took the first plane out at 6:15 in the morning to Oakland. Why did I need to get there seven hours before the game? It was probably because I knew I wouldn't be able to sleep the night before so I might as well get to the airport. The airport bar wasn't even open, much to the chagrin of the passengers of that particular plane [who were all Raiders fans]. It was an amazing sight. We were all standing outside the gate before they opened the airport before 6:00 a.m. on Sunday. There was nobody else there. The security line looked pretty strange because it was full of people with black shirts on—and the funniest thing was the reaction of the people who just happened to be on that flight and didn't know what was going on. They were just flying to Oakland maybe to connect to somewhere else and the looks on their faces, you know, looks of unease. There was a gentle muttering behind newspapers, "What is occurring?" You know, "Who are these people? Are we safe? Can we be safe? Should I take the next flight instead? Today could be a bad day."

I just remember going to the back of the plane, which I always do, and I made the mistake of sitting next to the problem trio who were demanding beer before the plane even taxied away from the gate. And what was shocking about it was that the flight attendant, using her best judgment, felt it was better to placate them rather than enforce the rules. You know, no alcoholic beverages before the plane takes off. And not only did she give them one beer, she gave them two beers each as she felt this would take care of the situation. Unfortunately, it only gave way to boisterous behavior, to say the least, to the point where there were complaints by the other passengers. As a Raiders fan, you are dressed in the colors and I felt excited [about the game] yet disappointed that this was occurring on the plane, because I was worried that we might not even get away from the gate. We might have had to return to the gate. At this point, most of the plane was chanting "Raiders!" and the plane just took off and going up, the pilot even greeted us, "Good morning, Raiders fans! Happy to have you aboard." The whole plane was chanting, "Raiders! Raiders!" That's something that sticks in your mind.

Getting from the airport to the Coliseum was an amazing experience. As soon as we left the airport you started seeing people waiting to get into the stadium, but they didn't open the gate for a while. Some people were there for a full week from the end of the prior game and the police were actually allowing them to park in the street. One lane was given to people to park in. [The drive to the Coliseum on the BART bus] was one of the most amazing sights I've ever seen. Fans had staked out their territory and were tailgating and partying and had created a mini tent city. It went for more than a mile. There were people set up in gas stations where the owners had let them park and put up their tents and the mini-malls were filled with people. There was just a sea of black-and-silver people. It was barbeques with all the smoke and the smells and music booming and excited, happy, happy people. Some of the other people on the bus obviously had no idea what was going on and it was really something else for them. I mean it said something for true Raiders fans, and it made me proud to be wearing the colors that day, without a question because everything was civil and yet people were having the time of their lives. And knowing what the city and the fans have gone through over the years, it was like a culmination of everything they had been waiting for.

There was a downside to being a Raiders fan as well:

Every year now [for over a decade] I've been going to the Raiders–Chargers game in San Diego. I always get there early to park and we just have our party. We don't get out of hand or do anything crazy, just a few beers. This one Sunday I had my Smoky Joe [grill] out and I needed some newspaper so I see this one couple, maybe in their fifties, reading the Sunday paper. And I walk over to them and say, "Hi, I forgot to bring a newspaper to start the chimney for my barbeque. Is there any way I can have a piece of newspaper from you, a part you don't want?" And the woman looks at me and said, "I'm sorry, you're a Raiders fan. I can't help you." And I said, "Really?" And that was it. That let me know where I stood in some people's eyes, you know? There was a feeling of disrespect and it let you know what's going on in [other fans'] heads when it comes to Raiders fans. It was just one of those things that you chuckle about. You try to make peace. I find myself constantly telling people, "We're okay." You keep on trying to justify yourself. It's like, "You don't need to be scared of us. I know there is an element out there, but . . ."

The crackdown in security is incredible now compared to what it used to be. A couple of years ago it was out of control because the Chargers fans were still the majority, but you were getting that hard-core L.A. fan base who were acting out. I still remember leaving the stadium one year after the Chargers had won a close game, and as we were exiting the stadium these two women got into a huge brawl and they were rolling on the ground and creating a storm. People started engaging in fisticuffs and a little one-on-one female brawling ignited this major spread of violence. I remember the fights at that game. It was just dominated by fights in the stands. People were paying attention to what was going on in the stands more that what was happening on the field. The game was almost secondary after awhile. It was just rows of people moving when a fight erupted, waves of people moving. It was clearly out of control. Everybody loves going to the game and seeing good-natured battling between the fans, verbally and whatnot. But when it turns physical, it's just no fun for anybody.

It was probably one of the scarier things I've seen. It was violent to the point where you just wanted to run the other way, get out of there as fast as possible and not get caught up into it because you are wearing the colors. [The cops] would just throw you in with the rest of them. That evening was like shades of *Apocalypse Now* with police helicopters hovering above the parking lot informing us that we had a certain amount of time to leave or be arrested. We were told to get in our cars and leave immediately. It felt like a police state. It had gone beyond the bounds of football. People had gone to the game to have fun and had ended up in a police state.

It was only a three days before Christmas and the sellout Monday Night Football crowd at the Coliseum was sprinkled with a myriad of black Santa's hats as well as a number of Green Bay cheeseheads playfully wrapped in silver tinfoil. Before the game we learned that Packers quarterback Brett Favre's father had died and that Brett had dedicated the game to his memory. As if in deference, the Raiders' defense handed Favre and the Packers an early Christmas present by allowing pass after pass to drift by the outstretched hands of a host of defenders into the grateful clutches of Green Bay receivers. The 41–7 Packers' trashing of the Raiders in front of a nationwide audience was the worst debacle I have ever witnessed in person. Merry Christmas to all, I said to myself, and to all a good night. After awhile, those of us who stayed developed a sense of humor about the ugly proceedings and noted that if we had to be slaughtered, why not by the Packers, the most Raiders-like team in the NFC with their own pack of rowdy, blue-collar fans who like to dress up and consume large quantities of Milwaukee's finest? Still, the relentless punishing stung. We stayed to the bitter end even as large portions of the Black Hole fled in horror. As we walked to BART after the game, Chuck asked, "Did that really just happen or was it a bad dream?"

Brawling Alone

Three days after the Green Bay massacre, our son was born on Christmas Day, putting all the petty mental anguish the Raiders had inflicted on us in proper perspective. After seeing my sweet little boy, Walter Henry Mayhew Miller, enter the world, I just couldn't get too worked up over the fact that Raiders punter Shane Lechler had been snubbed and left out of the Pro Bowl. Even the Raiders' record-setting worst season after playing in the Super Bowl couldn't get me down. In the big picture, not much of what people get exercised about in their daily lives really matters. The prospect of heading to the Raiders game after a week of nearly sleepless nights in the hospital brought to mind a quote from the other great American transcendentalist I named my son after, Henry David Thoreau:

> The mass of men lead lives of quiet desperation. What is called resignation is confirmed desperation. From the desperate city you go into the desperate country, and have to console yourself with the bravery of minks and muskrats.

A stereotyped but unconscious despair is concealed even under what are called the games and amusements of mankind. There is no play in them, for this comes after work. But it is characteristic of wisdom not to do desperate things.[1]

Nonetheless, on Sunday, I would go to the game with the hospital bracelet still on my wrist.

The headlines going into the annual Raiders–Chargers contest were traditionally fearful stuff like "Wary San Diego Hopes This Raid Is Peaceful," "San Diego Hopes to Keep Order," and "They Can't Stem the Silver and Black Tide." This year the *San Diego Union-Tribune* was more staid, announcing plainly, "Security Tightens for Chargers–Raiders." The report detailed the greatest hits of high arrest totals and reminded readers that last year even a San Diego sheriff's deputy had been nabbed on suspicion of assaulting a security guard. Still, there had been no murders like the one at a recent Padres game, the paper assured its readers. This year, fans would be subject to hour-long lines, increased monitoring, and pat-down searches all in the service of "a safer family environment for fans and employees."[2]

King Stahlman Bail Bonds got into the act as well, rerunning its famous local Emmy Award–winning "The Raiders Are Coming" ad that had received considerable coverage during the previous Super Bowl. When we called King Stahlman to ask if the game really did help their business, his son-in-law, Mike Hardwick, told us that the ad was intended to be a joke. "We were playing on the perception of Raiders fans," he told us, "That they're nuts." The ad was shot the day after the Raiders made the 2003 Super Bowl, and they were surprised when some people took it seriously. Ironically, Hardwick told us, his business did *not* see an uptick in business as a result of arrests during Raiders week. At first, Mr. Stahlman didn't like the commercial, we learned, fearing an onslaught of angry Raiders fans—but that never happened. The office did, however, receive a visit from *The Best Damn Sports Show Period* after the commercial ran.

When we checked back in with the staff of Rock Bottom Brewery, we learned

458

that, after a season of cursing, groping, and brawling, the local Raiders fan club had not renewed its arrangement with the establishment. "I hate having negative feelings about any group. I resist feeling prejudiced," said Rock Bottom waitress Bethany, "but the Raiders fans bring it out in me." Interestingly, I had thought the new Raiders fan club digs were pretty gentrified compared with the place they used to hang out in. Back in the eighties, when I watched every game with the Silver and Black legions at College Billiards, a rowdy polyglot of bikers, blue-collar types, street denizens, and pool hustlers used to gather to watch the Raiders on a single fuzzy big screen. I remember enjoying the wildly diverse crowd of whites, blacks, Samoans, Vietnamese, Latinos, and Raiders nuts of all sorts happily mingling amid the sea of covered pool tables. The same bunch would show up every week, and there was a rough, warm camaraderie that brought together people who might normally never speak to one another. My old friend and Raider Nation expatriate Jon Cariveau of Guayaquil, Ecuador, was my companion in those days. When we looked him up recently he recalled:

> Starting in the early eighties, the College Billiards Center on El Cajon and 54th was the headquarters of the San Diego Raiders Fan Club. It was always a good crowd at the Billiards Hall, with Raider fans of all stripes, everyone in silver and black. The standard game fare was the half-pound extra-greasy cheeseburger and fries plate and, of course, pitcher after pitcher of beer. Everybody got along and we would all get progressively louder as the beer flowed, but generally a reasonable amount of order was maintained. After a Raiders victory, people would usually hang out for a while and celebrate, drinking and talking about the game. But after a loss, the place tended to clear out pretty quickly. I remember after one particularly tough loss, things got a little scary. There was this very big guy who used to wear a Raiders hat with black tape streaming down from under it. He looked like an NFL lineman, that kind of size. After this loss, he was a little wasted, pissed off, yelling and screaming until the staff managed to get him to leave. My buddies and I were leaving, and I remember seeing him on the way out, walking down El Cajon

Boulevard, smashing out windows of parked cars with his bare, bloodied fist. Then he went around behind the pool hall and started slamming into the trash Dumpster in the parking lot. He was slamming into this huge metal Dumpster like it was a tackling dummy on a practice field. We got out of there pretty quick. Obviously, this guy was very passionate about the team.

Sometimes stuff like this can give Raiders fans a bad name, but my experience is that this is the exception to the rule. Raiders fans care about the team and do get pissed off at times, but we generally don't get out of control. There's a lot more goodwill than obnoxious behavior. I remember one time I had shared a table with a guy named Terry a couple of times. Got to know him a little. One game we were at a table with him and I was putting down a lot of beer. The game ended and we took off before him. I was working graveyard at the time at a supermarket, so I went home and crashed out, and when I got up to go to work at midnight, somewhere between still buzzed and hungover, I realized I didn't have my wallet. I figured I must have left it on the table at the bar, so it was probably long gone. Then I remembered Terry had mentioned he worked at a post office branch up near College and El Cajon Boulevard. I figured maybe he found my wallet at the table after we left. I didn't really know him too well, but after work in the morning, I took a flier and went up to the P.O. branch he said he worked at. Sure enough, there he was, looking about as hungover as I felt. As soon as he saw me come in, he pulled my wallet out of his pocket and handed it to me. I thought that was pretty damn cool. I offered him ten bucks for helping me out, but he wouldn't take it. That's more like the Raider fan brotherhood I'm used to.

Throughout the eighties, the San Diego Raiders Fan Club once or twice a year would organize a bus trip up to the L.A. Coliseum to see a game. There was a woman at the Billiard Center who was in charge of things and would always remind everyone to sign up for the trips. It was a great deal. For twenty-five bucks you would get round-trip bus fare, a tailgate party with food and beer before the game, and a decent ticket. These things were a blast. The bus rides were party central. Everyone brought their favorite beverages for the ride. The one problem I remember is that you had to be at a shopping center parking lot in Clairemont at 5:30 in the morning to catch the bus. That could be a little early for a Sunday morning, so I remember that in the true Raiders fan spirit, we usually decided it was easier to just stay up partying Saturday night than to get up that early. Occasionally this may have required some minor chemical assistance to pull off, which made for some long, interesting game-day experiences.

One year on the trip I went with two friends. The bus was full, so they sat together and I sat a few rows away next to a Latino guy I'd never met before. We both had small coolers full of beer for the ride and we soon found out we had both brought pint bottles of Bacardi to smuggle in for the game. We had a good time on the way up, drinking beer and nips of straight rum, talking about the team. A big black woman I knew a little from the pool hall was sitting across the aisle from us and heard us talking about sneaking in the pint bottles. She told us we were doing it the wrong way. She said, "Check out my binoculars" and handed me her big, clunky old-style binocs. They felt a little too heavy. Then she reached over and started unscrewing the focus button. Immediately I smelled wine. "Go ahead," she told me, and I took a sip out of the binocs. "This is the way to get stuff into the stadium," she told us.

The Raiders lost that day, so everyone was pretty quiet getting back on the bus. We all took the same seats because we'd left our coolers on the bus during the game. I got there first and took the window seat. Soon my new buddy came in. He was totally ripped, could hardly walk but somehow managed to stumble into the seat next to me. I said something about it being a tough game, too bad they lost, and he couldn't even talk, just sort of mumbled back to me. The bus got rolling, and my new friend kept sort of mumbling and leaning his head onto my shoulder and sort of drooling. I kept trying to kind of push him away and get him to sit up straight. After a little while, he suddenly reached down for his cooler on the floor and got it partly open before belching out a veritable waterfall of foul-smelling puke. He got most of it into his cooler, but some of it got onto the floor, my shoes, and my pants. When he finished, he pretty much passed out and kept on leaning into me, puke dribbling down his chin with me trying to make him sit up straight. This was a little hard to take, especially being that I was in a pretty intoxicated state myself. I wanted to get the hell out of there but I was pretty much stuck.

I tried at least standing up a little to get away from the smell. My woman friend across the aisle was talking, saying how gross it was and so on. After awhile she stood up and told me I needed some more wine, offering me her binocs again. I said no, but thanks anyway, and I clearly remember her standing there in the aisle and saying to me "You havin' a weird experience. You got a cooler full of puke at your feet, this guy keeps leanin' on you and I'm standin' here drinkin' wine outta binoculars. You ain't never gonna forget this bus ride." I had to laugh—and it turns out she was right.

While I ruminated about the old days, I thought of the famous line from Dr. Samuel Johnson, "He who makes a beast of himself gets rid of the pain of being a man."

As game day approached there were the requisite local news stories about the Raiders invasion, and one station interviewed a sports psychologist whose sage wisdom was that "fans of losing teams are more likely to vent their anger." By this logic, I thought, Bengals fans must occupy half of an Ohio state penitentiary. Truly violent Raiders fans were a tiny minority, and most people with any sense could easily avoid conflict with them. In my sleepless delirium, I thought it might be useful to compose a list of guidelines for Chargers fans or others who feared for their safety. Something like "ten ways to avoid be pummeled by an angry Raiders fan." With my lifetime of experience in Raider Nation I had observed a few things that I thought might help:

1. Understand that aggressive Raiders fans, like the thanes in *Beowulf,* operate by the principle "wergild" or "man price," which means that any insult or challenge to their pride must be answered in kind, otherwise they must forfeit their life or one of their relatives.

2. Know that as good patriotic Americans, aggressive Raiders fans have also adopted the Bush doctrine of preemptive strikes. Consequently, an angry fan may deem it necessary to take aggressive action as a way of stopping you from insulting them before you even have the chance to do so. They are generally unrepentant about faulty intelligence.

3. Don't call guys with tattooed tears on their faces "Fucking losers." In fact, avoid using the f-word with them at all costs and consider not engaging them in conversation at all. Generally avoid eye contact.

4. The tailgate is the mead hall. Respect the aggressive fan's mead hall. Hosting the opponent's flag next to a mead hall or carelessly strolling by in the enemy's colors may be perceived as a direct challenge to Raider National Security. For God's sake, stand down!

5. Remember that even though only a very small percentage of Raiders fans are violent felons, even mild-mannered construction workers from Pacoima don't take kindly to being flipped off and may have to kick your ass.

6. Avoid slurs of all kinds, particularly those related to race and class. Remember that you are a mild-mannered suburbanite who works in an office park. You are not tough and 99 percent of Raiders fans can kick your ass. Even the women who you think are safe to flip off can beat you up.

7. Your status as a security guard in a yellow windbreaker does not strike fear into the heart of Raider Nation. Don't be an idiot or a bully or they will kick your ass.

8. If the Raiders win, take the harassment from aggressive Raiders fans good-naturedly and you will win over your hated enemies. Otherwise, well, you know . . .

9. Remember that, as the Center for Aggression Management explains, "It is . . . important to understand that aggression begins when any individual becomes unable to cope with their anxiety. At this juncture, the mind perceives this anxiety as a threat and the body responds by producing the fuel

to aggression: adrenaline. Thus begins a spiral of aggression that can, all too often, result in violence. As spectators observe their favorite players conducting themselves in an aggressive way, they too become aggressive in the stands, especially when these elements are exacerbated with the introduction of alcohol. Contemporary research in the field of 'mirror neurons' has demonstrated that individuals watching an action movie experience to some degree the same fear and aggression as if they were actually experiencing that action. Whether athletes, spectators, vendors, participants in gaming establishments or worker-on-worker aggression, the Sport, Leisure & Entertainment Industries provide a prime setting for potential aggression." Translation: If the Raiders lose, be afraid. Be very afraid.[3]

10. It is not safe to cut off Raiders fans or flip them off from the alleged safety of your expensive land tank. The aggressive Raiders fan will happily jump over the median and kick off your side view mirror as punishment for this kind of infraction.

On game day, I met my Raiders buddies Chuck, Hector, and Brad, as well as a few of their friends, in the parking lot before the sold-out Raiders–Chargers game. Here I was, back at the scene of the crime, where the hideous nightmare that was 2003 for the Raiders began. There was a kind of evil symmetry to it, but I was disengaged, still basking in the afterglow of my son's birth. After some beer and doughnuts, I left my friends to do one last tour of the tailgates and found my Silver and Black brethren to be in remarkably good spirits, despite the Raiders' dire circumstances. It was four hours before the game and the lot was full with Raiders fans clearly outnumbering Chargers adherents. I ran into a nice Filipino family, two parents with two cute little girls, all decked out in Raiders gear. Their dad, a navy man who was riding a tiny bike, had a big Raiders tattoo on his upper arm and told me that he was trying to start a Raiders fan club in Okinawa. After the family, I ran into some people I'd met in the Black Hole who'd driven their motor home down from Oakland and a bunch of guys who'd come down from East L.A. It was a beautiful day and the mood was festive. There wasn't a hassle in sight. When I came upon the San Bernardino Raiders Fan Club group, one of the members told me, "It's not about winning and losing. It's about family. We're about family." Not a very scary crew, I thought.

At one point, a police car rolled up and when I asked for a comment on Raiders fans from the cops, they told me to turn the tape recorder off, but then one of them said:

> I don't think this game lives up to the hype. There is a spike in fights, but I just think it's the proximity between the two cities. Back in Philly, where I'm from, the rivalries are similar. Here in San Diego, they almost never win, so people blow this game up. It's a big thing for Chargers fans every year, but I'd say Raiders fans are no worse than Vikings fans or any other fans. Maybe a little bit more fired up, but not that bad. I don't know what it is exactly, but people make a big deal out of this game, more than they should.

I thought it was interesting to hear this from a cop who, unlike the local media, actually had to deal with the rough stuff. It confirmed my theory that when one factors in the good, the bad, and the ugly, Raiders fans are indeed not nearly as nasty as their reputation. Everybody has their crazy story, but, for the most part, Raiders fans are pretty good people. The real dirty secret of Raider Nation may be that the majority of Silver and Black fans are average working- and middle-class people who enjoy basking in the Raiders mystique and having a little tongue-in-cheek fun on the weekend. And Raiders fans like to party hard and let it all hang out. But while many of them might enjoy their status as urban folk devils, they are nothing compared to the Chicago Cubs fans of 1900 who celebrated a 4th of July double header with fire crackers and gunfire, yelling "Load! Load at will! Fire!" when the Cubbies won. As has been noted previously, the occasional violence at Raiders games is not historically unique in America, nor does it come close to the wreckage left by their European or South American sports fan counterparts. What the existing violence does threaten to do, however, is kill the party for everyone, since the fear of the unruly crowd fuels the puritans and the enemies of free public space who want to turn every corner of America into a lame, boring G-rated movie with a heavy police presence.[4]

Back at our tailgate, my friends were hitting the tequila and chatting it up with the group next to us who had driven up from L.A. By the time we were ready to get to our seats, the line to get in was wrapped halfway around the stadium. As our bladders filled to painful levels and the line moved at a snail's pace, I noticed security personnel with cameras standing on top of the entrance above the crowd. I thought back to the Super Bowl nightmare as the minutes ticked away relentlessly. Chuck and I had gotten separated from the rest of the group and, after an hour and a half, we had missed most of the first quarter. It was clear that the Orange Alert combined with the Raiders invasion had inspired the authorities to make everyone's life miserable in order to keep us safe from one another. For a moment, I had the temerity to be outraged that I had paid good money for this privilege. I wondered if herding cranky football fans like cattle on the way to slaughter was an effective aggression management strategy. After the first quarter ended and we were just about to call it a day and go listen to the game on the radio, the gate appeared before us. Chuck, who was a little buzzed but far from a menace, gave me an "I love you man" hug in celebration as we approached the elusive gate. Then he almost tripped on a cord that was taped to the ground and had to steady himself on the rail by the entrance. That was it. The SDPD swooped in and cuffed him, no questions asked. When I asked what was going on, the cop said, "You want to go with him?"

After the game, Chuck reported that the cops had kept him in handcuffs in the holding cell in the bowels of the stadium for four hours without allowing him to pee or telling him why he was there. Some of our Raiders brethren were less polite, kicking the walls, and cursing the cops for the whole time. I spent the second quarter looking for a pay phone so I could call Chuck's wife and let her know what had happened. It certainly didn't seem like a good idea to risk talking to the cops. After I got a hold of Sharon, I went to my seat to watch the Raiders lose the game 21–14 to the Chargers. It was a fitting end to a nightmare of a season. On the way out, I heard a woman in a Chargers jersey say, "Now I can tell that Raiders bitch at work, 'Fuck you!'" For the first time in several years, I didn't see a single fight. The Prison Entertainment Complex, it seemed, was a rousing success.

The next day I read that Charles Woodson and Charlie Garner had missed a team meeting and that Coach Callahan had benched them just before the game, nearly provoking an unprecedented team walkout. This might have been a better way to go down as the Raiders' only scores came from kick runbacks in a game where third-string quarterback Rick Mirer was forced out due to an injury, leaving the team in near-total chaos. It was a marvel that they lost by only 7 points. "They quit playing for him," a Raiders official said of the team's reaction to Callahan's move, "You saw that today." As the *Oakland Tribune* put it, "Call it a mercy killing." With the games out the way, the soap opera continued as speculation raged about which players would leave and when Callahan would be fired and who would replace him. Raider Nation had fallen apart. It was the worst collapse of any Super Bowl team in NFL history, and they didn't even earn the first draft pick. Nonetheless, we knew that, as the last group of fans I spoke with in the parking lot said, "We'll be back."[5]

The Decline and Fall of Raider Nation?
Sadly for the small, rain-drenched contingent of 31,000 Raider Nation diehards who endured the Silver and Black's ugly 13–6 loss to the Jacksonville Jaguars in their final game of the 2004 season, the pride-and-poise boys did not come back. Instead, they let Hall of Fame shoe-ins Tim Brown and Jerry Rice go and the team went nowhere. Having lost starting quarterback Rich Gannon in the third game of the season, the Kerry Collins–led Raiders faltered badly, finishing 5–11 to complete the worst back-to-back pair of seasons in team history. After the Raiders finally exorcised the 2003 Super Bowl demons by defeating Jon Gruden's Tampa Bay Buccaneers in front of a delirious sellout crowd in Oakland to start out 2–1, Collins threw interception after interception in the games that followed, and the defense bled points all year long in loss after loss. Midway through the

season, in the second quarter of yet another brutal home field pummeling at the hands of the hated Denver Broncos, the soggy sellout crowd of Raider Nation loyalists let the team have it and kept booing all game long as the Raiders were humiliated by the Broncos 31–3 in a hellish mud bath. Never have I heard a hometown quarterback being booed as loudly and relentlessly as Collins was that day. "Our fans sucked," whined Raider Barry Sims after the game. It was, as the *Oakland Tribune*'s Monte Poole put it, "Raiders vs. Raider Nation."[6]

While Sims and other Raiders would later make nice and Collins would begin to play better, the boos continued all year long along with chants of "Tui! Tui!" (for backup quarterback Marques Tuiasosopo) every time the offense faltered. Besides the Broncos game in Oakland, other 2004 lowlights included losing to the hapless New Orleans Saints at home, getting absolutely crushed by the San Diego Chargers on the road, and blowing late leads to the archrival Kansas City Chiefs in a pair of home-and-away choke jobs, the latter one on Christmas day in front of a national television audience. Only a stunning upset of the Broncos in a blizzard in Denver stood out as a beacon of hope in the dark night of the soul that the last two seasons had become for the Raider faithful. Well, that and the emergence of bootleg "Revolutionary Raider" t-shirts featuring the iconic image of Che Guevera in a black beret sporting a pirate shield.

Off the field, Raider Nation suffered further. Late in that ill-fated season, excessive revelers were targeted during a police dragnet dubbed "Just Drive Sober, Baby" that yielded thirty-one drunk drivers, twenty-one unlicensed drivers, fifty-two impounded cars, a kidnapper, and one loaded .357 caliber handgun. In the courtroom, Al Davis was handed another defeat when a judge ruled that the McGah descendants had rightfully inherited a partnership in the Raider franchise, virtually guaranteeing future legal squabbles over revenue. The players, however, both present and former, were engaged in the most dramatic fiascos. Raiders defensive standouts Charles Woodson and Marques Anderson were busted for public intoxication near Oakland's Jack London Square in December, raising the spectre of a second NFL drug policy offense for the superstar Woodson. The Raider soap opera continued as troubled ex-Raider All Pro center Barret

Robbins was arrested in San Francisco for punching a guard at the Sir Francis Drake Hotel after the man brought Robbins the glass of water he requested; the guard had found him wandering near the Starlight Room Bar on the 21st floor of the hotel at 7:00 a.m. It appeared that Robbins's emergence from the depths of his bipolar disorder and alcoholism had been short-lived, as only weeks later he was shot and seriously wounded in a tragic confrontation with Miami police.[7]

If all of this was not enough, the bizarre arrest of ex-Raider kicker Cole Ford for a drive-by shootup of famous Las Vegas illusionists Siegfried and Roy's compound rounded out the 2004 Raider rap sheet. Ford, who left football soon after losing his job with the Raiders, quickly went on a downward spiral into homelessness and schizophrenia. Living on and off in cheap Vegas strip motels and occasionally camping in the desert, Ford's strange behavior first resulted in his being banned from the Monte Carlo Resort and Casino for scribbling notes on paper while apparently plotting a lawsuit against the establishment that demanded he be paid for every bet the sports book had accepted on every college and professional game in which he had played. After losing the suit, Ford went on to pump four shotgun blasts into the magicians' mansion from the safety of a white minivan while yelling, "We need to get these [expletive deleted] out of our country!" No one was injured, however, and the police have ruled out a hate crime against magicians or Germans as a motive. Upon his capture, the once clean-cut USC grad's mug shot evoked comparisons to Charles Manson and the Unabomber. As of this writing, Ford's attorneys are contemplating an insanity defense. The placekicker's NFL decline began when, in 1996, he missed a chip-shot field goal against Tampa Bay that lost the game and knocked the Raiders out of the playoffs. Perhaps the unfriendly sign posted by Raider Nation in the Coliseum at a subsequent game signaled his impending run of bad luck. It read: "FORD=Found On Road Dead."[8]

All of this seems to add up to some seriously bad mojo for Raider Nation as the team emerges from yet another horrendous season just in time to try to convince their beleaguered personal seat license holders to renew them for 75 percent of the original cost. Will Raiders season ticket holders sign up for another ten years of this torture? The jury remains out. With many fans realizing how much cheaper it is to purchase tickets to one or two big games a year and watch the rest on TV (or listen on the radio if it's not sold out), it might take a miracle to resell them all. Even if this happens, the Oakland-Alameda Coliseum complex would still be almost $100 million in debt. Hence, it seems harder and harder to imagine a new golden era for Oakland Raiders football. Still, the faith persists. Many of our Black Hole neighbors insist they'll be back even if the team isn't. As we marveled at the generosity of our Raiders fan cohorts who gave up their dry seats to stand in a cold pouring rain so we could sit under the overhang with our year-old baby at the Jacksonville game, I surrendered to hope. Maybe the Norv Turner era would bring back the glory years after all. Sure, Kerry Collins's multiple gut-wrenching interceptions and drive-killing fumbles were not encouraging, but the young receivers were promising. If we could only pick up a durable running back and entirely retool the league's worst defense. It seemed impossible, but as veteran safety Ray Buchanon put it, "In this organization, the weirdest thing that can happen usually happens. So you never know what's going to happen."[9]

Afterword

Rebels of Oakland

So what, after all, is the meaning of Raider Nation? What would fuel fans to come back after such a miserable season? To put it in academic terms, Raider Nation is a polysemic signifier, a symbol that means different things to different people. When fans put on the pirate shield, they imagine that it stands for hyper-masculinity, bad girl flair, street toughness, working-class pride, gangster menace, Oakland pride, Los Angeles pride, ethnic identity, rebellion, persistence, a strong work ethic, cut-throat competitiveness, family tradition, freedom, individuality, community, hegemonic domination, seventies nostalgia, ironic affiliation with the bad guys, old school football, a social Darwinist corporate ethos, a counter-cultural party scene, a sign of the little guy, the outsider getting one over on the favorite sons, and any number of other things.

Perhaps the most interesting aspects of Raider Nation are its contradictory meanings as an imagined community. Raider Nation is a place where fans go for community connection that transcends barriers of race, gender, and class, and it is a site of vicious competitive individualism and petty exclusionary tribal-ism. It is a family, and it is a place to get away from the ties that bind. Raider Nation valorizes discipline and excess. It is an imaginary land of authenticity, and it is a mass-marketed, trademarked commodity. Raider Nation celebrates working-class grit even as it valorizes the dominant values of a market economy that has ravaged the American working class. But most compelling of all, it is an embattled desire for some kind of community in an age when community is in decline.

The team's past moves and its perpetual threats of future moves have broken the firm ties it has had with the city of Oakland, but it will always be haunted by the ghost of Oakland past. As Monte Poole observed after viewing *Rebels of Oakland*, a fine documentary about the Raiders in the seventies, the current Raiders have lost the "ability to bond with the community," as have the players, "whose contracts have taken them well beyond even the most liberal interpretation of blue collar." Poole goes on to note that "Today's Raiders—and pro athletes in general—prefer the suburbs, isolated from the guy who carries a lunch bucket. Investments tend to remain under cover. There are thousands of restaurants, lounges and retail establishments in the Bay Area and [as opposed to the players of the seventies] not one Raider has his name out front." The consequence of all this, according to Poole, is that "while the Raiders fan might be knee-deep in disappointment as the team stumbles to the finish, it could be worse. Your identity is not at stake, and the agony is not likely to reach down into your soul."[1]

Although the notion that there ever was a time when professional teams really did have a genuine connection with the community is probably a myth of a golden era, it is a powerful one nonetheless. Sports fans strain against the notion that they are simply rooting for the interests of one corporation against another, even as team owners brazenly move, raid public funds, and do everything they can to shatter the illusion that community interests have anything to do with their bottom lines. And it is this phenomenon of "corporate delocalization" that defines the experience of contemporary sports fans and that particularly hits Raiders fans both in Oakland and Los Angeles who have had their team taken from them and have had to stare the naked truth of American sports and indeed America itself straight in the face. As Robert Putnam argues in *Bowling Alone*, with the "gradual but accelerating nationalization and globalization of our eco-

No cash refunds

nomic structures" has come, "[t]he replacement of local banks, shops, and other locally based firms by far-flung multinational empires" which "often means a decline in civic commitment on the part of business leaders." The trend is clear, "As Wal-Mart replaces the corner hardware store, Bank of America takes over the First National Bank, and local owners are succeeded by impersonal markets, the incentives for business elites to contribute to community life atrophy." In the case of professional sports teams, they are no longer even vaguely interested in representing "communities." What sports owners want are "markets" full of "corporate supporters" whose interests are, in turn, to sell products to other "markets" of affluent consumers. It hardly matters where these "markets" are as the real money is generated by television contracts making the regular fans in the stands little more than props whose input pales in comparison to the luxury suite set.[2]

Why do the Raiders seem to loathe Oakland? As a recent *USA Today* article pointed out, "At least six teams are at a 'significant disadvantage because of their venues' and several others have trouble keeping pace with richer teams. . . . [T]he Denver Broncos' annual operating income, boosted by a new stadium, is at least $60 million more than the AFC rival Oakland Raiders."[3] Thus, despite the fact that there is "not a single franchise that is not profitable," the rules of the game dictate that the Raiders need even more profit to "Just Win, Baby," city, tradition, and fans be damned. The Raiders organization is a corporation marketing itself to other corporations, as are all the other teams in American professional sports. Just like other American corporations that have deemed it necessary to value "flexibility" over loyalty to their employees or even a minimal sense of social obligation and have demanded unprecedented control over our politics without giving much back to the body politic itself, professional sports teams have gotten into the game of bilking and screwing over their fans and then demanding more from them. And we are suckers for it because sport is, in our imaginations, a mythic space "outside" of history, economics, and politics. We know this isn't true, but our hearts lead us astray time and again.

Hence the nostalgia that permeates Raider Nation is, for me, a yearning for the days when Ken "the Snake" Stabler was my childhood hero, and I didn't know anything except that he played by his own rules, won the Super Bowl, and was the coolest guy in the league. For many more fans, it is a yearning for a golden era when the team was connected to a place and you could root for your working-class heroes without much cognitive dissonance. It is a yearning for a utopian imagined community that brings everybody together. It is a desire for something other than "one market under God." And even that yearning is strained, as one fan pointed out: "You know, with professional football, like basketball, baseball, or any professional sport, you are required to suspend a great deal more disbelief on both sides—as both a player and a fan. I mean you look at these professional football players now. The game ends. They play together. They clearly like each other more than they like their fans." Still, we want to be part of something that, if just for one moment, makes us feel we are bigger than ourselves.

Acknowledgments

We owe a special debt to Rosalie Kramm and Chris Jordan, without whose technical assistance this book would not have been possible. In addition, thanks goes to Colin Robinson, Abby Aguirre, Lizzie Seidlin-Bernstein, Maury Botton, and everyone else at The New Press for all their help with this project, as well as to Steve Hiatt for his fine editorial, design, and typesetting work. Our friend and photographer extraordinaire, Joe Blum, also deserves a medal for letting us drag him through Raider Nation and its hinterlands.

Special thanks also go to Jim Zamora, Monte Poole, Dave Newhouse, Michael Oriard, Chris Rhomberg, and Mike Davis, for their contributions and advice.

We are also particularly indebted to Bobby Davis; Michele Clark; Dennis Smith; Mark Henderson; Renay Jackson; Hank Mahler and family; Joe and John Spinola; Kevin, Menish, and the firefighters; Scott Schillo; Megan Bauer; Ricky and Bob Ricardo; Jimbo; Amanda and Carrie Donnelly; Chris Eaton; Carlos Canal; Lizet Gonzalez; Mychal Odom; Hector Martinez; Danny Widener; Chuck and Sharon; Bradley Bang; Jim Mahler; Rick Cassar; Jon Cariveau;

Jennifer Cost; Roberta Alexander; and Alys Masek.

Raiders players Roland Williams, Mo Collins, Brad Badger, Eric Johnson, Rick Mirer, John Parella, Frank Middleton, Charles Woodson, Teyo Johnson, and Tom the security guard at training camp all graciously gave us a few minutes of their time as well.

We are also grateful for the input from Mike Sheehan, Randy Leppard, Victor Cotto, Mark Shelton, Jim Freeman, Brad Richardson, Andrew Miller, Patty and Pedro, John Dreisbach, Michel Hines, Bernard Anderson, Griz Jones, Tony Pizza, Nicole Joyner, Singh Shady, Malcolm, Mikie Valium, Darth Raider, Mike Rosaker, Dan Bartolomeo, Buck Allred, Eugene Jeffers, J.A. Miller, Stephanie Sandlin, David, Kerry Smith, Stephen Dixon, Gary Glasser, Terry Gartner, Mohamed Noor Ahmed, David Slack, Kris Snider, Daniel Chen, Marc Lein, Steve Lamoreaux, Margaret Caraway, James Shock, Tim Bryner, Mark Bryant, Mary Anne, Shawn Utterback, Jan Frost, Scott MacCarroll, Tony Lara, Larry Mastin, Peach, BlackHole Mike, StonerDude and Raiderhed, Slackenloader, Marc Guitierrez, Jeff Childs, Guadalupe Loera, Amanda Briggs, Nancy Machianado, Clifford Bolden, Bonesaw, Steve Clark, Dale Pendexter, Anthony Nardi, Lee Hutchinson, Steve Waite, Steve Poland, Derek Ryce, Paul O'Shanassy, Artur "Fred" Chielowiec, Massimo Corsi, Mark Phillips, Barujo, Elva Salinas, Jim T, Jeff Haldeman, Jeff Clark, Dave Laughlin, Amanda Logan, W.S. Song, Mark Wilson, Bonnie McDonald, Phil and Angel Ramirez, Traci the Raiders Cat, Larry the Raiderman, Mike and Jenny, Donovan and Jack, Mark "Gorilla Rilla" Acasio, the "Oaktown Pirates" (Azel, Kimmy, and Melvia), Mario Garcia, Frank and Trinity Klein, Chains and Lady Chains, Malcolm, Señor Raider Man, Lee "the Flea," "Shieldhead," Gus Cardenas, George and Anthony, "the Raidiator," "Skull Lady," Raider-Gloria, Kim and Trotter, Bonnie, Robert, Dino, Jersey John, Roberto, Joyce, Ron, Pat, Beth at Rock Bottom, Mike Hardwick, Bethany, William McHugo, Charles F. Pollock, Tim Bartlett, Ron Snow, Raider John of Rhode Island, David Surpanch, Amin Badruddin, Derek Ottman, David Gramp, Dave Nesbitt, Justin Schummer, Dennis Meier, Dave Kostka, Chris Muntz, Scott Luck, Clint Hedges, James Shook, Andrew Conner, Debi, Warren, Terry

Johnson, Rex Krohn Jr., Henry T. Zukowski, Brian Stransky, Steve Cilurson, Ray, Keith Kaczmarcyk, Michael Lupton, Phil Nemeth, Dave McFarlin, J.B., Jeff Sturgill, Tony Lamonica, Douglas Gordon, Rayda Joe, Scott, Anthony Penn, Donald Dold, Kenny Sapp, Mark Calet, David Schiller, Bernie "the Coach" Nace, Shawn Simpson, Josh Kitzerow, RaiderMadness, Tim Smith, Big Cory, Timothy Puett, Doug Hopkins, Steve Childers, Glen Citerony, Leon Satz, Jeff Corman, Rich Castro, Hofer, David Walsh, Corey Oliver, Mike Pulis, Rich, Jose Tolentino, Marty Rogers, Brad "Woody" Woode, Mike Reynolds, Amy Collins, Paul Garille, Mark Lawless, Angelo Bottoni, James Goodell, Yvonne Lara, Carl Scheel, LeRon Beason, Leroi Archuleta, Bobbie Joyner, Christie, Kris Olson, Dave Keys, Veronica Valdez, Brandon Castillo, Glenn Heinrich, Mary and Gary Degler, RedDog, Charles Tinsley, Richard Webb, Brad Kopp, and the hundreds of other fans who sent us e-mails and gave us anonymous interviews over the last two years.

Special thanks go to our Black Hole neighbors who tolerated our cameras and note-taking for the entire 2003 season: Al, Colleen, Carrie, Monroe, Charles, Shawn, and their friends as well as the hundreds of anonymous fans who universally responded to our requests for interviews and pictures with openness and generosity.

We are also grateful to the bartenders and wait staffs at Ricky's, the Pacific Coast Brewing Company, the Fat Lady, Heinold's First and Last Chance Saloon, Eli's Mile High Club, Yoshi's, and the bar with no name in the midst of the produce market for tolerating our turning their workplaces into interview central, letting us use the phone, and always being warm and welcoming.

Finally, we would like to thank Al Davis for over forty years of the good, the bad, and the ugly.

Notes

Preface: Paradise Lost

1. *Paradise Lost,* ed. M.H. Abrams et al., *The Norton Anthology of English Literature,* vol. 1 (New York: W.W. Norton, 1979), book 1, lines 254–63.
2. Ibid., "The Argument"; lines 106–10.
3. *San Diego Union-Tribune,* Jan. 17, 2003.
4. *Oakland Tribune,* Jan. 21, 2003.
5. *San Francisco Chronicle,* Jan. 20, 2003.
6. *Oakland Tribune,* Jan. 19, 2003; *San Diego Union-Tribune,* Jan. 17, 2003.
7. *Song of Myself,* ed. Harold W. Blodgett and Scully Bradley (New York: W.W. Norton, 1968), section 16, lines 346–49.

Introduction: Raider Nation as an Imagined Community

1. Michael Oriard, *Reading Football: How the Popular Press Created an American Spectacle* (Chapel Hill: University of North Carolina Press, 1993), 2, 34; Pete Williams, "Can Football Now Be Considered America's Pastime," *Street and Smith's Pro Football 2003 Yearbook,* June 2003, 42; *New York Times,* July 10, 2003.
2. As Oriard puts it: "Imagine our receiver is black, the defender white. Or one of them from Notre Dame, the other Brigham Young; one from the Big Ten, the other from the Southeastern Conference; one a candidate for a Rhodes Scholarship, the other a known drug-user; one a street kid from the inner city, the other the son of a wealthy cardiologist; one a well-known volunteer for the Special Olympics, the other an arrogant publicist of his own athletic brilliance. Certain teams have their own distinctive images: think of the Cowboys, the Bears, the Raiders, the 49ers in the National Football League" (Oriard, *Reading Football,* 3).

3. Ibid.

4. One can usefully view football as an allegory of American culture in that an astute observer can read in it one of the central ideological contradictions of American society—the simultaneous embrace of the values of extreme competitive individualism emblematic of late capitalism and a utopian embrace of the very community that capitalism erodes. In his second book, *King Football: Sport and Spectacle in the Golden Age of Radio and Newsreels, Movies and Magazines, the Weekly and Daily Press*, Oriard himself makes a similar point as he notes football's "simultaneously integrative and exclusive" function: "It represented the racial, class, gender, regional, and religious values and prejudices of a diverse people, while at the same time providing a common interest where those people came together, their prejudices in tow." This is clearly not the only story that football and its fans tell, but it is a central and compelling one.

   In *Reading Football*, Oriard insists that football is a "multiply interpreted text" that is part of "a diverse, contested, yet still ideologically freighted American culture." It tells many stories about gender, race, class, work, play, and violence. While it is about "many things," he continues, "what precisely it says depends in part on its many interpreters: the fans or viewers." Football can't mean just anything because the game defines its own boundaries of meaning without determining the specific meanings within those boundaries. Its cultural power, Oriard maintains, resides in its "framing" of certain questions and not others, while the freedom of the fan depends on "interpretive possibilities." Interestingly, after this intensive effort to negotiate between what he calls a reading of football as a mass cultural "allegory" and an impossible effort to determine the "specific interpretations of a million readers," Oriard settles on analyzing sports writing as a mediation between the contest and its audience and leaves any serious consideration of fans behind. Importantly, Oriard completely neglects the fact that fan identity is not simply a product of how fans "read the game" but also of how they see themselves as fans and how others see them. In some ways, fan identity, particularly among the most passionate adherents, is partially autonomous from the game itself. All Oriard has to say on the matter is that it is indisputable that there is a "collective nature" to watching football and that "whether the sense of community that results in these situations is spurious or real can be endlessly debated." It is our contention that Raider Nation is indeed a "real" community of sorts and that it is obviously tied to but not always totally dependent on the "contest." (Michael Oriard, *King Football: Sport and Spectacle in the Golden Age of Radio and Newsreels, Movies and Magazines, the Weekly, and the Daily Press* [Chapel Hill: University of North Carolina Press, 2001], 15; Oriard, *Reading Football*, 8, 16, 18, 19; Oriard, *King Football*, 17)

5. Dean Chadwin, *Those Damn Yankees: The Secret Life of America's Greatest Franchise* (New York and London: Verso, 1999), 39, 40.

6. Ibid., 55.

7. Ibid., 57.

8. In addition to overcoming differences of social, political, or economic interest, the imagined community transcends time and space. Anderson notes that the imagined community as we know it came about in the eighteenth century with the birth of "homogenous empty time" that developed with advent of the novel and the newspaper, which allowed people to represent "the kind of imagined community that is a nation." Central to this was the notion of simultaneity:

> The idea of a sociological organism moving calendrically through homogenous empty time is a precise analogue of the idea of the nation, which also is conceived as a solid community moving steadily down (or up) history. An American will never meet, or even know the names of more than a handful of his 240,000-odd fellow Americans. He has no idea of what they are up to at any one time. But he has complete confidence in their steady, anonymous, simultaneous activity.

One of the factors that helped create imagined communities as we know them was "the almost precisely simultaneous consumption ('imagining') of the newspaper as fiction." Indeed, Anderson notes Hegel's suggestion that the morning newspaper had come to serve as a substitute for morning prayers, a meaning giving "mass ceremony" of imagining performed privately "in the lair of the skull" by millions of people: "Yet each communicant is well aware that the ceremony he performs is being replicated simultaneously by thousands (or millions) of others of whose existence he is confident, yet of whose identity he has not the slightest notion." The incessant repetition of this ceremony created a "vivid figure for the secular, historically clocked imagined community." In addition to the repetition of the ritual, the newspaper reader's observation of other people sharing in the consumption of "replicas of his own paper being consumed by his subway, barbershop, or residential neighbors" continually reassured him "that the imagined world is visibly rooted in everyday life."

A final example of simultaneity points to another payoff one receives for membership in an imagined community—unisonance: "Take national anthems. . . . No matter how banal the words and mediocre the tunes, there is in this singing an experience of simultaneity. . . . At precisely such moments, people wholly unknown to each other utter the same verses to the same melody. The image—unisonance." And the payoff of unisonance is a feeling of becoming part of something larger than oneself. This sense of harmonious connection, of belonging is perhaps the greatest pleasure of an imagined community. As Anderson puts it, "How selfless this unisonance feels! If we are aware that others are singing these songs precisely when and as we are, we have no idea who they might be, or even where, out of earshot, they are singing. Nothing connects us all but imagined sound." And yet it connects us powerfully. (Benedict Anderson, *Imagined Communities* [London: Verso, 1983] 5, 6, 7, 25, 26, 35, 35–6, 145)

9. Robert D. Putnam, *Bowling Alone: The Collapse and Revival of American Community* (New York: Simon and Schuster, 2000), 287.

10. As Dunning puts it: "In short, in modern societies, sport has come to be important in the identification of individuals with the collectivities to which they belong; that is, in the formation and expression of their "we-feelings" and "we-I" balances. Through their identification with a sports team, people can express their identification with the city that it represents or perhaps with a particular subgroup within it such as a class or ethnic group. There is even reason to believe that, in the context of complex, fluid, and relatively impersonal modern industrial society, membership of or identification with a sports team can provide people with an important identity-prop, a source of "we feelings" and a sense of belonging in what would otherwise be an isolated existence within what Riesman . . . called the 'lonely crowd.'" (Eric Dunning, *Sport Matters: Sociological Studies of Sport, Violence and Civilization,* [London: Routledge, 1999], 6)

11. Ibid.

12. As Rowe observes, "A 'values vacuum' has been created whereby many people feel alienated, no longer believing deeply in anything, identifying with anyone, or feeling committed to any cause outside the immediate interests of themselves and their immediate relatives. An opening exists, therefore, for enterprising parties to engage in the 'consciousness' trade . . . to help supply the meaning and commitment that rapid social change under late modernity or postmodernity has evacuated from many lives. But what phenomenon has the emotional force to bind symbolically the fragmenting constituents of society, especially where there is abundant critical self-reflection, cynicism and a seeming 'exhaustion' of novelty? Not surprisingly, the answer is . . . media sport." (David Rowe, *Sport, Culture, and the Media: The Unruly Trinity,* [Philadelphia: Open University Press, 1999], 69)

13. Rowe, *Sport,* 70; Dunning, *Sport Matters,* 6.

14. *Oakland Tribune,* Jan. 19, 2003.

15. Oriard, *King Football,* 148, 219–20, 221, 345.

16. Dunning insightfully argues that "in the everyday life of the relatively 'civilized' advanced industrial societies of today, routines and controls . . . tend to be conducive to the regular generation, not only of simple boredom but, perhaps more importantly, of feelings of emotional 'staleness' as well." Consequently, many people turn to sports as "a search for pleasurable and de-routinizing emotional arousal." Sports delivers this kind of "de-routinizing emotional arousal," as Dunning puts it, big time. Thus the rush of feeling may come from Raiders quarterback Rich Gannon scrambling for a game-winning touchdown or from watching him writhe in pain beneath fat Baltimore Ravens defender Tony Siragusa in the 2002 AFC Championship game, but the intensity of the true fan's state of being at such moments is undeniable. Dunning outlines the contours of the sports fan's emotional landscape as follows: "Sports can also be said to be a form of non-scripted, largely non-verbal theatre, and emotional arousal can be enhanced by spectacular presentation, the emotional 'contagion' which derives from being part of a large, expectant crowd, and from the 'performances' which spectators and not just athletes put on." Of particular note here

is Dunning's comparison of sports and "theatre" in that it illustrates both how knowledge of the formal aspects of the performance enhances the spectators' pleasure and how one must "suspend disbelief" in order to fully engage the show. His reference to the emotional "contagion" of the crowd is central since it addresses the fundamentally collective nature of sports consumption and the central role of that collective emotional expression in fans' connection to sports. Dunning's point about the performances that *spectators* put on is crucial as well. (Dunning, *Sport Matters*, 3)

17. Dunning goes on to say, "In order, as it were, for the 'gears' of one's passions fully to engage, one has to be *committed*, to want to *win*, either as a direct participant for one's own sake because one's *identity* is at stake, or as a spectator because one *identifies* with one of the individual performers or competing teams." Questions of identity and identification are of critical importance both for the routine functioning of sports and for some of the problems recurrently generated in connection with them. (Dunning, *Sport Matters*, 3)

18. Ibid., 4–5.

19. Glen Dickey, *Just Win, Baby: Al Davis and His Raiders* (New York: Harcourt, Brace, and Jovanovich, 1991), 167.

20. John Matusak with Steve Delson, *Cruisin' with the Tooz* (New York: Franklin Watts, 1987), 209; Dickey, *Just Win,* 189; Jim Plunkett and Dave Newhouse, *The Jim Plunkett Story: The Saga of a Man Who Came Back* (New York: Arbor House, 1981), 221; Ira Simmons, *Black Knight: Al Davis and His Raiders* (Rocklin, Calif.: Prima Publishing, 1990), 202 and 198; John Lombardo, *Raiders Forever: Stars of the NFL's Most Colorful Team Recall Their Glory Days* (Chicago: Contemporary Books, 2001), 1.

21. Lombardo, *Raiders Forever,* 7; Simmons, *Black Knight,* 197; Mark Ribowsky, *Slick: The Silver and Black Life of Al Davis* (New York: Macmillan, 1991), 277.

22. Simmons, *Black Knight,* 316-17; Ribowsky, *Slick,* 341.

23. Lombardo, *Raiders Forever,* 7.

24. *Oakland Tribune,* July 2, 2003, July 1, 2003, May 23, 2003; Simmons *Black Knight,* 298.

25. *Oakland Tribune,* May 23, 2003, Aug. 15, 2003.

26. By this time the trial had been moved to Sacramento, California.

27. *Oakland Tribune,* Aug. 5–7, 2003, Aug. 15, 2003, Aug. 17, 2003, Aug. 27–30, 2003; *San Jose Mercury News,* Aug. 11, 2003; *San Francisco Chronicle,* Aug. 27, 2003, Aug. 30, 2003; www.raiders.com, accessed Aug. 26, 2003.

28. *San Francisco Chronicle,* Aug. 27, 2003; *Oakland Tribune,* Aug. 29–31, 2003, Sept. 1, 2003, Nov. 12, 2003, Dec. 30, 2003, Feb. 5, 2004, March 16, 2004. As of this writing, there has still been no final resolution in this case.

29. *Oakland Tribune,* Oct. 10, 2003, Oct. 29, 2003, Nov. 14, 2003, April 3, 2004; *San Francisco Chronicle,* Aug. 27, 2003, Oct. 16, 2003.

30. Ribowsky, *Slick,* 294.

31. Dickey, *Just Win,* 249.

32. As cultural studies scholar Stuart Hall once pointed out about the way people consume the ideology that comes with televised media, some people swallow the "dominant-hegemonic" message (or party line) whole, others take an "oppositional" position and resist the message, and many more in the middle negotiate a position that accepts some of the ideology while rejecting other aspects of it. Transferring this model from the realm of television consumption to the realm of football fandom helps illustrate how the "meanings" of football are not totally constructed by the game's owners and then unproblematically accepted by the fans. We will not argue, as some cultural studies scholars have, that the consumption of popular culture (in this case sports) constitutes an act of serious political agency, but on the other hand, it is not simply indoctrination either. (Stuart Hall, "Encoding, Decoding," in *The Cultural Studies Reader,* ed. Simon During, [New York: Routledge, 1993], 90–103)

33. *Los Angeles Times,* Dec. 2, 1995.

34. *San Francisco Chronicle,* Jan. 22, 2003.

35. Ribowsky, *Slick,* 316; Dickey, *Just Win,* 245.

36. Mike Davis, *Magical Urbanism: Latinos Reinvent the U.S. City* (London: Verso, 2000), 43–4.

37. Chris Pink, "End Zone 67," *Raider Mystique,* Jan. 10, 2003, available from www.nflfans. com/raiders/article, accessed July 17, 2003.

38. Dick Hebdige, "Subculture," in *The Subcultures Reader,* ed. Ken Gelder and Sarah Thornton (London: Routledge, 1997), 130.

39. Ibid.

40. Hebdige, "Subculture," 131; Dickey, *Just Win,* 239, 246; Simmons, *Black Knight,* 270; Jo Sparkes, "Horsehair Jerseys," Arizona Sports Fans Network, Nov. 27, 2002, available from www.arizonasportsfans.com/storypage, accessed May 25, 2003; *Oakland Tribune,* Nov. 17, 2003; for his discussion of class consciousness and "Otherness," see also Hebdige, "Subculture," 133.

41. Hebdige, "Subculture," 139.

42. Rowe, *Sport,* 162.

43. Ibid., 68.

44. Ibid., 70.

Chapter 1: Bin Laden Is a Raider Fan

1. Sadie Plant, *The Most Radical Gesture: The Situationist International in a Postmodern Age* (London: Routledge, 1992), 26.

2. Hunter S. Thompson, "Back in the Day," www.espn.com, April 21, 2003, available from http://espn.go.com/page2/s/Thompson, accessed July 7, 2003; Thompson, "The Last Super Bowl."

3. *San Diego Union-Tribune,* Jan. 22, 2003 and Jan. 25, 2003; "INS Kicks Off 'Operation Game Day': Agents Arrest Dozens in Security Sweep Tied to Super Bowl," *World Net Daily,* January 24, 2003, available from http://www.worldnetdaily.com/news, accessed July 31, 2003.

4. Plant, *Radical Gesture,* 26.

5. *Oakland Tribune,* Jan. 30, 2003.

6. *San Diego Union-Tribune,* Jan. 28, 2003; *Oakland Tribune,* Jan. 27, 2003; Jan. 28, 2003; Feb. 2, 2003; June 12, 2003.

Chapter 2: Oakland's Burning

1. John Krich, *Bump City: Winners and Losers in Oakland* (Berkeley, Calif.: City Miner, 1979), 71; Gary Rivlin, *Drive By* (London: Quartet Books, 1996), 11.

2. Beth Bagwell, *Oakland: The Story of a City* (Novato, Calif.: Presidio, 1982), 205–6; Marilynn S. Johnson, *The Second Gold Rush: Oakland and the East Bay in World War II* (Berkeley: University of California Press, 1993), 83, 84.

3. Abbie Wasserman, ed., *The Spirit of Oakland* (Carlsbad, N.M.: Heritage Media Corporation, 2000), 89.

4. Rivlin, *Drive By,* 35–6; Wasserman, *Spirit,* 89, 87, and 79; Ishmael Reed, *Blues City* (New York: Crown, 2003), 87; Chris Rhomberg, *No There There: Race, Class, and Political Community in Oakland* (Berkeley: University of California Press, 2004), 199.

5. *Oakland Tribune,* July 18, 2003; Rhomberg, *There,* 184, 199; Rivlin, *Drive By,* 19.

6. *Oakland Tribune,* June 3, 2003; July 25, 2003.

7. *Oakland Tribune,* June 16, 2003.

8. *Oakland Tribune,* June 28, 2003, May 14, 2003, July 27, 2003; Rhomberg, *There,* 186.

9. James Diego Vigil, *A Rainbow of Gangs: Street Cultures in the Mega-City* (Austin: University of Texas Press, 2002), 20, 22, 26.

10. *San Francisco Chronicle,* Jan. 21, 2003.

11. *San Francisco Chronicle,* Jan. 27, 2003; *Oakland Tribune,* Jan. 27, 2003; ER, "OPD Uses Tear Gas in Post–Super Bowl Maneuvers," www.sf.indymedia.org, Jan. 27, 2003, available from http://sf.indymedia.org/news, accessed July 3, 2003; *San Francisco Chronicle,* Jan. 20, 2003; *Oakland Tribune,* Jan. 28, 2003.

12. *San Francisco Chronicle,* Jan. 27, 2003; *San Jose Mercury News,* Jan. 26, 2003; *San Francisco Chronicle,* Jan. 27, 2003; www.sf.indymedia.org, Jan. 27, 2003.

13. *Oakland Tribune,* Jan. 28, 2003, Feb. 1, 2003.

14. Krich, *Bump City,* 75; Johnson, *Gold Rush,* 168; Ishmael Reed, "Living at Ground Zero," *Image,* March 13, 1988, 11; Ishmael Reed, *Airing Dirty Laundry* (Boston: Addison-Wesley, 1993), 102; *Oakland Tribune,* July 17, 2003; July 2, 2003, June 26, 2003, July 29, 2003, Sept. 9, 2003, Oct. 1, 2003, Oct. 2, 2003, Nov. 1, 2003.

15. *Oakland Tribune,* Jan. 31, 2003.

16. Ibid.
17. *Oakland Tribune*, Feb. 6, 2003.
18. www.sf.indymedia.org, Jan. 27, 2003 and Jan. 28, 2003.
19. Ibid.
20. Ibid.
21. Rhomberg, *There,* 54, 56–57, 99.
22. Johnson, *Gold Rush,* 169; Bagwell, *Oakland,* 240–41.
23. Johnson, *Gold Rush,* 165.
24. Amory Bradford, *Oakland's Not for Burning* (New York: David McKay, 1968), 2, 6.
25. Ibid., 191.
26. Ibid., 200–1.
27. Ibid., 212.
28. Jeffrey L. Pressman and Aaron B. Wildavsky, *Implementation: How Great Expectations in Washington Are Dashed in Oakland* (Berkeley: University of California Press, 1973), 4, 5, xi, 154,149–51; Rhomberg, *There,* 169.
29. Rhomberg, *There,* 184.
30. Reed, *Airing Dirty Laundry,* 213.
31. Vigil, *Rainbow,* 168–9; *East Bay Express,* July 23, 2003.
32. Barry Glassner, *The Culture of Fear: Why Americans Are Afraid of the Wrong Things: Crime, Drugs, Minorities, Teen Moms, Killer Kids, Mutant Microbes, Plane Crashes, Road Rage, and So Much More* (New York: Basic Books, 1999), 72.
33. Dunning, *Sport Matters,* 170-73.
34. Dunning, *Sport Matters,* 172; Bill Buford, *Among the Thugs* (New York: Vintage, 1993), 205, 249.
35. Gustave Le Bon, *The Crowd* (New York: Penguin, 1960), 16, 32, 30.
36. Jean Baudrillard, "The Mirror of Terrorism," in *The Transparency of Evil: Essays on Extreme Phenomena* (London: Verso, 1993), 76, 75; *Oakland Tribune,* Jan. 28, 2003; Baudrillard, "Mirror," 75.
37. Baudrillard, "Mirror," 76, 76–77; *Oakland Tribune,* Feb. 1, 2003.
38. *Oakland Tribune,* Jan. 27, 2003; Baudrillard, "Mirror," 77.
39. Baudrillard, "Mirror," 79, 80; www.sf.indymedia.org, Jan. 27, 2003 and Jan. 28, 2003.

Chapter 3: We Are Everywhere

1. *Oakland Tribune,* March 10, 2003.
2. Rowe, *Sport,* 168.
3. www.silverandblackattack.com.
4. Putnam, *Bowling Alone,* 173, 175, 176, 178.
5. Tom Frank, *What's the Matter with Kansas?: How Conservatives Won the Heart of America* (New York: Metropolitan, 2004), 113.

6. www.knumbskullrecords.com.
7. www.roxie77.com/blackout/lyrics.
8. www.cdbaby.com/cd/deadriver.
9. www.smokealotrecords.com.
10. Luniz, "Oakland Raiders," *Silver and Black*, compact disk, Rap-A-Lot Records, 2002.
11. *San Francisco Chronicle*, June 16, 2003.

Chapter 4: Training Camp

1. Rob Huizenga, *"You're Okay, It's Just a Bruise": A Doctor's Sideline Secrets about Pro Football's Most Outrageous Team* (New York: St. Martin's, 1994), 92, 105; Lombardo, *Raiders Forever*, 116.
2. Ken Stabler and Berry Stainback, *Snake: The Candid Autobiography of Football's Most Outrageous Renegade* (Garden City, N.Y.: Doubleday, 1986), 76; Lombardo, *Raiders Forever*, 64, 184, 108; Ribowsky, *Slick*, 193, 225–6; Jack Tatum with Bill Kushner, *They Call Me Assassin* (New York: Everest House, 1979), 39.
3. Joe Queenan, *True Believers: The Tragic Inner Life of Sports Fans* (New York: Henry Holt, 2003), 54.

Chapter 5: What a Long, Strange Trip It's Been

1. *Oakland Tribune*, August 8, 2003.
2. www.singhshady.net.
3. Hunter S. Thompson, "Fear and Loathing at the Super Bowl," 75–6.
4. Krich, *Bump City*, 77.

Chapter 6: Crying Won't Help

1. Reed, *Blues City*, 28, 183; Lee Hildebrand and Michelle Vignes, *Bay Area Blues* (San Francisco: Pomegranate, 1993), 8; Albert Vetere Lannon, *Fight or Be Slaves: The History of the Oakland-East Bay Labor Movement* (New York: University Press of America, 2000), 96.
2. Rivlin, *Drive By*, 4; Reed, *Blues City*, 20–22; *Oakland Tribune*, Aug. 20, 2003, Sept. 1, 2003, Sept. 3, 2003.
3. Sadly, the 2000 return of the blues to Oakland would last only a few more months: Eli's has changed hands twice as of this writing and is no longer a blues club.
4. *East Bay Express*, Aug. 20, 2003.
5. *Oakland Tribune*, Aug. 21, 2003, Aug. 24, 2003, Aug. 26, 2003, Aug. 27, 2003, Aug. 29, 2003. Aug. 31, 2003; *San Francisco Chronicle*, Aug. 26, 2003.

Chapter 7: At Ricky's

1. Lawrence Wenner, "In Search of the Sports Bar," in *Sport and Postmodern Times*, ed. Genevieve Rail (Albany: State University of New York Press, 1998), 324–8.

2. Ibid., 318–22.
3. Ibid., 302.
4. Putnam, *Bowling Alone*, 113.

Chapter 8   Working-Class Heroes

The chapter epigraphs are from Robert O. Self, "California's Industrial Garden: Oakland and the East Bay in the Age of Deindustrialization," 178, in *Beyond the Ruins: The Meanings of Deindustrialization,* ed. Jefferson Cowrie and Joseph Heathcott (Ithaca, N.Y.: Cornell University Press, 2003); Joe Blum, "Degradation without Deskilling: Twenty-five Years in the San Francisco Shipyards," in *Global Ethnography: Forces, Connections, and Imaginations in a Postmodern World,* ed. Michael Burawoy (Berkeley: University of California Press, 2000), 129–30; and Renay Jackson, *Oaktown Devil* (Oakland: La Day Publishing, 1998), 10–11.

1. Rhomberg, *There,* 74, 106, 107, 111; Lannon, *Fight or Be Slaves,* 108–11; George Lipsitz, *Rainbow at Midnight: Labor and Culture in the 1940s* (Urbana: University of Illinois Press, 1994), 150.
2. Self, "California's Industrial Garden," 165, 177.
3. *Oakland Tribune,* Sept. 14, 2003.
4. *Oakland Tribune,* Sept. 15, 2003 and Sept. 16, 2003.

Chapter 9: Raiders Rage

1. David Cordingly, *Under the Black Flag: The Romance and the Reality of Life among the Pirates* (New York: Random House, 1995), 241.
2. *New York Times,* Sept. 26, 2003 and Sept. 28, 2003; *Oakland Tribune,* Sept. 28, 2003 and Oct. 2, 2002.
3. *Oakland Tribune,* Sept. 29, 2003.

Chapter 10: Monday Night Lights

1. Peter Stallybrass and Allon White, "From Carnival to Transgression," in *The Subcultures Reader,* ed. Ken Gelder and Sarah Thornton (London: Routledge, 1997), 294–5, 296, 297.
2. *Oakland Tribune,* Nov. 17, 2003.
3. Susan Faludi, *Stiffed: The Betrayal of the American Man* (New York: William Morrow, 1999), 158, 205.
4. Greil Marcus, *Lipstick Traces: A Secret History of the Twentieth Century* (Cambridge: Harvard University Press, 1989), 99.
5. Ibid., 98–9, 99, 104–5
6. Dunning, *Sport Matters,* 1–2.
7. Michael Oriard, review of Susan Faludi, *Stiffed: The Betrayal of the American Man, Mother Jones Magazine* (September 1999).

8. *Oakland Tribune*, Oct. 21, 2003.

Chapter 11: Real Women Wear Black

1. *Oakland Tribune*, Nov. 4, 2003, Nov. 7, 2003, Nov. 8, 2003, Nov. 9, 2003, Nov. 10, 2003, Nov. 11, 2003.
2. Ibid., Nov. 4, 2003.
3. Michael Messner, *Power at Play: Sports and the Problem of Masculinity* (Boston: Beacon, 1992), 15.
4. Oriard, *Reading Football*, 191.
5. Faludi, *Stiffed*, 154.
6. Jenkins, 79.
7. Ibid., 5, 79-80, 80.
8. Alysse Minkoff, "Sweetheart of the Hole," www.espn.com, Sept. 27, 2003, available from http://espn.go.com/page2/s/minkoff, accessed Sept. 29, 2003.
9. Meaghan Morris, *The Pirate's Fiancée: Feminism, Reading, Postmodernism* (London: Verso, 1988), 1–3.

Chapter 12: Los Malosos

1. *Oakland Tribune*, Nov. 13, 2003, Nov. 15, 2003, Nov. 17, 2003, Nov. 20, 2003; www.espn.com, Nov. 16, 2003.
2. *Oakland Tribune*, Nov. 15, 2003, Nov. 16, 2003, Dec. 10, 2003.
3. Ibid., Nov. 17, 2003.
4. Ibid.
5. Ibid., Nov. 19, 2003, Dec. 9, 2003, Jan. 4, 2004.
6. *Los Angeles Times*, Sept. 28, 1990, April 16, 1992, April 17, 1992, Jan. 8, 1998, Jan. 23, 1998.
7. Ibid., May 19, 1991.
8. *Seattle Times*, Jan. 21, 2003.
9. Mike Davis, *City of Quartz: Excavating the Future in Los Angeles* (New York: Vintage Books, 1990), 270.
10. *Los Angeles Times*, Sept. 6, 1996, Dec. 15, 2001.
11. Davis, *City of Quartz*, 304.
12. *Oakland Tribune*, Nov. 21, 2003, Nov. 23, 2003, Nov. 24, 2003, Nov. 27, 2003, Nov. 28, 2003.
13. *Oakland Tribune*, Nov. 29, 2003, Nov. 30, 2003; *East Bay Express*, Nov. 26, 2003.
14. *Oakland Tribune*, Dec. 1, 2003.

Chapter 13: Just Lose, Baby

1. Henry David Thoreau, *Walden and Other Writings* (New York: Modern Library, 1981), 7.

2. *San Diego Union-Tribune*, Dec. 27, 2003.

3. www.aggressionmanagement.com.

4. Dunning, *Sport Matters*, 166–7.

5. *San Francisco Chronicle*, Dec. 29, 2003; *Oakland Tribune*, Dec. 29, 2003.

6. *Oakland Tribune*, Jan. 4, 2005, Nov. 11, 2004, and Oct. 28, 2004.

7. Ibid., Dec. 23, 2004, Nov. 11, 2004, Dec. 21, 2004, and Dec. 26, 2004.

8. *Los Angeles Times*, Dec. 24, 2004; *Las Vegas Review-Journal*, Dec. 7, 2004; *Magic News*, Dec. 28, 2004, Dec. 18, 2004, and Dec. 28, 2004.

9. *Oakland Tribune*, Dec. 28, 2004 and Jan. 4, 2005.

Afterword: Rebels of Oakland

1. *Oakland Tribune*, Dec. 10, 2003.

2. Putnam, *Bowling Alone*, 282–3; *USA Today*, July 5, 2004.

3. *USA Today*, July 5, 2004.

Index

Oaktown Pirates, 142–43, 184
Oliver, Chip, 116
Operation Game Day, 51–52
Oriard, Michael: *King Football*, 10, 19, 231–32, 237, 239
Ottman, Derek, 40
Otto, Jim, 100, 159, 163, 220

Pacific Beach, Calif., 64
Pacific Coast Brewing Company, 197, 201
Paramount Theatre, 134
Parella, John, 122
Park, Richard K., 27–28
Parker, Craig: *Football's Blackest Hole*, 133
Peach, 94, 105–6; and www.Raiderslinks.com, 94
Pendexter, Dale, 106
Perales, Jorge, 255–56
Perez, Francisco, 88
Peter Krist, 145
Philadelphia Eagles, 108
Phillips, Lee "The Flea," 173–74
Phillips, Mark, 108
Pirate Saq's Pirate Ship, 94
Pittsburgh Steelers, 274
Plummer, Jake, 273
Plunkett, Jim, 24
Poland, Steve, 107
Poole, Monte, 22, 29, 64, 75, 298, 302
Porter, Jerry, 118, 121, 123, 238, 254
Pressman, Jeffrey: *Implementation: How Great Expectations in Washington Are Dashed in Oakland*, 82
Proposition 13, 83–84
Proposition 21, 84
Putnam, Robert: *Bowling Alone*, 17, 95–96, 167, 171, 302–3

Qualcomm Stadium, 57–60, 258
Queenan, Joe, 117

Raiders. *See* Oakland Raiders
Raider, Augusta, 186
Raider Bandit, 4, 38, 249, 256–57
Raider Empire Listserv, 233
Raider Fan Radio, 98
Raider-Gloria, 185–86, 246
Raiderhed, 99–100, 193

Raider Image, 111–12
Raider Nation, 1–7, 9, 10, 12–14, 16–22, 30, 36–42, 44–47, 53, 55, 61–62, 71, 73, 75, 77–78, 84–86, 91–109, 111–12, 118–24, 127–28, 135–53, 178, 184–93, 201, 221, 232–35, 272, 292–94, 299–305; blue-collar origins, 4–5, 12, 37–38, 42, 44–45, 131, 302; as carnival, 149–50; charity, 46, 92–93; class in, 96–97; crimes by, 255–58; deadheads, similarity to, 146–51; diversity in, 5–7, 10–12, 37, 41, 44–46, 73, 137, 144, 178, 185, 266, 275–76, 289; as family, 44–46; fear of, 3–4, 84–85; gangs and, 258–66, 277; geographic distribution of, 47, 95, 103–9; haters, 12, 39, 85; Hispanic culture and, 259, 270–71; identity and, 21–22, 40, 71; as imagined community, 5–6, 9, 13, 19–21, 36, 39, 45, 75, 92–94, 128, 171–72, 184, 301–2; inclusivity of, 45–46; ironworkers and, 197–200; Jimbo and, 233–35; in Los Angeles, 263; loyalty of, 21, 25, 29–30; music of, 98–102; origin of term, 233–34; rebel image of, 2, 5, 41, 131, 182, 210; relationship with Raiders organization, 22–30, 33, 35–36, 195; religion in, 18–19; in San Diego, 260, 262–63; stereotyping of, 3–4, 39–42, 84–86, 189, 267; subcultures, 40; transcendentalism, 44–46; tribalism in, 5, 292–94; as virtual community, 94–97; violence and, 21, 38–40, 135, 187, 216–17, 228, 286, 292–94; white collar, 12, 41–42; women in, 45, 242–47. See also *fans*
Raider Rooter Booster Club, 98
Raider Shack, 95
Raiders for Life, 95; BlackHole Mike, 95, 139–41
Raiders gang, 256
Raiders of the Far North, 103
Raiders 'Till Death, 95
Ramirez, Phil, 139, 184
Ramirez, Angel, 139, 184
Ratto, Ray, 28
Reed, Ishmael: *Blues City*, 69, 74, 83, 155; "Living at Ground Zero," 156
relocation of sports teams, 23–24
Rhomberg, Chris; *No There There: Race, Class, and Political Community in Oakland*, 69–70, 79, 83, 182–83, 200–1